School Leaders' Sensemaking and Sensegiving

Educational Leadership and Leaders in Contexts

Series Editor

Philip Quirke (*Higher Colleges of Technology, UAE*)

Editorial Board

Laila Boisselle (*Trinidad and Tobago*)
Amparo Clavijo (*Universidad Distrital Francisco José de Caldas, Colombia*)
Alex Gardner-McTaggert (*University of Manchester, UK*)
David Gatewood (*The Chair Academy, Worldwide Leadership Development in Higher Education, USA*)
Gowri Ishwaran (*Global Education and Leadership Foundation (GEL), India*)
David Lees (*Kyoto University, Japan*)
Rosina Merry (Te *Rito Maioha ECNZ Director Teaching & Learning and Research, New Zealand*)
Ada Omile (*E.L. Africa magazine, USA*)
César Taboada Varela (*Ecola de Arte e Superior de Deseño ESAD Director Departamento de Programas Internacionales, Spain*)

VOLUME 8

The titles published in this series are listed at *brill.com/ellc*

School Leaders' Sensemaking and Sensegiving

By

Judith Norris

BRILL

LEIDEN | BOSTON

Cover illustration: "Heart of the Alpine", photograph by Scott Leggo

All chapters in this book have undergone peer review.

The Library of Congress Cataloging-in-Publication Data is available online at https://catalog.loc.gov

Typeface for the Latin, Greek, and Cyrillic scripts: "Brill". See and download: brill.com/brill-typeface.

ISSN 2666-7746
ISBN 978-90-04-51718-9 (paperback)
ISBN 978-90-04-51719-6 (hardback)
ISBN 978-90-04-51720-2 (e-book)

Copyright 2022 by Koninklijke Brill NV, Leiden, The Netherlands.
Koninklijke Brill NV incorporates the imprints Brill, Brill Nijhoff, Brill Hotei, Brill Schöningh, Brill Fink, Brill mentis, Vandenhoeck & Ruprecht, Böhlau and V&R unipress.
All rights reserved. No part of this publication may be reproduced, translated, stored in a retrieval system, or transmitted in any form or by any means, electronic, mechanical, photocopying, recording or otherwise, without prior written permission from the publisher. Requests for re-use and/or translations must be addressed to Koninklijke Brill NV via brill.com or copyright.com.

This book is printed on acid-free paper and produced in a sustainable manner.

Contents

Preface IX
Acknowledgments XIV
List of Illustrations XV
List of Abbreviations XVII
About the Author XVIII

1 All in the Same Field 1
  1 The Need for This Book 2
  2 Purpose and Aims 2
  3 Metaphors 5
  4 Ecology and the Human Condition 5
  5 The Eucalyptus Tree—Its Attraction 6
  6 Australian Indigenous Peoples' Reciprocity with Trees 6
  7 Going Forward 7

2 Problem, Trigger, Conjectures 8
  1 The Underpinnings of the Model 9
  2 The Theoretical Model 11
  3 Core Category 1: Making Sense 16
  4 Core Category 2: Giving Sense 18
  5 Relationship between Making Sense and Giving Sense 19

3 Problem Re-namers 23
  1 Sensemaking 24
  2 Sensegiving 28
  3 Sensebreaking 39
  4 School Leaders' Sensemaking and Sensegiving in Accountable Times 40
  5 The Theory of Planned Behaviour 41
  6 Application of Leadership to the Theory of Planned Behaviour (TPB) 43
  7 Bringing the Re-namers Together 45

4 Context: Not Everything, But Something 51
  1 Impact of Public Purpose on School Leaders' Work 51
  2 Global Actors Impact on School Leaders' Work 54
  3 National Actors Impact on School Leaders' Work 57

4	State and Jurisdictional Actors	59
5	Secondary Schools in Australia: Changing Times	61
6	Faith-Based: Dual Bind or Single Resolve?	69
7	Principals' Interpretations of Their Accountability: Clashing Times	72
8	Policy to Practice Gap	74
9	School Leader Identity Formation	79

5 Educational Accountability: New Normal or Site of Struggle? 80

1	Introducing Educational Accountability	80
2	The New Normal: Site of Struggle?	81
3	Typology of Accountability in Education	82
4	Defining Educational Accountability	87
5	Rationale for Accountability in Australian Schools	89
6	The Mechanisms	91
7	Accountability Stakes Drive into the Hearts of Educators	96
8	Effects of Educational Accountability on School Leaders	98

6 '... Somehow Frame Accountability to Make Sense of It' 100

1	Contextualising	102
2	Prioritising Referents: Account for What, to Whom and How	107
3	Anomaly: Terence Prioritises Performance Results	110
4	Anomaly: Prioritising the DeCourcy Instrument of Analysis	119
5	Anomaly: The School System Expectations	121
6	Conceptualising	126

7 The Lady of Light 135

1	Sensegiving Acts: Persuading Teachers	135
2	Anomaly: Principals Manage Demands by 'Cherry Picking'	141
3	Anomaly: Principals Manage Demands through Target Setting	141
4	Sensegiving Acts: Enacting the Leader Learner Identity	143
5	Sensegiving Acts: Creating Cultures of Coherence	147
6	Anomaly: Aspiring for Grades as Brilliance	155
7	Anomaly: Principals Set Performance Results as Targets	156
8	Sense Leaders: Sammy, Charmaine, Barry, and Leonie	157

CONTENTS VII

8 Not How It Is, But How I See It Is 166
1 Not How It Is, But How I See It Is 166
2 Constraining, an Authoring Act 173
3 School Leaders Framing Their External Demands 180

9 Credibility, Persuasion and Coherence 187
1 Persuasive Devices: Narratives, Metaphors and Mantras 189
2 Sensegiving Act of Articulating a Vision for Learning 191
3 Sensegiving Act of Modelling Expertise 193
4 Sensegiving Act of Facilitating Professional Learning Conversations 194
5 Sensegiving Act: Reconciliation 195
6 Sensegiving Act: Leaders Creating Coherence 197
7 School Leaders Give Sense by Articulating Perspective 198
8 Two Moderating Factors of School Leaders' Sensegiving 201
9 Theoretical Relationship between Leaders' Sensemaking and Sensegiving 206

10 Sense Leaders: Ready for Any Catastrophe 215
1 Eucaus Announces Nation-Wide Testing 215
2 The Theoretical ELM in Situ 218
3 Contributing to Further Research 221
4 Implications and Recommendations 222
5 Researching into the Future 227
6 A Metaphor for School Leaders' Sensemaking and Sensegiving 228
7 Closing Remarks 229

References 233
Index 264

Preface

The drive for performance results over the last 15 years has impacted the work of students, teachers, school leaders and school system advisors, across the globe. The risks with such drives have morphed some schools and school systems from innovative cultures of learning to mechanical cultures of performativity. The principal is the key agent influencing this impact, acting as a fulcrum, managing up and down. School systems' advisors, both government and non-government, expect principals to demonstrate how teachers in their schools implement these prescribed practices from data informed evidence to improve student performance scores. These expectations are built into their performance goals.

Such expectations have created certain tensions and challenges for not only principals but all senior school leaders. This book is about a theoretical model which demonstrates a new approach to understanding the ways in which school leaders react to such tensions, and in particular conflicting expectations and demands. While this book draws on leadership examples from Australia, the reader may find parallels with their own international jurisdictions.

Most Australian school leaders are held to account by school system wide programs and processes. Teachers and principals over the last 5 years are expected to be skilled and hold contemporary understandings about teaching and learning. They need skills erecting data walls (Sharratt & Fullan, 2012); sowing high yield strategies (Marzano, 2009); 'walking the walk' and 'talking the talk' of the observational and instructional tours (Zepeda, 2017); applying visible learning practices (Hattie, & Zierer, 2019; Maitlis & Lawrence, 2007) and; creating professional learning communities to optimise collective teacher efficacy (Donohoo, Hattie, & Eells, 2018; Donohoo, O'Leary, & Hattie, 2020). Each practice is to be implemented, monitored, and then evaluated. The practices themselves are evidence based and hold value if they work. However, a worst-case scenario for educators in the field, is when these practices are an affront to their professional beliefs. Teachers' and school leaders' beliefs are compromised when the practices are narrowly measured in terms of student achievement on external assessment mechanisms. In Australia, such mechanisms include the National Assessment Program–Literacy and Numeracy (NAPLAN) or final year measurements such as an Australian Tertiary Admission Rank (ATAR). However, it needs to be acknowledged there has been some movement which holds a semblance of congruence between an educator's professional beliefs and what the system regulator is demanding. For example, Australian school leaders now experience the instructional leader being reconceptualised from a prescribed rigidity, such as the instructional rounds, to modelling and coaching as a means for influencing teacher practices (Thessin, 2019).

Measurements of impact are the devices employed by stakeholders, such as school systems and parents, through the public disclosures of results to hold, in the first instance, Australian principals to account. Principals depend on teachers in this accountability milieu. The nature of the dependency relationship between senior school leaders and teachers has never been more essential. No longer is the principal distant from teaching and learning, masking in roles of administrators, marketing and/or business managers. The need for an influential dependency relationship with teachers calls on principals to be engaged in the work of teachers intimately. These changing expectations raise the question of how school leaders traverse such changes in their school communities. This book responds to this question.

Australian studies have been carried out on the tensions between school leaders' beliefs and regulatory requirements (Gobby, Keddie, & Blackmore, 2018; Smeed, Spiller, & Kimber, 2009; Thompson & Mockler, 2016), challenges in terms of autonomy, equity and access (Eacott et al., 2020) and with Gurr and Drysdale continue to give much value to the field from historical perspectives (Gurr & Drysdale, 2020b), especially with regards to the challenges of high velocity events, such as the consequences of the pandemic COVID-19 for school leaders (Gurr, 2020; Gurr & Drysdale, 2020a). From policy (Lingard, Thompson, & Sellar, 2015) to critical and theoretical perspectives (Eacott, 2017; Gobby et al., 2018; Heffernan, 2018; Kemmis et al., 2014) all these scholars offer diverse perspectives on the challenges of educational leaders in the field of educational leadership in Australia (see Section 7 in Chapter 1). This book offers a framework for navigating some of these challenges. The model proposed here explains and, under certain conditions, predicts how school leaders are likely to act when confronted with contradictory expectations and demands.

The model, named the Eucalypt Leadership Model (ELM), is fully described at the beginning of the book with the remainder of the book showing the model's practical application. School leader practitioners are likely to relate to the applications as they tell the human story of principals managing their external accountability demands with the realities and significance of honouring teachers' and students' work. While the examples provided are from the perspective of a principal, they can relate to any school leader. The principals are from two Australian school systems, one rural and the other metropolitan in the State of New South Wales (NSW), Australia. Both School Systems are Catholic. The governance and regulatory arrangements for these School Systems hold common jurisdictional requirements. Should the reader wish to know more about the methods of data collection and analysis, they can refer to my thesis (Norris, 2017).

Chapter 1 presents the need, aims, purpose and the utility of metaphors in the book. Chapter 2 presents the theoretical ELM, demonstrating how principals' interpretations of their accountability expectations, and any expectations for that matter, can predict the likely ways they will implement such expectations. The ELM exposes the psycho-social processes that educational leaders are likely to negotiate when faced with external accountability demands. Weick's sensemaking properties (Weick, 1995) and sensegiving premises (Gioia & Chittipeddi, 1991) along with the well-respected Theory of Planned Behaviour (Ajzen, 1991) are the theoretical foundations drawn upon to develop the model. The ELM importantly pinpoints effective leadership practices required when principals make sense of their external demands, simultaneously meeting their internal school commitments. It also demonstrates the effectiveness of principals/school leaders being skilled in two processes: sensemaking and sensegiving. Underlying these two interdependent processes is a psychological one. Namely, the leader's own self-belief about their influence on teaching practices.

The ELM is useful on several fronts. One, it provides insights about the reasons why school leaders may or may not meet expectations. Such insights may guide school system leaders in the most effective ways when placing expectations on school leaders. Two, it may provide formation for school leaders, notably early career leaders, or aspirant leaders developing their professional identities when managing increasing external demands, or critical events. Hence, it could be a source of understanding for those who regulate and those who are 'being regulated.'

The ELM is applied to principals' experiences of their accountabilities. There are two points that the reader may like to consider. One, the accountabilities as described in these principals' contexts are novel and involve high stakes, so could be termed high velocity events. Two, the reader may consider that these accountabilities are not limited to principals or school leaders but extend to the experience of teachers. What is important is that these principals' voices, at times provocative, offer the realities of the turmoils, and simultaneously provide insights into how educators can eloquently act as negotiating agents between reconciling external demands with the reality of changing teaching practices. Pragmatically, it is a cascading effect of how a principal or school leader makes sense of external demands, impacting the work of teachers, and importantly reaching students and their learning.

The three theoretical lenses from which the ELM has been developed are introduced in Chapter 3. These lenses theorise human behaviour: sensemaking;

sensegiving; and planned behaviour. There is sufficient detail about these lenses to understand how they contribute to the model. These lenses explain the reasons and predict how school leaders may go about interpreting and enacting external demands.

Chapter 4 explores the context in which school leaders find themselves working, at the macro and micro levels. The exploration is carried out in two ways. First, through examining the implications of the public purposes of Australian education and second by introducing the external actors who, in each of their own ways, contribute to the accountability demands placed on school leaders. Global, national, state and school system actors and their evolving impact presents new challenges for school leaders performing in the dazzle on the global and national stages. In turn principals, as key agents in their school communities, are interpreting their external demands into 'something' meaningful and palatable for teachers and their practices. The local context of the Australian school system is examined in so far as demonstrating the impact of this context on principals' role expectations, introducing the potential effects of role expectations in high accountability cultures on principals' professional identities.

The types of accountability mechanisms are explored in Chapter 5, juxtaposing how school educators and scholars adopt preferential terms for educational accountability. It clearly defines the term educational accountability by examining what the system regulator is asking of school leaders and how the regulator evaluates leaders' performances.

Chapters 6 and 7 demonstrate the applicability of the ELM. They tell the principals' stories in managing their accountabilities for performance results. Principals with the capital 'P' indicate the Principals partaking in my study (Norris, 2017). All references to principals indicate principals or school leaders in general. Chapter 6 presents the Principals' interpretations of their accountabilities with Chapter 7 extending the ways the Principals enact these interpretations.

Given these applications, Chapters 8 and 9 compare the extant literatures and align the three theoretical lenses. In Chapter 8 school leaders' sensemaking is examined; the ways they interpret external demands; the ways they lead teaching and learning; and the influences on school leaders' interpretations in their leading of teaching and learning. Chapter 9 explores the notion of school leaders being key agents in enacting their external demands. Three sensegiving tasks which enable their agency are: composing persuasive accounts; facilitating teaching and learning systems; and creating coherence in their communities.

In episodes where school leaders are faced with an external demand such as a demand for favourable student results the following factors are likely to influence their interpretation of events:

1. World views about what learning represents and how that learning is measured.
2. Knowledge and skill base in teaching and learning.
3. Levels of self-efficacy in teaching and learning processes.
4. Levels of self-efficacy in influencing teachers and their teaching.
5. Career stages and historical pathways in educational leadership; and
6. Professional identities as leaders.

The final chapter tests the ELM's capacity. Chapter 10 begins with a hypothetical case in teasing out its applicability to the model. The underpinnings of the ELM with its application of the Principals' stories and the hypothetical case propose that effective school leaders are agile and adaptable. The metaphor of the Eucalyptus tree is introduced here to represent a school leader's adaptability to their environment. The metaphor points to several recommendations for school leaders and those conducting school leader formation and tertiary programs.

Acknowledgments

First and foremost, I wish to acknowledge the First Nation peoples of Australia who over the thousands of years have had and continue to hold a deep spirituality and 'dialogue' with the land. Of note are the Aboriginal stories and their different meanings of trees on 'Country' (Arnold, Atchison, & McKnight, 2021). Pertinent to this book is the Eucalyptus tree and its special place in the Australian Indigenous peoples' way of being (Gifford, 2010). Judith Wright is one of Australia's most esteemed poets. Her poem 'The Eucalypt and the National Character' aligns with the major themes in this book (Wright, 2016). Excerpts from the poem are courtesy of and permission from HarperCollins Publishers Australia Pty Ltd.

This book is based on my dissertation, *From Metaphors to Mantras— Principals Making Sense of and Integrating Accountability Expectations: A Grounded Theoretical Model* (Norris, 2017). The principals interviewed were frank, honest, and trusting. I thank them for their willingness and commitment in contributing to such important perspectives about their work. I trust that the model developed here reflects their experiences, and I hope that it helps to support other principals, aspirant school leaders and teachers.

Week by week writing sessions and annual retreats have kept me focussed and on track. So, I thank my consistent writing buddy and generous colleague Dr Tonya Rooney, along with her daughter Tilda for the figures in the book.

The cover image "Heart of the Alpine" is taken by Australian artist Scott Leggo. It is an "eucalyptus pauciflora," a snow gum, which dominates sub-alpine woodlands, mountains of the south eastern Australian mainland, at the altitudinal limit to tree growth. Forests and woodlands of snow gums can look uniform from a distance, but they have unique characters.

The publishing team at Brill has also been generous and supportive to me as an early career writer. They have provided support and encouragement all along the way, even when there have been hardships in their own regions during our pandemic, 2020–22.

I thank my family, Connie and Jia Li for their support and wisdom.

Illustrations

Figures

1 Mud map of the interaction between sensemaking and sensegiving in a school context (adapted from Maitlis & Lawrence, 2007). 10
2 The Eucalypt Leadership Model (ELM). 21
3 Processes involved in the initiation of a strategic change (from Gioia & Chittipeddi, 1991, p. 444). 30
4 The critical role of moderators in leaders' sensegiving (from Kraft, Sparr, & Peus, 2015, p. 310). 34
5 Moderating forces in educational leaders' sensegiving practices (adapted from Kraft et al., 2015, p. 310). 34
6 Ajzen's Theory of Planned Behaviour (TPB) (from Ajzen & Fishbein, 1980). 42
7 Integration of sensemaking, TPB and sensegiving. 47
8 The shifting balance in the role of the secondary school principal. 70
9 Principals' interpretations of their accountability expectations. 102
10 Linking views: Beliefs about learning, purpose of schooling and objects of account. 111
11 Principals' criticisms of their accountability mechanisms. 114
12 Self-efficacy levels in meeting dual expectations. 124
13 Framing educational accountability. 132
14 Principals making sense of accountability. 133
15 Principals' agency in managing accountability. 136
16 Principals giving sense to accountability. 157
17 A sample in the cycle of a school leader's sensegiving practices. 188
18 School leaders' sensegiving acts and moderators (adapted from Kraft et al., 2015). 207
19 Snow gums, snowy mountains, Australia (contributor David Bigwood, Alamy, https://www.alamy.com/search/imageresults.aspx?imgt=0&qt=Snow+gums+david, used with permission). 229

Tables

1 Theory of planned behaviour authenticating sensemaking and sensegiving. 20
2 Aligning Weick's sensemaking properties with educational leaders' accountabilities. 27

3	Literature, sensemaking, sensegiving and the TPB. 49
4	Typology of accountabilities in education. 86
5	School leaders enacting educational accountability. 89
6	Representing the objects of account. 108
7	Subjects of the account: Frequency and excerpts. 113
8	Summary of principals' educational accountability: To whom, what and how. 123
9	Leaders' metaphors, mantras and narratives. 137
10	Diverging views: Building credibility with teams. 144
11	Relationship between principals' understandings of accountability and their practices. 158
12	Summary of findings. 162
13	Aligning Weick's sensemaking properties with leadership examples. 175
14	Application of the TPB to case examples. 212
15	Examples of the impact of leaders' sensemaking on sensegiving practices. 216

Memos

1	The descriptive story. 14
2	Making sense of accountability demands. 15
3	Julie, the Juggler and Charmaine, the Cheerleader: Differences. Why? 104
4	Beliefs about learning, post school and accountability. 111
5	Numbers on a page: Faces on results link with faces on data? 117
6	Peer relationships. 118
7	Faces on data: Faces on results. 129
8	Constructing cognitive schemata. 131
9	The power of influence for the right reasons. 154

Abbreviations

ACARA	Australian Curriculum, Assessment and Reporting Authority
AIS NSW	Association of Independent Schools of New South Wales
AITSL	Australian Institute for Teaching and School Leadership
ATAR	Australian Tertiary Admission Rank
CEO	Catholic Education Office
COAG	Council of Australian Governments
ECP	early-career principal
ECDF	Every Child Deserves a Future
ELM	Eucalypt Leadership Model
GT	grounded theory
HSC	higher school certificate
ICSEA	Index of Community Socio-educational Advantage
KLA	key learning area
LCP	later-career principal
MCP	middle-career principal
NAPLAN	National Assessment Program—Literacy and Numeracy
NESA	NSW Education Standards Authority
NSW	New South Wales
OECD	Organisation for Economic Co-operation and Development
PBMS	performance-based mechanisms
PISA	Program for International Student Assessment
SMART	School Measurement, Assessment and Reporting Toolkit
TALIS	Teaching and Learning International Survey
TPB	Theory of Planned Behaviour
UK	United Kingdom
UNSW	University of New South Wales
USA	United States of America

About the Author

Judith Norris
is a senior lecturer in educational leadership studies at Australian Catholic University, Australia. She has been a school practitioner with 30 years' experience as a teacher in primary and secondary schools, faculty coordinator, assistant principal, campus head, principal, and senior school system advisor. Judith continues her work in Australian schools and school systems when they are facing critical events and major structural changes.

The inspiration for this book was derived from Judith's professional interests in the ways school leaders manage their external demands, particularly when these demands compromise their own professional beliefs and internal school commitments.

CHAPTER 1

All in the Same Field

There have been many moments of excitement as a teacher leader when I have been working with school leaders and aspirant ones in their post graduate tertiary studies. One of these moments has been students' high levels of engagement with conceptual frameworks and models. I too, have found frameworks to serve as anchors, particularly to ground my own leadership decisions. They offer a lifeboat in somewhat treacherous seas. Additionally, my excitement has been the keenness of students, once realising that there is no silver bullet to their leadership endeavours, to embrace theoretical ideas that may help them identify their problem and apply a framework to create resolutions to such challenges. Several theoretical ideas, what I term frames, are the works by Weick (1995), Gioia and Chittipeddi (1991) and Ajzen (1991). Over recent years I have learned from my students about the ways they engage with these theorists. Students are now finding theories such as sensemaking particularly helpful for their leadership cognition and practice. This book attempts to bring together the work of these theorists to create a theoretical model that has practical applications for school leaders in a variety of contexts. Never have school leaders, with their complexities, uncertainty and increasing demands, more needed a framework to create order out of very fluid environments. Outside of collective teacher efficacy (Donohoo et al., 2020), the practices of school leaders are the second most influential in-school determinant for student achievement (Hattie, 2015). School leaders' work is essential.

An intriguing observation about school leaders' work is their way of adapting to new demands. Some leaders are active agents in making sense of these demands. They reflect on previous experiences, evaluate the consequences of their future actions, and simultaneously integrate these demands within their own school contexts. The observation of these school leaders' agility in sometimes adverse conditions is inspirational, to say the least.

For school leaders to adapt to new demands they need to make sense of them, particularly when they are conflicting. School leaders' work is relational (Branson & Marra, 2019; Sanders, 2018; Smit & Mabusela, 2019). Their sensemaking occurs within a social context (Weick, 1995). Sensible meanings tend to be those for which there is 'social support, consensual validation, and shared relevance' (Weick, 2001, p. 461). Once sense has been made, the leader needs to give this sense to the different social groups in the community. This sensegiving is a back and forth process (Gioia and Chittipeddi (1991). As simple as this

© KONINKLIJKE BRILL NV, LEIDEN, 2022 | DOI:10.1163/9789004517202_001

may sound, it is a complex social process of influence (Bush, 2003). This is a process in which school leaders can achieve various levels of effectiveness.

This book centres around this complex social process. It builds a theoretical model from a different perspective to understand how school leaders may react to conflicting expectations and demands. It incorporates the theoretical understandings of the two psycho-social processes of sensemaking (Weick, 1995) and sensegiving (Gioia & Chittipeddi, 1991) along with the Theory of Planned Behaviour (TPB) (Ajzen, 1991). The Eucalypt Leadership Model (ELM) offers a pathway to help school leaders, aspirants and teacher leaders manage the increasing and sometimes volatile demands of their work. Metaphors and narratives as sensemaking devices are employed intermittently. This introductory chapter describes the need, purpose and aim of the book. The Eucalyptus tree, with its reciprocal relationship with Australian Indigenous peoples, is presented as a metaphor for school leaders at the end of the chapter.

1 The Need for This Book

There is widespread concern about school leaders in the challenges they face. In Australia, for example, there is an escalating disquiet about school leaders' deteriorating mental and emotional health. "An alarming percentage of school leaders (83 in 100) continue to be subjected to at least one form of offensive behaviour in the last 12 months" (Riley, See, Marsh, & Dicke, 2021, p. 7). This recent study, along with studies by Earp and Riley (2018) and Riley (2019), found that school leaders are increasingly at risk of violence, burnout, stress and self-harm. The book does not diminish school leaders' risks in their role. Instead, it offers understandings and a framework through such risks. Moreover, they are facing escalating levels of accountability which seem to be a 'stubborn one-way direction flow' (Henebery, 2021). These challenges for school leaders are significant. There is a timely need here.

2 Purpose and Aims

The book proposes a model of how school leaders manage the demanding and often contradictory circumstances. For example, leaders need to manage expectations for high student scores, while honouring the learning growth of students with low scores. Apart from managing such a contradiction, they are committed to meeting their professional moral and ethical beliefs (Shipps, 2012), to empower students and staff in their joy of learning. While the ELM is theoretical, there is a practical application of principals' experiences from the context of two school systems. The ELM demonstrates several moderating factors which may impact how school leaders manage these competing demands. These factors include school leaders' levels of self-efficacy to influence teaching practices and their credibility with teachers.

The aim of this book is to offer possibilities in adverse conditions for school leaders, aspirant school leaders and those who prepare their professional programs. Over the last decade, the school leader's role and notably their functions have lost some appeal. High velocity events, including the consequences of the COVID-19 pandemic, have certainly prompted many aspirant leaders to rethink the next steps in their career. High velocity events are increasing in schools where information is often ambiguous and unclear, and normal approaches no longer work (Salicru, 2018). In 2020–21, home learning and precarious security in future routines hampered school leaders' practices. The toll on all educators at the time was significant. Included in this toll was the school leader. They continue with "diminishing resources and support, greater pressure to deliver academic excellence, and increasingly complex technologies" (Hasinoff & Mandzuk, 2018, p. 19).

Teachers observing the principal's current role and its complex demands see first-hand the weariness and sheer exhaustion of their leader. Late nights, parental complaints, litigation, and staff resistance all lead to many hours of work. "School leaders continue to work long hours, working an average of 54.5 hours per week, over the 14 hours longer than the standard 40-hour workweek" (Riley et al., 2021, p. 6). Teachers observing the principal's current role demands, seriously question whether to further pursue their leadership career pathways.

However, the role of the school leader has never been so critical for student success. Empirical research into effective leadership by district and school system leaders now informs system wide strategic directions in ways to lead (Australian Institute for Teaching and School Leadership (AITSL), 2017; Kenneth Leithwood, Sun, & Mccullough, 2019). School leaders are pressured. They are accountable for employing data informed practices with prescribed and nuanced ways to lead (Holloway, Nielsen, & Saltmarsh, 2018). School leaders are expected to act upon their school system's research trends. For example, research on collective teacher efficacy (CTE) as now the most influential in-school determinant of student achievement (Hoogsteen, 2020), compels school leaders to be skilled in facilitating positive team cultures to bring about higher levels of CTE. This includes leaders knowing how to set up teams and manage them when they break down (Thessin & Louis, 2020).

In a broad sense, school leaders are responsible for fostering positive, inclusive, and caring cultures (McMillan, 2020; Ryu, Walls, & Seashore Louis, 2020).

They are expected to create highly effective data teams (Wayman, Midgley, & Stringfield, 2017). Developing a common vision and shared purpose with teaching teams is also crucial. Moreover, school leaders need to 'know' their teachers. Empathy, mutuality and emotional reciprocal relationships for developing teachers' agency are common competencies for school leaders across the globe (Qian & Walker, 2021). Understandably, knowledge of their teachers' motivations and needs is pivotal in a school leader's ability to influence teaching practices.

The principal's role has changed. No longer are they the administrator, facilities, or business manager. The principal is the lead in teaching and learning (McMillan, 2020). To be successful, Bush argues they need to be "increasingly focused on learning" as the core purpose of the educational enterprise (Tony Bush, 2019, p. 13). They are held accountable for student results. These results depend on their teachers' agency. Hence, school leaders need to be credible to influence teaching practices. Building credibility, while a complex responsibility, requires the school leader to know about and be skilled in teaching and learning processes. School leaders may feel isolated and vulnerable in the face of these expectations (Du Plessis, 2017). The theoretical components of the ELM presented in this book are useful frames in navigating these multi-faceted challenges. The ELM has the potential to strengthen school leaders in their effectiveness in managing the challenges, but also for their own professional growth as leaders. Self-investigation is essential in the fluctuating world of school leadership (Brazer, 2019). The growth in becoming aware of how school leaders engage in sensemaking within, and importantly, how sensegiving in its potential for social reciprocity can be a powerful and authentic influence for change. While the ELM is theoretical, the application in Chapters 6 and 7 provides examples of Principals' reactions (Norris, 2017) to external demands. The chapters are in essence theory in practice.

These reactions to external demands in the Principals' experiences are in line with other researchers, including Spillane, Shipps and White. Spillane (2002) found that school leaders adopted, adjusted, or ignored expectations. The Shipps and White (2009) study found that some of their principals were disappointed when their professional beliefs were compromised in highly regulated regimes aiming for top grades. The Principals' sensemaking in the book's examples also aligns with other research, such as Ganon-Shilon and Schechter (2019b) and Kruse (2019). It is here that the ELM is reflected in its application. There were distinct characteristics of those Principals who appeared to be flourishing and adapting well. Even when the odds were against them, they faced the 'new' demands with confidence in their tough school conditions with tight regulatory external expectations in competitive demographics.

3 Metaphors

Metaphors are employed on several levels in this book. They are used as a sense-making device for the psycho-social processes of school leaders in general, in the ELM and, for the two cohorts of principals. Weick (1989) himself points out that representations such as metaphors in middle range theories "are inevitable, given the complexity of the subject matter" (p. 516). School leaders spontaneously draw on metaphors about themselves when making sense of events (Kihlberg & Lindberg, 2021). Leaders when adopting metaphors are, albeit possibly unconsciously, developing their social identity (Ganon-Shilon & Schechter, 2017). School leaders developing their metaphors do so in context, and the metaphors emerge as a way to manage complex situations. Panzer (1989) purports that the metaphor is so powerful that individuals may become their metaphor. As a therapeutic sensemaking device, metaphors may enable individuals to reconcile contradictory or "stuck situations" (Nardon & Hari, 2021).

However, the name of the metaphor itself is only a signal of its meaning. A metaphor can hold multiple meanings. The narrative or story about an individual's chosen metaphor is more beneficial than the name of the metaphor itself. The application of the ELM with Principals' experiences utilises metaphors for each Principal. More broadly, this book concludes with drawing on the Eucalyptus tree as a metaphor for school leaders. The narrative presented about the Eucalyptus describes how the tree's characteristics have much in common with school leaders as they exist interdependently within their environments. Australia's harsh climate and arid conditions holds many challenges to the Eucalyptus trees, and there are distinct similarities in the context in which school leaders are now working.

4 Ecology and the Human Condition

Australia is not the only country where a tree holds an emotional significance. The Cherry Blossom tree in Japan, the Witch tree in the Netherlands, the Ginkgo tree in China and the Maple tree in Canada—all have their significance not only for the tree itself, but also for the tree's relationship with its ecology, with other flora and fauna, and, above all, with the people.

Judith Wright, a well-known Australian poet, wrote the poem 'Eucalypt and the National Character' (Wright, 2016). Judith may not have recognised the continued importance of this poem for our ecology. She may not have realised its importance for the reciprocal relationship between Eucalyptus trees and cultures of our Australian indigenous peoples. Gifford (2010) in his critique of the poem points to the determination of the poem. The malleability of the Eucalyptus signifies a way of life with the conditions of the continent, which Aboriginal culture has already made effective, with the evidence of our need to live and lead with our developing planetary conditions (Gifford, 2010). Importantly for this book, Judith may also not have known her portrayal of the Eucalyptus would be utilised in depicting the essence of a school leader's character and context today.

5 The Eucalyptus Tree—Its Attraction

The attraction of the Eucalyptus to the general Australian is their mysterious recovery and beauty after bush fires. Rich, vivid green and tender shoots emerge contrasting their blackened trunks, amassing multiple gums across saddles in mountainous wild bushlands. The Eucalyptus is also appreciated for their diversity in species, their glistening leaves in the often-harsh Australian sun, the shade and respite they bring, and for children, the offering of the gum nut, leaves and branches for their play.

There are over 800 species of eucalyptus trees (Australian Government National Parks, 2009). The trees grow in their natural habitat in many climatic conditions. Named by a French botanist, the word Eucalyptus, from the Greek, *eu*, means well, and *calyptos* meaning covered (Brooker, 2002).

6 Australian Indigenous Peoples' Reciprocity with Trees

Some Indigenous peoples maintain that there is a deep reciprocal relationship between humans and trees and that relationship impacts an individual's wellbeing. "Yuin ontologies assert trees and humans are actors in the world, but who are constantly and always in reciprocal relationships with all beings" (Arnold et al., 2021, p. 132). Reciprocity is central. This reciprocity is expressed through the extension of the body, connecting in a physical and spiritual sense with trees. School leaders hold emotional, physical, and spiritual connection to their communities. Uncle Max (elder from Yuin Country) compares trees to people to highlight their similarities—how trees need other trees, just as leaders need other leaders to support their growth. The school leader's identity shapes their community. Ideally, and in turn, with an ethos of reciprocity the community shapes the leader's identity; they cannot be separated. This is a reciprocal relationship.

7 Going Forward

Chapter 2 presents the theoretical ELM that acknowledges the necessity of reciprocal relationships in school leadership. Often obscure, school leaders' psycho-social processes of sensemaking and sensegiving, along with the TPB, are theoretically embedded in their work with their school communities. These processes are ideal for school leaders who are in constant relationships of influence with multiple social groups in their school communities.

The propositions on which the ELM is based contribute to the study of the cognition and behaviour of school leaders. Although these contributions are theoretical, the applications of the two cohorts of school leaders attempt to demonstrate the capacity of the ELM. In its practical application it offers likely moderating factors. The reader is invited to engage critically with the proposals. The lenses used for this theoretical ELM may not align with some researchers in the discipline of educational leadership. However, an insight by Johnson and Kruse (2019) provides wisdom in the importance of diversity to promote the discipline. At the risk of mixing analytics here, this chapter closes with their insight about appreciating diversity: "Individuals are at work in different parts of the educational field. Some are planting, some are watering, while others are harvesting or enriching the quality of the soil—all in the same field" (Johnson & Kruse, 2019, pp. 8–9). The reader is invited to engage critically with the ELM and make their decision as to what work in the field the ELM contributes to, and at the same time hopefully crystallising their own thoughts about school leadership.

CHAPTER 2

Problem, Trigger, Conjectures

> The quality of theory produced is predicted to vary due to the accuracy and detail present in the problem statement that triggers theory building, the number of and independence among the conjectures that attempt to solve the problem, and the number and diversity of selection criteria used to test the conjectures.
>
> WEICK (1989, p. 516)

∴

Chapter 1 presented multiple challenges facing school leaders in our current times. The problem here is how leaders manage their challenges. We need models or frameworks to help school leaders. This is the 'trigger' for this theory construction. The conjectures are situated within several other theoretical premises: sensemaking, sensegiving and Theory of Planned Behaviour. This theoretical Eucalypt Leadership Model (ELM) is deliberately dissociated from a validation process. Based on Weick's (1989) argument, "we cannot improve the theorizing process until we describe it more explicitly, operate it more self-consciously, and decouple it from validation more deliberately" (p. 516).

This current chapter presents the ELM which explains how school leaders make sense of external demands, and how they provide sense to their communities about those demands. It starts with a brief introduction to the theories behind sensemaking and sensegiving, with a mud map showing how they could intersect (Figure 1). This is followed by the rationale for including and applying the Theory of Planned Behaviour (TPB) (Ajzen, 1991). The rest of the chapter takes the reader through the genesis of the ELM to the core categories and subprocesses. The chapter concludes with a justification of the relationship between sensemaking and sensegiving through the TPB (Table 1), followed by an illustrated figure of the ELM itself (Figure 2). Since this theory has an interpretative aspect of its genesis, the first person is appropriated in the relevant sections.

© KONINKLIJKE BRILL NV, LEIDEN, 2022 | DOI:10.1163/9789004517202_002

1 The Underpinnings of the Model

In the school community, the school leader relies on teachers to achieve student success. Therefore, the way a school leader makes sense of external demands must be credible, especially from the perception of their teaching teams. Both sensemaking and sensegiving are processes that leaders engage consistently, sometimes with little consciousness, yet more often when faced with complex and high velocity environments their processes are deliberate; disseminating new understandings to the community to influence their 'sensemaking-for-self' (Eisenhardt, 1989) "The basic idea of sensemaking is that reality is an ongoing accomplishment that emerges from efforts to create order and make retrospective sense of what occurs" (Weick, 1993, p. 635). Sensemaking, as originally theorised by Weick, describes it as a process in which the individual develops a new reality of the event, they are trying to make sense of (Weick, 1995). Sensemaking is a cognitive act (Maitlis & Christianson, 2014). When a school leader articulates or acts upon their sensemaking to the community it is a sensegiving act. Sensegiving is an act of translation by the leader to the community (Gioia & Chittipeddi, 1991). A school leader's sensemaking, which progresses to a sensegiving act to the community, is an iterative process. Optimistically, the process does not end at this point. The community engages with the school leader's sensegiving with their own sensemaking. In turn, the community gives meaning to the leader again. This giving sense back is also an act of translation by the community members (Maitlis & Christianson, 2014). Hopefully, and in exchange, the school leader is responsive to the community's sensegiving. Ideally, the school leader will make amends or adjust their own sensemaking. This description of sensemaking and sensegiving briefly describes the relationship between the two processes that underpin part of the theoretical ELM. Figure 1 is a simple mud map illustrating the interactive relationship between the two. Although there is some coverage of sensemaking and sensegiving below, Chapter 3 explains in more detail the theoretical components of both processes.

Making and giving sense can be examined through several theoretical premises. Karl Weick (1995) proposes seven properties to examine how individuals can make sense of events. Gioia and Chittipeddi (1991) propose four phases in the sensegiving process. Sensemaking and sensegiving are often unconscious acts (Maitlis & Christianson, 2014). Yet they are made visible when individuals are interrupted in their unconscious sensemaking and sensegiving, when they cannot create order or when routines or approaches no longer work. High velocity events are understandably ones which precipitate overt sensemaking

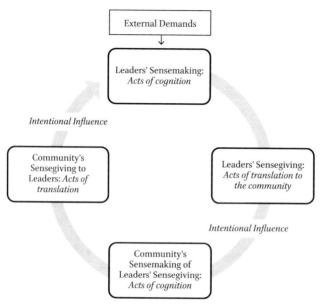

FIGURE 1   Mud map of the interaction between sensemaking and sensegiving in a school context (adapted from Maitlis & Lawrence, 2007)

and sensegiving for school leaders. However, persistent, and conflicting external demands may also be triggers.

Sensemaking is triggered when there are perceived or anticipated gaps in their sensemaking (Maitlis & Lawrence, 2007). These processes are deliberate to disseminate new understandings to the community to influence the community's own 'sensemaking-for-self' (Eisenhardt, 1989). "Sensemaking as a cognitive phenomenon is an everyday occurrence that happens inside an individual's head when they 'make sense' of something" (Giuliani, 2016, p. 4). Sensemaking, as an act of cognition, is a common event, but from a theoretical perspective, it is more complex (Weick, Sutcliffe, & Obstfeld, 2005). First, sensemaking is more than understanding or interpretation. The individual actively plays a role in assembling a new reality from the event they are trying to make sense of (Weick, 1995). Second, a school leader's sensemaking occurs as an interplay with the community (Snook, 2011). It includes sensemaking at the relational group and societal levels of meaning. School communities, as relational groups, are making-meaning microcosms in themselves. School microcosms often reflect broader society. Sensemaking in school communities therefore seeks meaning with substantial layers of interaction. While sensemaking can be covert, sensegiving is overt.

Sensegiving practices are "the symbolic constructions used to create meaning for others (i.e., to give sense)" (Gioia & Chittipeddi, 1991, p. 448). Sensegiving

PROBLEM, TRIGGER, CONJECTURES

acts are the visibility of a school leader's cognition in their own sensemaking. The potency of a school leader's sensegiving will influence community members in their own sensemaking. As such, sensegiving acts can be considered political and influential processes (Maitlis & Lawrence, 2007). More detailed explanations of sensemaking and sensegiving as influential processes are found in the following chapter.

What is relevant here is that the sensemaking of the school leader must be meaningful to the community, especially when complex events occur in the school environment. Such environments, now common in schools and school systems world-wide, are 'hypercompetitive' due to rapid and continual changing expectations (Salicru, 2018, p. 130). Individuals may feel frustrated, anxious, or confused when routines, successful structures and processes no longer meet the needs of the present condition.

The ELM on which this book is based proposes how school leaders make sense of these conditions in the face of contradictory conditions, and how their 'sensemaking-for-self' can be translated into acts of self-giving for others. Hence, it is possible that from sensemaking to sensegiving, there is an intentionality of influence. The relationship also involves the school leader's decision-making and action. A well-recognised theory that supports the theoretical relationship of an individual's decision-making and action is Ajzen's Theory of Planned Behaviour (TPB) (2012). Ajzen and Fishbein (1980) examined this relationship to understand the key determinants of behaviour. If intentions influence behaviour (Ajzen, 2012), an individual's intention is a precursor for their behaviour (Ajzen, 1991). These intentions are based on three conceptually independent determinants (Ajzen, 2012): attitude, subjective norm, and perceived control (Ajzen, 1991). In varying contexts, these three determinants are the predominant influence on an individual's intention. Chapter 3 provides the detail about these determinants.

2 The Theoretical Model

2.1 *Overview*

> ... the final theory is a representation of both participant and researcher. Another individual could take the same data and by placing a different emphasis on the data to construct a different theory ..., however this emphasis does not lessen the theory's contribution. ... whatever theory is produced provides another insight and understanding. (Corbin & Strauss, 2014, p. 29)

The Eucalypt Leadership Model fulfills one of the purposes of this book, creating a theory that provides answers to the "what, how, when, where, and why of something" (Corbin & Strauss, 2008, p. 55). The ELM positions and describes the relationships between sensemaking and sensegiving for school leaders. It explains how school leaders may interpret their policy expectations. These interpretations are likely to affect their intentions when implementing external demands, under certain conditions. The intentions and enactments of school leaders are aligned with the Theory of Planned Behaviour (Ajzen, 1991). The organising scaffold of the ELM adopts the terminology from Straussian grounded theory (Corbin & Strauss, 2014). Terms including core category and sub processes are the various components of the ELM. Core category means a substantial recurring idea. Sub-processes of the core category mean the important elements that build the core category.

The theoretical components of the ELM are substantive. They are considered the probable experiences of school leaders in the context of administrative and regulatory school systems. An example of a comparable leadership experience would be where school leaders, who are ultimately responsible for making sense of policy expectations, also have the responsibility to make decisions about how to implement policy in their school communities. Formal theory, which is different from substantive theory, is developed from the investigation of a phenomenon, as in these examples of educational responsibility, in various situations in which theory may have a broader application (Corbin & Strauss, 2014; Strauss & Corbin, 1990, 1998). As such, this theoretical ELM is described as substantive, not formal.

Comparing the existing literature with the applications of Principals' experiences with the ELM (Chapters 7 and 8), these cohorts of Principals have much in common with other senior school leaders. Moreover, principals devolve their tasks to other senior leaders: "I leave it to them, they know more about it than I do" (Principal). Therefore, this ELM uses the term school leaders, which also includes principals. In the development of this theoretical ELM pejorative terms are adopted, including educational responsibility, capturing the nuances of it, and yet coined as external demands.

The two major components that describe school leaders' engagement with external expectations are making sense and giving sense. These components are the two core categories. They represent school leaders' likely interpretations and descriptions of their professional practices in their responses to external demands, respectively.

The applications in Chapters 5 and 6 indicate that school leaders may understand their external demands in their unique ways, which influence the ways they explain themselves at 'their best' in their leadership practices. They are making sense of their external expectations. Their interpretation of their school environments and the priorities and constraints they give to one expectation over the other are influenced by their previous leadership experiences, beliefs in teaching and learning, their expectations of students, their self-efficacy in mobilising their teaching teams, and their peer-leader networks and relationships with the school system. Theoretically, their interpretations are described as making sense of their external demands. Weick's (1995) sensemaking properties closely align with a school leader's likely ways of interpreting external expectations. The process of making sense influences their intentions. Their intentions to act vary. These may range from pursuing a moral purpose to coherence in their school communities, including reconciling external demands with internal obligations. Importantly, the enacted intentions are to give sense to the community, in this instance, their external demands.

Theoretically, school leaders' practices in response to their own sensemaking can be described as sensegiving. Chapter 9, through a hypothetical case, teases out in a practical sense, the theoretical relationship between school leaders' interpretations of their intentions and resultant behaviours. The theoretical relationship aligns with Ajzen's (2012) determinants of behaviours. Understandably, school leaders vary in their ability to make sense and give sense to expectations simultaneously, as well as meeting internal commitments and agendas. However, I propose there are probable commonalities in the relationships between school leaders' sensemaking and sensegiving in their ability to manage external demands and meet their internal commitments.

2.2 *Genesis*

My interpretations underpin the emergence of this theoretical ELM. It is not unusual for a theory to have a story. In this theory, the descriptive story emerged mysteriously and compellingly early, as if it had to be remembered.

2.2.1 The Descriptive Story

I was immersed in the data for some time before asking myself some broader questions: What jumps out of the page? What comes through the data, even if not directly (Corbin & Strauss, 2008)? I use the descriptive story technique guided by Strauss & Corbin (1990) to capture the highlights. Memo 1 tracks my thought processes, where I create a metaphor to explain the processes I experience in my observations. The Eucalyptus tree emerges, representing images of adaptability and durability in a school leader's experience of interacting with their external environments.

Memo 1: The descriptive story

One striking and consistent thread that knits together variations of a school leader's experience of their external demands is their adaptive process. Their adaptive processes suggest they are active agents in making sense of the expectations, evaluating the consequences of their future actions, and sometimes simultaneously integrating their environments with these expectations. Their adaptability reminds me of the big Australian Eucalyptus tree in both its hardiness and beauty, as the tree's organic nature adapts to the regularity of the weather and seasons as well as to the irregularity of fire, drought and flood intrusions. The Eucalyptus, as if recognising and absorbing changes, evolves in its structure, bending and twisting, at times seeping and yet shooting out tendrils to ensure its growth. Mysteriously, yet assumedly, the ways in which the Eucalyptus adapts is unique, even though the surrounding eucalypts may have been planted at the same time, near and in the same bushland. The Eucalypt, like most large trees in the Australian landscape, have interconnectedness that is not readily visible. The roots of large trees are so interconnected that damaging one tree may impact on another. Like the underground interconnectedness of the eucalypts, school leaders are interconnected with each other in making sense of external demands.

Integrating, according to Strauss and Corbin (1990, 1998), is making a choice for a core category followed by developing the story around this and using the categories and concepts that are emerging. This descriptive story assisted me to integrate the main components into a "unified theoretical explanation" (Corbin & Strauss, 2008, p. 107). Namely the core category of sensemaking.

However, the descriptive story only captures part of my thinking. What is not represented here are the art forms that are at play when some school leaders may integrate demands seamlessly. They absorb their external expectations within their existing school structures, their teaching and learning goals and their broader agendas. Moreover, the effective school leader stresses the importance of understanding teaching and learning and 'knowing' their teachers. They have high expectations of teachers' and students' capabilities, finding perspective and balance about the priorities from external demands, and always honouring the learning story. These school leaders are likely to integrate the external demands with their internal commitments effortlessly. As I compare this ELM to the literature, I find parallels with other research about this apparent seamless and effortless integration. Carnoy, Elmore, and Siskin (2003) and Elmore (2005), along with Roche (2004), found that schools with weak or non-existent internal school based processes are unlikely to be able to respond in a coherent way with external demands. I would add here that if the internal processes were not designed or agreed by teachers this hinders the success of such an alignment. Thus, school leaders who develop shared, collective, and agreed internal processes and systems are likely to be able to give sense to the external expectations incorporating, even advancing, their internal school commitments.

Making sense and Giving sense hold explanations for school leaders' interpretations of their expectations and the ways these interpretations influence their leadership practices. The analyst should also 'find references in the data' to reflect the central elements, along with their properties (p. 111). When Owen the Principal reported a 'making sense' it triggered my thinking about 'Making sense' as a key element (see Memo 2 below). Making sense was initially selected as central because it was difficult to ignore. Similarly, Glaser (1992) discovered that at times, words can leap out from the page and as coding continues, become difficult to ignore. This Principal's views initially triggered my thinking about school leaders engaging in processes of adaptability: '… I think it's a personal thing how you see accountability … I think if you have an understanding of what you're about yourself as a principal and what's your agenda, then you can somehow frame accountability to make sense of it ….'

Memo 2: Making sense of accountability demands

Since my interview with Owen, I wonder about his ideas about making sense of accountability. When I read and reread his text data, making sense continues to stay with me. It is difficult to ignore. His ideas encourage me to source studies around sensemaking. There is a whole body of literature around sensemaking. It is now difficult to block this idea of sensemaking out as I continue to analyse the data: I am afraid that I am experiencing my own sensemaking as I analyse!

However, Sensegiving as a grouping concept arrived later. Conceptualising sensegiving emerged through this book. Part of this larger concept of sensegiving was 'integrating.' The term 'integrating' is an overt action of a school leader, where they implement all or part of an external demand to meet their school's internal goals. Because the act is overt and in a school context, carried out with others, it is reasonable to judge it as an act of sensegiving. Its alignment with sensemaking holds an appeal. It aligns well with Weick's sensemaking, and the phases of sensegiving work well in school communities, whereby the school leader to enable their leadership—is in and depends on social relationships with others. Sensegiving is revealing. The act captures the actual leadership practices, and if authentic, reflects the school leader's own sensemaking. Sensegiving crystallised my thinking and its usefulness in the ELM and had begun to make sense.

Hence Giving sense is adopted as Core Category 2 because of its capacity to demonstrate the task before school leaders whereby their sensemaking of their external demands, are overtly acted upon; through their discursive skills they devise and articulate persuasive accounts, facilitating school processes and structures in response. A sensegiving act does not necessarily need to be an agent of change, for example it can be as simple as making sure that the external expectations do not create another layer of 'busy work' for teachers. From an educational leadership lens Giving sense involves the school leader making visible their own sensemaking in the relational cycle to the school community. In high volatility and complex environments, the purpose of giving sense is to manage disruptive events for the community. The disruption for example could be high stakes accountability; the sensegiving acts aim to influence and persuade teaching teams to make sense of the expectations and make decisions to act (see Table 1). Like the Eucalyptus, school leaders adapt their interpretations of external demands where their actual form is changed.

The next two sections explain the core categories and the theoretical subprocesses in more detail.

3 Core Category 1: Making Sense

3.1 *Description*

Making sense of external expectations is defined as the process where school leaders take notice and make meaning of pertinent factors in their school environments, prioritising certain expectations over others, constraining external influences, and settling on frames in which to act upon, in response to external demands. This process of Making sense considers who the leaders are; their beliefs about schooling, which are influenced in turn by their beliefs about teaching and learning. While school leaders interpret their expectations in different ways, their common experience is their adaptive processes in interpreting their expectations.

3.2 *Explanation*

Making sense is adopted because of its power to integrate school leaders' experiences of external demands (Corbin & Strauss, 2008). Weick's properties,

PROBLEM, TRIGGER, CONJECTURES   17

along with those of other scholars (Dunford & Jones, 2000; Helms Mills, Thurlow, & Mills, 2010; Watson, 1995) contribute to the processes and are applied here because of their explanatory and integrative power (Corbin & Strauss, 2014).

The phenomenon of school leaders *making sense* of external demands occurs through three sub-processes:

- *Contextualising external expectations* is the process where school leaders take notice of factors over others in their school environments, given their interpretations of policy expectations such as enrolments, performance results, discursive competition, student demographics, teacher receptivity or parental and school systems' expectations. Weick's properties of 'social context' (Weick, 1995) aligns with the process of *Contextualising,* whereby educational leaders seek support and consensual validation and relevance with their school communities about the policy expectations. The validation and relevance for members in the community act as social anchors. The process of *Contextualising* is also historical in nature. School leaders, like the principals' stories (see Chapter 6 for the application), look to the past to make sense of present events in a way that is like Weick's explanation of the 'retrospect' property. Weick asserts that retrospect is weakened when individuals do not appreciate or recall the past (Weick, 2001). Notably, school leaders are likely to draw upon empirical and historical data from local and global peers about similar policy expectations, such as the consequences of high-stakes national testing. There is a strong likelihood that when external expectations jeopardise or compromise school leaders' beliefs about learning, such as a number not being an adequate measure in the representation of learning, policy interpretations will not be interpreted as the policy makers may intend. One influence that fuels this compromise is benefit. School leaders need to perceive that a change from imposed policy expectations can create a positive outcome for teachers, students, or themselves.
- *Constraining expectations* occurs when the school leader makes sense of the event by placing boundaries on some portion of the flow. Weick describes the setting of boundaries as *constraining.* Sensemaking diminishes when boundaries are loosened (Weick, 2001). In the context of school leadership and external demands, such as accountability for learning outcomes, *Constraining* involves school leaders placing boundaries (Weick, 2001) around what content of the demands may be applicable (*account for what learning*), to whom it may apply (*accountable to whom for learning*) and how it is to be implemented (*how learning is accountable*). The Principals' experiences as told in Chapter 6 make these 'boundary decisions' in light of their current expectations in their role function as school leaders.

- *Framing expectations*, in the context of accountability for learning outcomes, occurs when school leaders personalise (*personalising accountability*), accept (*accepting accountability*), may frame expectations as a responsibility (*accountability as a responsibility*) and may frame expectations as an enactment (*accountability as an agency*). In a similar way to Weick's property of 'social context,' individuals seek sensible meanings about the policy expectations. They also develop stories that, according to Weick, have 'plausibility,' with a sense of reasoning and credibility. Aligning Weick's properties here, it is hypothesised that school leaders frame their policy expectations in a similar fashion to the Principals' experiences presented in this book, whereby they tell stories, develop schemas and mantras about their interpretations of their expectations to make sense to themselves and give sense to their communities.

4 Core Category 2: Giving Sense

4.1 *Description*

School leaders' *Giving sense* to their community, in this case about external demands, involves leaders making visible their sensemaking, through communicative and non-communicative acts. In the context of accountability demands, their sensegiving acts aim to influence, persuade, and mobilise teaching teams and students to meet their overall learning commitments.

4.2 *Explanation*

Giving sense is adopted because of its theoretical understandings which easily align with the experiences of school leaders' work with their communities. The underpinnings of these understandings are sited in the communal cycle of sensemaking to sensegiving (Gioia & Chittipeddi, 1991); a leader's discursive ability in their persuasive accounts and processes of facilitation (Maitlis & Lawrence, 2007; Thayer, Goldhaber, & Barnett, 1988), including sensegiving moderators (Kraft, Sparr, & Peus, 2015).

The phenomenon of school leaders *Giving sense* to their communities in response to external demands occurs through three sub-processes:
- *Composing persuasive accounts* involves school leaders creating and articulating convincing accounts to sway the thinking and actions of others in their community. School leaders' discursive abilities hold the potential to create positive frames for school communities when faced with unsurmountable challenges. Their discursive abilities are anchored in their oral narratives, such as storytelling or mantras. These are devices enabling a leader's sensegiving. A moderator of a leader's persuasive skills is their role

identity. Metaphors used by school leaders are windows for others demonstrating how leaders see and shape their role. The utility of metaphors can be a highly internalised and normalised process (Panzer, 1989).

– *Facilitating teaching and learning systems* as a sensegiving act involves school leaders responding to external demands through the teaching routines, practices and structures (Maitlis & Lawrence, 2007). The efficacy of this act is the extent to which the school leader can integrate the external expectations with their existing internal learning and teaching goals. Their integration (or non-integration) is moderated by the school leader's perceived practical and empirical knowledge base about teaching and learning; their self-belief in being able to influence the teaching and learning processes; and their self-perceived capability in cultivating credibility with teachers and students.

– *Creating cultures of coherence* involves school leaders' abilities to bring a consistency and a sense of collective and consensual agreement in response to imposed external demands. These abilities are witnessed through articulating and modelling. Again, they employ discursive skills to articulate desirable practices, such as encouraging perspective taking and balance. Their modelling practices are seen when they act in ways, they expect their teachers or their leadership team to do, such as working closely with and alongside their teaching teams, analysing data and developing implementation plans, distributing leadership tasks and for the minority, building aspirational and performative cultures.

5   Relationship between Making Sense and Giving Sense

School leaders' ways of *Giving sense* about external expectations are influenced by their *Making sense* of these expectations. The process of *Sensegiving* combines the capability of school leaders creating coherence within themselves and with their communities and designing and implementing teaching and learning systems to integrate the external expectations with their internal school commitments. However, these sensegiving acts are dependent on their sensemaking. The leaders contextualise, constrain, and frame their expectations. To justify this theoretical relationship of influence, Ajzen's (2012) behavioural and subjective norms and the perceived behavioural control are applied to the theoretical sub-processes (Ajzen, 1991, 2012; Ajzen & Fishbein, 1980). Table 1 demonstrates through example how Ajzen's TPB validates this theoretical relationship of influence (Ajzen, 2012). The contents of Table 1 move from left to right, demonstrating how Weick's (2001) sensemaking properties are aligned with the three processes of *Making sense*, which then move on to influence leaders' three processes of *Giving sense*. Ajzen's (2012) intentionality

TABLE 1   Theory of planned behaviour authenticating sensemaking and sensegiving

Sensemaking (Weick)	Core category 1: Making sense		Theory of planned behaviour	Core category 2: (Maitlis & Lawrence, 2007)	Giving sense
Properties	Sub-processes	Leaders' interpretations	Attitude, norms, and control	Sub-processes	Leadership practices
Social context— 'social anchors'; Plausibility	Contextualising expectations	High parental expectations for high performance results	Subjective norms	Composing persuasive accounts	Capacity to influence teachers through perspective taking, educates and tells good news to parents; possibly through declarations and at times testing the waters through oration
Retrospect		Effects on enrolments			
Enactment		Effects on teacher pay scales			
		Teacher receptivity			
Ongoing projects	Constraining expectations	Higher priority given to parental expectations over policy expectations	Attitude	Facilitating teaching and learning systems	Capacity to set clear and collective internal learning goals; to articulate a vision and implement a school-wide pedagogy
Salient cues	Framing expectations	Capacity to evaluate policy expectations and options, considering parental constraints and enrolments; evaluates their own capacity to act	Attitude	Creating coherence	May employ selected parts of the expectations, as an agency for change
Personal identity			Perceived behavioural control		These actions are dependent on school leaders' self-efficacy judgements

of attitude, norms and perceived control, aligned in the central column, demonstrates the relationship between *Making sense* and *Sense giving*. Given certain conditions, it is reasonable to see how a school leader's intentions would likely form and how these intentions may influence their ways of enacting on the external demands significantly.

The display of the theoretical ELM in Figure 2 illustrates the two central processes that school leaders are likely to engage when faced with conflicting demands—*Making sense* and *Giving sense*—and positions their relationship with the external demands. The ELM identifies the likely sub-processes of school leaders' in *Making sense* of external expectations: *Contextualising, Constraining* and *Framing* the expectations. It illustrates the likely sub-processes at play for school leaders' processes of *Giving sense: Composing Persuasive Accounts, Facilitating Teaching and Learning Systems* and *Creating Coherence*. Importantly, the two key phenomena, *Making sense* and *Giving sense* intersect as Table 1 demonstrates. The moderators of *Giving sense* as depicted are school leaders' beliefs about teaching and learning and their beliefs about their levels of self-efficacy in mobilising their teaching teams (cultivating credibility being high on the list). While school leaders *Making sense* is a covert cognitive act, their *Giving sense* here is an overt act of translation to the school system authorities and to the school community. The ELM forms the culmination of

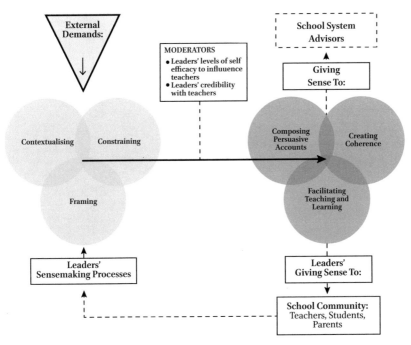

FIGURE 2   The Eucalypt Leadership Model (ELM)

the several demonstrations that align Weick's Sensemaking Properties and Ajzen's Theory of Planned Behaviour. In this figure they are aligned as a strategy to demonstrate support for the theoretical propositions presented.

It is hoped that the ELM presented in this chapter has aroused interest, is viewed as reasonable and novel to the point of uncovering unanticipated relationships and is also responsive to the problems described in Chapter 1 for school leaders. Concluding as the chapter began with Weick (1989), he proposes that

> a good theory is a plausible theory, and a theory is judged to be more plausible and of higher quality if it is interesting rather than obvious, irrelevant, or absurd, obvious in novel ways, a source of unexpected connections, high narrative rationality, aesthetically pleasing, or correspondent with presumed realities. (p. 517)

The reader's judgment will determine the ELM's plausibility and quality. Part of its plausibility and quality is its ability to be applied and its alignment with other literature. Chapters 6–9 aim to do exactly this. Chapter 3 now moves to a more detailed explanation of Weick's (1995) properties of sensemaking, the phases of sensegiving by Gioia and Chittipeddi (1991), and Ajzen's TPB (1991).

CHAPTER 3

Problem Re-namers

The special wisdom that leaders seem to possess lies not in their achievement of a superior verbal knowledge of things, but in their willingness to remain forever in pursuit of understandings that lie beyond language ... The leader is not so much a problem-solver as a creative problem re-namer ...

THAYER (1988, p. 254; 1995)

∴

School leaders are often in the process of reconciling divergent viewpoints as they make decisions about how to enact their regulated responsibilities. It may be as simple as 'fight or flight,' specifically in disruptive contexts (Brimm, 1983; Shapiro & Gross, 2013). While this reconciling process could be a specific event, it can reflect a more general phenomenon when individuals make decisions to behave in certain ways. One of the needs the school leader may have been to make sense of the demand at the same time as predicting how the demand may be played out or be embedded in their school context and importantly whether they deem they have the capabilities to give sense to the community members about the demands. As Thayer purports their making sense may not be so much as problem solving but creative problem re-naming. A desirable skill for the democratic school leader is being a creative problem re-namer.

School leaders in their re-naming may be determined by not only their own sensemaking (Thiel, Bagdasarov, Harkrider, Johnson, & Mumford, 2012) but also their own values and beliefs (Ajzen, 1991), levels of self-efficacy (Bandura, 2006), and particularly their expertise in their 'sensegiving' practices (Maitlis & Lawrence, 2007). Hence, two fields of knowledge, the properties of sensemaking and phases of sensegiving are presented here as useful lenses. Another lens is the well-respected Theory of Planned Behaviour (TPB) (Ajzen, 1991) which notably, given certain contexts, is a predictive tool to an individual's behaviour. The TPB provides a credible view on predicting the Principals' behaviours.

Sensemaking and sensegiving are treated here separately, yet they are conceptual twins. Thayer (1988) demonstrates the interrelationship of sensemaking and sensegiving where the leadership involves redefining problems (sense-making) and creating new frames of reality for others (sensegiving):

> The art of leadership lies in redefining the problem, of creating other possibilities for seeing, of creating possible 'alternities,' of creating different meanings of things. In a very critical way, which seems in retrospect always to have been inevitable, the leader is a sense-giver. (Thayer, 1988, p. 254)

This interrelationship is considered later in this chapter.

1 Sensemaking

When faced with external expectations of accountability, school leaders are likely to hold similar experiences to any individual faced with external stimuli. A new stimulus requires adjustments by the individual. A process that describes such adjustments by individuals is 'sensemaking' (Caughron et al., 2011). Some of the popularity of the literature about sensemaking is because its application makes sense. Weick's (1995) theoretical proposition of sensemaking has given scholars the opportunity to examine groups of sensemaking practices within a range of contexts, from organisations (Johnson et al., 2013) to literary texts (Hunt, 2020). This includes the ways that leaders (and particularly school leaders) make meaning of imposed policies or external stimuli (Spillane, Diamond, et al., 2002; Spillane, Reiser, et al., 2002; Werts & Brewer, 2014) and integrate, in various adaptations, such impositions within their school environments and organisations (Thiel et al., 2012; Werts et al., 2013). Combining sensemaking literature with ethical decision-making frameworks demonstrates the importance of sensemaking strategies in the daily work of school leaders, especially when making ethical decisions (Bagdasarov et al., 2015; Thiel et al., 2012). The process of sensemaking enables individuals to work out the possible causes of the situation, the likely outcome of the situation and how they as individuals may influence the progression of the situation (Weick, 1995). Weick et al. (2005) explain that sensemaking starts when an individual realises that a foreign experience/event is happening and the sensemaking finishes when the individual comprehends the experience enough to allow them to make a decision to 'act, monitor, or ignore' the situation (Caughron et al., 2011, p. 353). In an organisational setting, when people are talking about sensemaking they discuss at least seven properties that have an effect on their efforts to 'size up what they face' (Weick, 2001, p. 461). Notably, part of the active sensemaking process is that the individual places constraints around the external

PROBLEM RE-NAMERS   25

stimuli (Weick, 1995, 2001). Weick presents a minimalist form in his development of his ideas about sensemaking, calling on the reader to rely on their "common-sense understanding of the terms employed" (Weick, 2001, p. 461). Weick explains his ideas about sensemaking through a scaffold of seven properties. Each of the properties of sensemaking is defined briefly below, followed by the implications when the strategy 'loosens.' Loosening occurs when the sensemaking is threatened or weakened, such as contradictory stimuli (Weick, 2001). The properties are drawn from Weick's (2001) publication *Making Sense of the Organization*, rather than Weick's (1995) landmark volume, because of the 2001 refinements and being cited more often in the sensemaking literatures (Allen & Penuel, 2015; Thiel et al., 2012).

1. *Social context:* Strategies in making sense of an event are influenced by the "actual, implied, or imagined presence of others. Sensible meanings tend to be those for which there is social support, consensual validation, and shared relevance" (Weick, 2001, p. 461). Weick names these sensible meanings as 'social anchors.' When social anchors seem to be absent or disappear for the individual, who then starts to feel isolated from others, the individual's grasp of what is happening loosens.

2. *Personal identity:* This sensemaking property describes an individual's sense of who they are, recognising their threats or enhancements in a setting. Loosening occurs when the "identity is threatened or diffused" (p. 461), such as in the early stages of a position within the group or losing 'a job without warning' (p. 461).

3. *Retrospect:* An individual is influenced by what they have noticed "in elapsed events, how far back they look, and how well they remember what they were doing" (p. 462). Loosening occurs when individuals do not appreciate or recall the past or "use it casually, where they put their faith in anticipation" (p. 462).

4. *Salient cues:* The individual uses their resourcefulness to elaborate on tiny indicators into full-blown stories, often shoring up an initial hunch. Loosening occurs when the cues become contradictory or unstable, the individual's preferences change, or because the situation is dynamic.

5. *Ongoing projects:* 'Experience is a continuous flow.' It is made a sensible event when the individual can place boundaries on some portion of the flow or when some interruption occurs. The individual loosens their grasp when they "lose their ability to bound ongoing events, to keep pace with them by means of continuous updating actions and interpretations, or to focus on interrupting conditions" (p. 462).

6. *Plausibility:* This sensemaking property is about individuals developing coherent stories, 'how events hang together,' a sense of reasoning and

credibility to explain the event. This property is influenced by the other six properties. Plausible sense "is constrained by agreements with others, consistency with one's own stake in events, the recent past, visible cues, projects that are demonstrably under way, scenarios that are familiar, and actions that have tangible effects. Loosening occurs when one of more of these sources of grounding disappears" (p. 462).

7. *Enactment:* The individual sees what they are "up against, tries a negotiating gambit, makes a declaration to see what response it pulls or probes something to see how it reacts" (p. 463). The old adages of 'testing the waters' or 'dipping one's toes in' possibly describe this property. Loosening the grasp occurs when no probing actions occur, or no declarations are made.

For the purposes of this book, Weick's seven properties are called the 'Sensemaking Framework.' A question at this point to ask is whether and how Weick's Framework is useful when investigating school leaders' interpretations of their accountability expectations. One way to answer this question is to evaluate whether the seven properties can be easily applied to principals' ways of making meaning of their accountability expectations, from a predicting sense along with an empirical sense. Table 2 aims to do this. It lists Weick's seven properties and develops operational definitions for each one of the properties as they align with the expected sensemaking from empirical support for principals and their work in resolving external accountability expectations.

What we know from the literatures is that principals make sense of their accountability environments (Shipps & White, 2009), yet with the consequences in some cases as having undesirable effects on learning outcomes for students (Stobart, 2008). Added to principals' own sensemaking of the expectations, thrown into this mix are in-school contextual considerations. One common experience is resistance from teachers at the same time principals are being pressured for better performance results by their superiors. Or similarly senior/middle educational leaders are pressurised for improving performance results by their principals at the same time they are faced with resistance from teachers. Such resistance is a considered stance by teachers, and often the drive for results jeopardises their moral compass (Bezzina, 2010) and may challenge their commitments in maintaining the balance between wellbeing and achievement for students (Willis, Hyde, & Black, 2019).

The bottom line is that the work of principals and school leaders is reliant on the work of teachers. Managing such pressure while simultaneously working with teachers requires careful and strategic attention from principals (Darling-Hammond, 2010a; Pineda-Báez, Bernal-Luque, Sandoval-Estupiñan,

TABLE 2   Aligning Weick's sensemaking properties with educational leaders' accountabilities

Property	Operational definition
1 Social context	The school leader seeks social support, consensual validation, and relevance with their communities, about the external accountability for performance results. Social anchors in principals' school communities relevant to their accountability expectations are considered. Examples of social anchors are the expectations about students' performance results from parents, students, and teachers.
2 Personal identity	School leaders form an idea of who they are in the accountability events. The accountability expectations may influence their identity as a principal. In this formation they recognise the threats or enhancements from their school contexts, which may determine their sense of efficacy where 'judgments of relevance and sense' emerge (Weick, 2001, p. 462).
3 Retrospect	The capacity for school leaders to notice elapsed events, going back and remembering what they or others have done to meet the accountability expectations. For example, principals may draw upon the way they managed the expectations from previous year's student performance data to make sense of their current expectations.
4 Salient cues	School leaders use their resourcefulness to pick out indicators from their accountability contexts to create meaning and coherence (Shipps, 2012). They shore up stories (Rigby, 2015) about the accountability expectations (Koyama, 2014). For example, leaders may draw upon empirical research of the negative consequences of national testing from other countries. Unfortunately, when these stories become contradictory, such as poor parallels of education systems, the making sense loosens.
5 Ongoing projects	School leaders make sense of the accountability expectations by constraining what, to whom and how they account (Spillane, Diamond, et al., 2002) and/or by updating their interpretations of the accountability expectations. They may negotiate and enact external accountability in ways that are creative and savvy (Koyama, 2014).
6 Plausibility	School leaders make sense by developing coherent stories (Elmore, Forman, Stosich, & Bocala, 2013) about their expectations. These stories hold certain levels of credibility and reasoning. The leader's level of coherence in the story is constrained by the agreements by their communities, their own stake in the expectations, familiar scenarios, action, and credible effects. They also create models which scaffold their stories (Darling-Hammond 2010; Kuchapski, 2001). Plausibility aligns with studies by Darling-Hammond (2010) and Shapiro and Stefkovich (2016) where school leaders create the coherent and convincing story that accountability is a collective responsibility.
7 Enactment	The school leader takes action to see what they may be up against, tries a negotiating gambit or makes a declaration (possibly in response to policy makers' expectations). The gambit becomes a reality when the principal's gambit is met with consensual agreement by the esteemed referents in their school community. Boundaries are tightened through such agreements and validation.

& Quiroga, 2019). Principals experience tensions between what they and the teachers value and what is expected of them (Shipps, 2012). Sensemaking strategies are essential for school leaders to make considered decisions for action. From empirical research principals experience potential challenges in making decisions in how they enact their responsibilities (Marks & Nance, 2007) at the same time as meeting the increasing demands for demonstrating and being accountable for pedagogical leadership practices (Brookhart & Moss, 2013; Fiarman, 2019). School leaders, like teachers, face directional complications when maintaining their moral compass and ethical commitments to themselves and their profession, when managing such tensions (Bezzina, 2010).

Some of these tensions materialise when principals' views about learning are under-represented through the accountability mechanisms (Goldschmidt et al., 2005; Stobart, 2008), exacerbated with the consequences of using a number to rank students and schools (Polesel, Rice, & Dulfer, 2014). These studies indicate the importance of the influences which may be at play in school leaders' sensemaking (Bagdasarov et al., 2015), such as their fundamental beliefs about the purposes of schooling, their world views about learning, motivations and their levels of self-efficacy in managing these tensions and challenges.

Taking seriously and broadly Weick's seven properties, they include emotional, bodily, spatial, and social practices in their most expansive forms (Balogun, Jacobs, Jarzabkowski, Mantere, & Vaara, 2014). Relevant to school leaders is the role of sensemaking in a school leader's professional identity. Weick embeds the personal identity property and as such implicates that when the individual (leader) defines an event they are also defining their 'leader self,' and in turn the event also defines the leader's self (Weick, 1995). Included in this sensemaking is the role and responsibilities and relations of the leader self with others (Chreim & Tafaghod, 2012). With this book's focus about Australian schools, the 'leader self' is in relationship with their school system supervisor, other senior leaders, and the teaching teams. How the 'leader self' negotiates defining their identity will impact on their practices with their community.

Being the twin of sensemaking, sensegiving is a body of knowledge, distinct, yet explains an individual's behaviour after making sense of an event.

2 Sensegiving

School leaders' capabilities in sensegiving may make or break the success of a school change or be instrumental in the school community coming to terms with critical events. As such, effective sensegiving leadership practices are fundamental to a school leader's effectiveness in mobilising and/or influencing members of the school community. The purpose of theorising about sensegiving is that it offers a feasible explanation of a different actuality. Importantly the intentionality of a sensegiving act is to influence another individual's thinking to accept it as their own or the collective (Gioia & Chittipeddi, 1991). It stands to reason that sensegiving literatures often are embedded in the field of management and leadership; the term provides an opportunity to be more explicit about the leader's role, or more inclusively the 'leadership activity' in the sensemaking process (Catasús, Mårtensson, & Skoog, 2009). If sensemaking is explaining and justifying, then a leader's sensegiving is the act of diffusing such explanations and justifications within the organisation (Green Jr., 2004). Sensegiving while normalising and legitimising certain realities and delegitimising others (Gioia & Thomas, 1996), also shuts down or constrains different interpretive meanings of reality (Voronov, 2008). Leadership activity is employed here as a term to include practices of influence by any member of the community, whether the member is in a formal or informal position. The term disarms the assertion that only the formal leader is the one to provide influence or in this case 'give sense.' In relation to others' sensemaking, a leader's sensegiving is the attempt to affect an employee's sensemaking (Kraft, Sparr, & Peus, 2018). For some, this attempt is seen to be 'a sender-centric view' of sensemaking. Corvellec and Risberg (2007) contest "it is non-sensical to speak of sense without referring to interpretation and, thus, to a living audience" (p. 322). This bypasses the sender's evaluation of where the audience accepts the meaning or not (Corvellec & Risberg, 2007). In its place they reason that sensegiving acts are the activities of persuading audiences in a desirable direction of a preferred reality, pointing out the interactive nature of sensegiving. Sensegiving is not simply 'done' to the other with blind acceptance; this illustrates the likely processes between leadership and teaching practices. The living audience in the school context is the teacher. The leadership 'activity' involves sensegiving acts to persuade teachers in their sensemaking with their intentions to act (teaching practices); in turn teachers are making sense of leaders' sensegiving practices—where they may change their teaching practices or not.

The process of educational leaders giving sense and teachers making sense about that sensegiving is what Gioia and Chittipeddi theorise as Phase 1 of sensegiving. Gioia and Chittipeddi (1991) organise the relationship between sensemaking and sensegiving into four phases (see Figure 3). The first phase as introduced in the previous paragraph is the Envisioning phase. The leader seeks to make sense of an event, this could be their own schema, shoring up a story or connecting to a previous event. Phase two is where the leader's schema is formed into communicative acts of sensegiving, called Signalling.

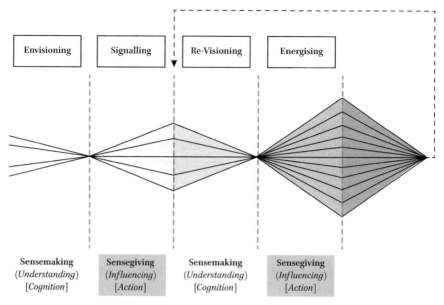

FIGURE 3   Processes involved in the initiation of a strategic change (from Gioia & Chittipeddi, 1991, p. 444)

Such acts are diverse and could range from storytelling to analogies of past events. These sensegiving acts may inject ambiguity or may 'stir the setting' in stable environments (Neumann, 1995). Such ambiguity calls for employees to make sense of what change is being promoted; this third phase of Re-Visioning may hold many different sensemaking properties, from plausible stories to identity fusion. These enacted sensemaking responses are fodder for further sensegiving, where the leader moves to the fourth phase of Energising, and like Signalling it is an influencing action. However, this Energising phase has more sway than the first Signalling because it includes modifications, adjustments to include the target audience's own sensemaking—or in the school context to include the teaching team's own sensemaking of the change or event.

2.1   *In Situ*

School leaders need to be credible, hold influence and persuasion in their relationships with their teaching teams, especially in challenging contexts of change or disruption. The new context for school leaders, during and post COVID-19 is complex, turbulent with disrupted social and economic realities. Sensegiving, in this new context, depends on school leaders' abilities to make sense of events for others in their communities and in giving sense they are communicating their sensemaking.

The Envisioning phase is where school leaders make sense of the event which involves understanding, a form of cognition. Once the event is understood by leaders, their sensegiving acts aim to influence and motion actions in teaching teams; this *Signalling* phase involves action. Gioia and Chittipeddi propose that at this point leaders seek to understand (a cognitive function) the impact of their influence with teachers (gaining information from teachers) and 're-sensemake,' moving to the *Re-Visioning* phase. In an ideal collaborative school environment, the more leaders seek to adapt or adopt teachers' own sensemaking, the less likelihood of rejection or resistance from teachers, and a greater likelihood of a strong *Energising* phase. The worst-case scenario is if the *Re-Visioning* phase is omitted. The influence by leaders may be diminished and the energising direction weakened or misapplied, or 'loosing sense.'

A school leader's sensemaking is as much influenced by their own 'leader self' as the school system regulators,' teachers,' students' or parents' sensegiving activities (Cornelissen, Holt, & Zundel, 2011; Kraft et al., 2018). As a sensegiving interpretive process individuals will exert mutual influence to affect others (Kraft et al., 2018) with a groundswell in a particular direction. Hence, sensegiving, unlike sensemaking, ideally is reflected in multiple mutual relationships.

Successful sensegiving acts result in a shared interpretation of an event (Balogun et al., 2014), which organise themselves in ongoing cycles of influence between sensemaking and sensegiving (Gioia & Chittipeddi, 1991). While the spheres of influence may not always be attributed to the designated leader's practices, generally those in formal positions call or dictate their role in sensegiving due to their hierarchical position (Ravasi & Schultz, 2006). In a school context, school leaders perceive they are obligated to give sense to others because of their compelling responsibilities. Despite the hierarchical positions of 'principal,' 'deputy,' 'assistant principal' or 'faculty head,' they do not dictate a leader's success or failures in influencing teachers' practices. There are many moderators of such successes. For example, a leader's communicative acts may determine their levels of influence.

Communicative acts are sensegiving practices (Huzzard, Hellström, & Lifvergren, 2014) employed by leaders to influence change with and within the community/organisation. In turn, these acts prompt the community members to 'sensemake,' that is remaking sense either individually or ideally as a shared remaking in mutual relationships. School leadership teams consistently face the challenge in changing and disrupting contexts of organising, and reorganising after teachers' sensemaking responses, resulting in the school leader reforming their sensegiving acts to maximise impact with their communities (Kraft et al., 2018; Stensaker, Falkenberg, & Grønhaug, 2008).

Yet, it needs to be considered that the school leader's sensegiving may not be aligned with teachers' sensemaking. It most likely will not be. In a study on organisational change Bartunek, Krim, Necochea, and Humphries (1999) found that the recipients' sensemaking was not the same as leaders' sensegiving. There were multiple and at times conflicting understandings of a change event, where understandings were evolving continually. In a school environment it is a complex process in coming to an understanding of a shared vision or direction for the school. Yet organisations such as schools can achieve high levels of sensemaking and reduce 'cognitive complexity when leaders connect sequentially with their communities "in dyadic sensegiving examples" (Maitlis, 2005, p. 47). Devices and linguistic acts are ideal companions for school leaders in realising such dyadic sensegiving.

2.2   *Devices, Linguistic Acts*

Some devices used by individuals in their sensegiving acts include metaphors, mantras, and storytelling. The use of metaphors by entrepreneurs has a long history of anchoring their sensegiving (Hill & Levenhagen, 1995). Mantras and storytelling (Salicru, 2018) are other sensegiving acts which translate events into plausible scenarios and images to persuade and influence others to take action (Salicru, 2018). The oral-aural traditions of school environments lend themselves for school leaders to give sense, through storytelling, and more generally, through linguistic acts. Storytelling is an effective sensegiving device which is used in diverse settings and cross-cultural leadership practices (Grisham, 2006). A theory to explain the power of stories called Narrative Parading Theory (NPT) was first developed by Fisher (1984). NPT regenerates the rational paradigm in the same way that sensemaking is not concerned with accuracy of facts but is rather about plausibility (Weick, 1995).

Other devices fall into the realm of linguistic acts of appeal. These communicative acts, which Weick (1995) would call enacted sensemaking, pertain to persuasive appeal. Bartunek et al. (1999) drew upon Johnston's (1994) theoretical language of sensegiving with persuasion, suggesting four tactics: (a) discharging linguistic acts that demonstrate logic and reason—consistent with Maitlis's (2005) findings that stakeholders' sensemaking increases when leaders behave in a procedurally fair manner; (b) employing praise and encouragement; (c) acts which appeal to the members' own values and norms (acts which identify with the in-group); and (d) building up a credibility story about the sender—being reasonable, ethical and for the common good. The original body of work on sensegiving by Gioia and Chittipeddi (1991) as described at the beginning of this section, is substantial. Their work has been a springboard for other research and models which further explain the relationships between sensemaking and sensegiving. For example, the body of work by Maitlis and Lawrence (2007) found that the trigger for leaders' sensegiving practices occurs when issues are ambiguous and involve multiple relationships. Leaders in their study were enabled to give sense when they thought they themselves had the appropriate knowledge and skill. In turn the enablers for the organisational members were also their knowledge and skill and in contrast, their trigger for sensegiving was when they thought the event was important to them. This finding about leaders having a knowledge and skill base is an important point about leaders and sheds lights on Norris's (2017) findings.

One credible model which extends the theoretical propositions by Gioia and Chittipeddi and yet sheds a different light on Maitlis's work, is the consideration of the moderators of a leader's sensegiving processes (Kraft, Sparr, & Peus, 2015).

2.3 *The Moderators*

Numerous managerial studies include sensemaking into their discourses about sensegiving (Catasús et al., 2009; Giuliani, 2016; Wong, 2019). Theoretically, sensemaking and sensegiving practices are a pair. The model by Kraft, Sparr and Peus (2015) is beneficial in understanding the processes about sensegiving and how it couples with a leader's sensemaking. It is also substantial as it is based on their well detailed literature review (Kraft et al., 2015) (see Figure 4).

The model in Figure 4 outlines a process of leaders' sensegiving and is appropriate for this book because it identifies empirically the moderators in leaders' sensegiving practices (Gioia & Chittipeddi, 1991; Kuntz & Gomes, 2012; Maitlis & Lawrence, 2007).

The reworked model 'Moderating Forces in Educational Leaders' Sensegiving Practices' (see Figure 5) aligns leadership sensegiving practices to a school context. The model demonstrates the reciprocal nature of the relationship between leaders' sensemaking and leaders' sensegiving practices.

Overall, the phases hold the fundamental premises proposed by Gioia and Chittipeddi. The senior leadership team internally makes sense of an event, then gives sense through language and actions of their sensemaking, to the school community members; reciprocally (in an ideal collaborative school world) the community members make sense of the leadership team's sensegiving practices to inform the next phases of Re-Visioning and Energising.

What is of interest here with Kraft et al.'s model compared with Gioia and Chittipeddi's theoretical underpinnings is that one, the model is from a leadership perspective and two, the model offers empirical detail about some moderating factors (descriptive acts) in both the leader's and the individual's sensegiving processes. The Kraft et al. model has the capacity to shed light

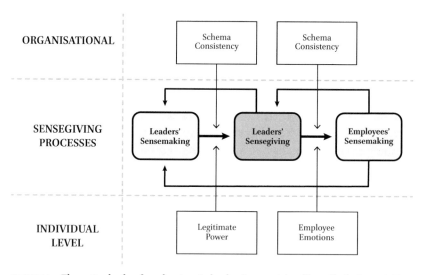

FIGURE 4 The critical role of moderators in leaders' sensegiving (from Kraft, Sparr, & Peus, 2015, p. 310)

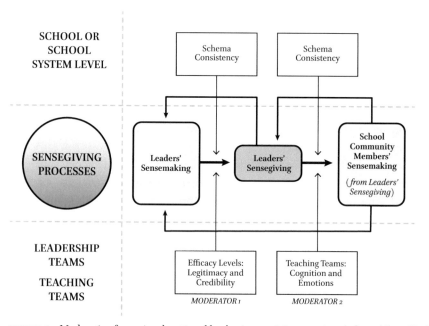

FIGURE 5 Moderating forces in educational leaders' sensegiving practices (adapted from Kraft et al., 2015, p. 310)

in a descriptive sense on the school context: the leadership team and teachers' sensemaking and sensegiving. It is for these reasons that this model is explained in detail in this next section.

2.4 Descriptors

The reciprocal loops in Figure 5 are represented as feedback loops. They illustrate the processes between the educational leader's sensegiving acts and the community members' sensemaking responses to those acts. In turn (and again ideally) the leader remakes sense from the school community's sensemaking practices. Notably community sensemaking is not limited to the leader's sensegiving, community members have their own schemata, but reciprocally in collaborative mutual relationships, they influence the further sensemaking and sensegiving (Gioia & Chittipeddi, 1991, and Kraft et al., 2015).

Two kinds of sensegiving strategies are identified by Kraft et al. (2015): Discursive and non-discursive strategies (Sonenshein, 2006). Discursive strategies, in a school context, could include communicative acts such as: staff meetings, newsletters, blogs, tweets and memos, video clips and emails. Non-discursive strategies, usually symbolic (Sonenshein, 2006) could involve rituals such as: the school assembly or religious rituals, special days such as harmony day or 'feast' days, stories, mantras, narratives along with narratives around symbolic objects such as trophies and religious artefacts, a statue or plaque.

2.5 Schemas

School contextual schemas contain understanding about the ethos or culture and character (Maitlis & Christianson, 2014) of a school and influence the choices from which an educational leader selects "differing segments to construct pathways for action" (Swidler, 1986, p. 277). Alongside, community members are organising their understandings about their school context in schemas. These organisational schemas direct their interpretation and understanding of events. For example, organisational schemas systematise understandings, such as teachers' attitudes about their responsibilities in response to their accountability for performance results.

2.6 Schema Consistency

At the organisational level, schema consistency is a relevant mediator for the relationship between a leader's sensegiving and the community's sensemaking. Bisel's and Barge's research (2011) unearths two major influential factors involving a leader's sensegiving practices through change. The first factor is that tangible events need to be incorporated into the sensegiving communicative acts. In the context of accountability for performance results, educational leaders may reason with their community that market accountability is triggered by national disclosures of performance results. The second factor is that these tangible events need to be aligned with what is agreed already about the school context and teachers' schemas. For example, and hypothetically a teaching team already accepts their accountability expectations around their students' performance results, due to the threat of their job security. Both these factors affect sensegiving as educational leaders communicate changes that are suitable for their teachers' sensemaking existing schemas (see Section 3.1 in Chapter 5).

Hence successful sensegiving practices, if they demonstrate coherency with existing schemas, are likely to "trigger top-down processing that does not aim to create new schemas but rather alters the existing ones" (Kraft et al., 2015, p. 319). However, new events, such as lockdown of schools resulting from the COVID-19 crises, often require bottom-up cognitive processing as existing schemas are no longer adequate. Therefore teachers, parents and students needed to understand the implications, create their schemas and 'manage-up' to help school leaders in their 're-sensegiving' through the crises. In the COVID-19 crises, teachers and students needed to inform consistently educational leaders how they were faring and what needed to be done to ensure the most effective remote learning practices. Added to the top down and bottom-up processing is that sensegiving practices which are consistent with prevailing schemas, safeguards a leader's influential positioning and maintains their power structures (Kraft et al., 2015).

In times of change "leaders often need to frame their sensegiving in a way that is inconsistent with existing schemas" (Kraft et al., 2015, p. 320). How these sensegiving practices 'make sense' to community members will determine their effectiveness. As such they signal what an educational leader needs to consider when 'scheming' their sensegiving acts, whether aligning with existing schema or sensegiving with new schemas.

2.7   *Legitimate Power*

The moderating factor of the leadership practices put forward by Kraft et al. (2015) and drawn from the power taxonomy by French and Raven (1959) is legitimate power. When providing examples from the school context the term legitimacy will be adopted, instead of power. Power is often viewed as a negative concept in school education. Legitimacy is more palatable and acceptable.

Some may think that legitimacy stems the formal authority beset by an educational leader's position in the school community, and anchored in policies, rules, and laws. This thinking suggests that the leader's sensegiving practices will be accepted without question. This is not the common experience for educational leaders. Historically, early to mid-20th century, teachers' work was relatively autonomous and carried out in isolation. Current practices encourage collaborative and subsidiarity decision making. Yet a leader's level of legitimate power is found to moderate both the choice of strategies and language in their sensegiving practices. Four studies identified by Kraft et al. (2015) demonstrated the moderating effect of legitimate power where managers with positional power more often employed confrontation strategies. Yet, leaders with low or without positional power more often relied on strategies in the 'what and how' to communicate to increase receptiveness. As such leaders with low legitimate power were more aware of differing perceptions among their employees (Leonardi, Neeley, & Gerber, 2012). These leaders are more likely to seek real time feedback to ensure their sensegiving acts are acceptable (Kraft et al., 2015, p. 316). They were more likely to engage 'team members in the interpretation process' (Leonardi et al., 2012, p. 98). Given teachers hold high levels of autonomy as they go about their work, it is logical that the moderating effect of legitimate power may mirror those leaders' strategies such us seeking real time feedback and to seek teachers' understandings on events (interpretation processes). Kraft et al.'s (2015) first proposition relating to legitimate power is thus:

> The level of legitimate power moderates the relationship between leader sensemaking and sensegiving such that: Leaders are likely to use indirect, multilateral sensegiving strategies if their level of legitimate power is low. (p. 316)

Levels of legitimate power moderate leaders' selection of sensegiving strategies along with their communicative acts, in several ways. One, leaders with low levels of legitimate power are likely to employ more hard fact justifications (for example, school enrolments will be jeopardised if results are poor) than leaders with high levels of legitimate power (Sonenshein, 2006). Those with high levels of legitimate power adopted the more familiar language of their employees.

Moreover, the level of power and the accompanying differences in the abstractness of information processing also influences leaders' choices in their sensegiving language. High levels of distance (cognitive or psychological) result in a leader's 'experienced abstractness' which in turn becomes an abstract communicative act (Magee, Milliken, & Lurie, 2009, as cited in Kraft et al., 2015) and suggests the likelihood of overlooking negative aspects (Magee et al., 2009). That is, if the educational leader is far removed from knowing and understanding the work of teachers and students the more likely their communicative acts of sensegiving will be abstract and hence the less likely the sensegiving acts will hold strength or meaning for teachers.

The second proposition regarding legitimate power:

Legitimate power moderates the relationship between leader sensemaking and sensegiving such that: (a) Leaders are more likely to use abstract, positive and normative language if their level of legitimate power is high. (b) Leaders are more likely to use concrete, negative and rational language if their level of legitimate power is low. (Kraft et al., 2015, p. 317)

In a school context if an educational leader's legitimacy is high, they are likely to hold positive discursive abilities with abstract and normative communication. The educational leader who employs factual, negative, and rational language is likely to have less legitimacy. The question this proposition raises is who determines the levels of legitimacy—the educational leader's self-perception, their perception of the community's perceptions or simply the community's perception of the leader's sensegiving acts?

2.8   *Emotions as a Moderator*

While this book's focus is on educational leaders' experiences of accountability it is worthwhile to attend to employees (teachers) because the employees' emotions can be examined considering how the educational leader may alter their communicative acts in response to their future perceived emotions of their teaching teams.

The role of emotions in sensemaking is important because they influence the whole sensemaking process (Weick et al., 2005). In terms of positive emotions in sensegiving practices, they can be advantageous (Maitlis, Vogus, & Lawrence, 2013). Emotions, a "transient feeling state with an identified cause or target that can be expressed verbally or nonverbally" (Maitlis et al., 2013, p. 223), act as a moderator in the relationship between a leader's sensegiving and an employee's sensemaking. Positive emotions result in a greater propensity to adjust existing instead of forming new schemas. Kraft et al. (2015) explain that emotions are differentiated according to their 'valence' (positive or negative) (p. 319). Enthusiasm for example is a positive emotion whereas distress is a negative emotion. Positive emotions increase the sturdiness of new founded schemas (Vuori & Virtaharju, 2012 as cited in Kraft et al., 2015). On the downside, emotions may inhibit sensemaking by decreasing the processing capacity of the individual (Maitlis & Sonenshein, 2010). This raises the question how educational leaders attend to or are attuned to the predicted emotions that their teaching teams may emit when change ideas are floated. Floating an idea is like Weick's (1995) property of enacted sensemaking of utilising the act by employing gambits. Educational leaders, likewise, to secure their influence, may well need to attend to their own emotional state.

A leader's expression of their positive emotions results in positive effects on employee sensemaking (Kraft et al., 2015). It is no surprise that genuine excitement and enthusiasm for a new project by the educational leader would influence teachers' feelings and attitudes towards a change in direction or facing a new event (Maitlis & Sonenshein, 2010), such as a leader championing or cheerleading their teams (Gioia & Chittipeddi, 1991). Equally Kraft et al. (2105) found that "employees' positive emotions also increase their receptiveness for sensegiving messages. In contrast, individuals experiencing negative feelings often evaluate their environment as problematic or dangerous" (p. 320). This indicates a detail-oriented bottom-up style for information processing, which is usually adequate or helpful to master difficult situations (Bless et al., 1996, as cited in Kraft et al., 2015).

The moderating effect of emotions is an important consideration for leaders initiating change. "Emotions influence the information-processing style by directing individuals' attention to the allegedly most adequate information at hand: existing knowledge structures versus new data" (Bless et al., 1996, as cited in Kraft et al., 2015, p. 320). In the school context therefore teaching teams will likely draw on the information most easily to integrate into their existing ways of going about their work, rather than create new schema.

In summary, Kraft et al.'s proposition considering the role of emotions in sensegiving is as follows:

> The relationship between leader sensegiving and employee sensemaking is moderated by employees' emotional state: (a) Leader sensegiving is more likely to trigger an alteration of existing schemas in employee sensemaking if employees experience positive emotions during sensereceiving. (b) Leader sensegiving is more likely to trigger an emergence of new schemas in employee sensemaking if employees experience negative emotions during sensereceiving. (p. 320)

Rounding up, the literatures on sensemaking and sensegiving have been explained and a new term called sensereceiving, was introduced. In contextualising this term to schools, sensereceiving could refer to teaching teams of taking in or 'being delivered' sensegiving messages from the leader(s). Another term which relates to the need for sensemaking and sensegiving is sensebreaking.

3 Sensebreaking

Sensebreaking occurs where the sensereceiver cannot make sense of an event at one particular point in time. The term 'break' means the gaps which occur "in the scanning, interpretation, and learning dynamics of the sensemaking process" (p. 221). Pratt (2000) refers to sensebreaking as the "destruction or breaking down of meaning" (p. 464). It occurs when "a person's process of sensemaking is disrupted by contradictory evidence" (Giuliani, 2016, p. 221). For example, when an educational leader first attempts to make sense of a new policy, and perceives there are ambiguous suggestions, there will be breaks in their sensemaking. The leader needs to seal it. Sensebreaking, or sense unmaking, involves the "destruction or breaking down of meaning" (Pratt, 2000, p. 464). Sensebreaking may need to occur before organisational members can give sense to it. Disrupted by contradictory evidence, the individual may experience 'breaks' in their sensemaking. Sensebreaking acts may take the form of reframing, redirecting, and offering new alternatives and learning (Maitlis & Christianson, 2014). Similarly, in ontological terms, Heidegger refers to this as the 'breakdown' in an individual's life (Koschmann, Kuutti, & Hickman, 1998). The breakdown, distinguished from a mental health breakdown, is a disruption to a domain or several domains in an individual's life. Effectively managing the breakdown provides the individual leader with opportunities for learning, redefining problems, creating new alternatives and different ways of seeing (Thayer, 1988) and being (Segal, 2010).

The initial experience by educational leaders to COVID-19 restrictions was breaking sense or the breakdown—a substantial disruption to the way teaching and learning would happen and their beliefs about the way teaching and learning 'should' be in their schools. How well they managed this breakdown, such as discovering new ways of teaching depended on leaders' and teachers' capabilities to seal the breaks in their sensemaking processes. For the individual to be predisposed to see the wonder in the breakdown/disruption is for the individual to welcome learning and opportunity from ambiguities or stuckedness.

4 School Leaders' Sensemaking and Sensegiving in Accountable Times

If an educational leader has reached the Envisioning phase with strong reciprocal sensegiving messages they are likely to have influenced teaching practices. Hypothetically school leaders will evaluate the external demands and expectations, such as accountability for high performance results, determining how much time they wish to invest, and notably how important their sensegiving messages will be to achieve a shared understanding of the demands with their teachers. Sensemaking and sensegiving are both crucial for the effectiveness of educational leadership in adapting their acts to be an influence with their school community members.

Sensegiving holds the intentionality to alter how individuals think and behave, yet a caution, with minimal assurance of that intention being adopted. The inquiry into sensegiving commonly stems from the inquiries into sensemaking literatures. Sensemaking and sensegiving are best conceptualised together, as treating them separately misses their interrelationship. Often enacted sensemaking is actually sensegiving. Gioia, Thomas, Clark, and Chittipeddi (1994) found 41% of the research codes labelled sensemaking were coded as influence (a sensegiving practice). As an aside there is an emerging research stream of positioning some leadership practices as unintentional sensegiving practices (such as ambiguous messaging or silence) (Wong, 2019). However, the key point for this book is that the sensemaking and sensegiving pair involves a reciprocal relationship.

To conclude, an educational leader's sensemaking guides the community, and especially for teachers, to develop meaning, and create new schemas if necessary, and serves as a leverage to mobilise teachers' work to meet external demands (Soshensian, 2007; Weick, 2009). Ideally, from this standpoint (of sensemaking/sensegiving), educational leaders are influencing how the community understand themselves, their work and their relations which assist at times in the necessary cognitive and emotional shifts—a vital leadership meaning-making responsibility in disruptive or ambiguous times.

Sensemaking and sensegiving can be described and explained in terms of strategic processes for change. Conversely, beliefs, motivations and attitudes also have a significant role in determining an individual's behaviour (Ajzen & Madden, 1986). An individual's internal decision-making processes and its influence on behaviour point to another body of knowledge which concerns beliefs and behaviours—the Theory of Planned Behaviour (TPB). In understanding the nexus between beliefs and behaviours provides the *likely* behaviours that educational leaders would engage, when faced with external demands for favourable student results. The premise provides a predictive capacity to a certain extent, to Norris's (2017) findings. A brief overview of the Theory of Planned Behaviour is presented in the next section encouraging the reader to see how TPB may forecast a leader's actions if we are clear about their intentions.

5 The Theory of Planned Behaviour

While the study of attitudes, beliefs and behaviours is a major field in social psychology, it is beyond the scope here to embark on a detailed study of this subject. However, the TPB, one of the most widely used theories, is useful in shedding light on a principals' intentions in this research and the way these might influence their behaviours. The TPB is based on the work of Ajzen (Ajzen & Fishbein, 1980; Madden, Ellen, & Ajzen, 1992; Ajzen, 2012). The fundamental proposition of the TPB is that behaviour is influenced by intentions (Ajzen, 2012). The theory is credible because empirical studies have shed light on health (Juraskova et al., 2012; Prestwich et al., 2014), corporate (Kautonen, Van Gelderen, & Tornikoski, 2013) and educational issues over the last 25 years (Bezzina, 1989; Dadaczynski & Paulus, 2015; Zolait, 2014). Moreover, the elements of this theory accommodate the research presented thus far regarding the likely behaviours in which school leaders may engage when faced with accountability expectations (certain conditions).

In 1985, social psychologists Icek Ajzen and Martin Fishbein researched the relationship between decision making and action, to understand the key determinants of behaviour (Lunday & Megan, 2004). If behaviour is influenced by intentions (Ajzen, 2012), an individual's intention is a precursor for their behaviour (Ajzen, 1991). These intentions are a function of three conceptually independent determinants (Ajzen, 2012): attitude, subjective norm and perceived control (Ajzen, 1991). These are shown in Figure 6. In varying contexts, these three determinants are the predominant influence on an individual's intention.

The first determinant is the attitude towards the behaviour and refers to the degree to which a person has a favourable or unfavourable "evaluation or appraisal of the behavior in question" (Ajzen, 1991, p. 189). Ajzen calls this appraisal 'outcome evaluation' (Ajzen & Fishbein, 1980). The second determinant is a social factor, termed a 'subjective norm' and 'refers to the perceived social pressure to perform or not to perform the behavior' (Ajzen, 1991, p. 189). Often, the social pressure is an individual and Ajzen (2012) calls these

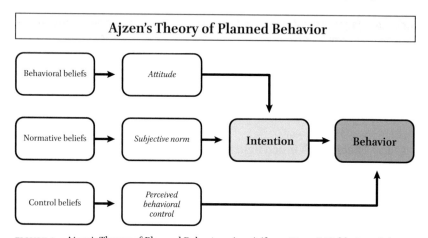

FIGURE 6   Ajzen's Theory of Planned Behaviour (TPB) (from Ajzen & Fishbein, 1980)

individuals 'social referents.' The third determinant of intention is "the degree of perceived behavioural control and refers to the perceived ease or difficulty of performing the behaviour and is assumed to reflect past experiences" as well as anticipated challenges (Ajzen, 1991, p. 189). However, perceived behavioural control not only influences behaviour indirectly, through intention, but has also been shown to have a direct effect on behaviour (Ajzen & Madden, 1986), as illustrated by the bold black line in Figure 6. Perceived behavioural control is most compatible with Bandura's (1977) concept of perceived self-efficacy, which concerns the judgements that individuals make in how well they think they can execute courses of action required to deal with future situations (Bandura, 2006).

Ajzen (1991) hypothesises that "as a general rule, the more favourable the attitude and the subjective norm with regard to a behavior, and the greater the perceived behavioural control, the stronger should be an individual's intention to perform the behavior under consideration" (p. 189). The importance of attitudes, subjective norms and perceived behavioural control is expected to vary across behaviours and situations. Hence, in some applications of the TPB, it may be found that only attitudes have a significant impact on intentions, whereas in others, attitudes and perceived behavioural control are sufficient to explain intentions. However, all three predictors make independent contributions (Ajzen, 1991; Ajzen & Madden, 1986).

In Ajzen's TPB, the determinants of an individual's intention can be demonstrated through the current understandings of principals' views and their enactments of accountability. Ajzen's three determinants for human action have been used as the framework for the following sections. Emerging bodies of literature pertaining to leaders' intentions and actions are critiqued within the TPB.

6 Application of Leadership to the Theory of Planned Behaviour (TPB)

This section applies Ajzen's theoretical components to the previous literature on principals' accountability to demonstrate its utility in the Norris study (2017).

6.1 Leaders' Accountabilities: The Determinant of Attitude

Ajzen and Fishbein (1980) outlined a process for the measurement of attitude using the three determinants. The first step was the identification of the person's beliefs about the behaviour in question, with beliefs representing the information individuals have about objects (Bezzina, 1989). The second step was determining the judgement that the individual makes as to whether or not the behaviour is favourable (Ajzen, 1991).

Ajzen's understanding of attitude as a determinant of intention is reflected in Shipps' (2012) research, whereby principals needed to make decisions whether to rely on external political resources in carrying out their accountability requirements. When we apply the determinant of attitude to Shipps's research, the principals identified that one of the possible consequences of relying on political resources in meeting their expectations may generate conflict among stakeholders. Although the principals may have seen this as being a negative outcome (outcome evaluation), they did not see it as likely to happen (likelihood of outcome). Thus, based on their evaluation and all other things being equal, principals would be likely to rely on external political resources. In this current research, some principals utilised these resources to the advantage of the school.

Conversely, applying the same determinant to the research study by Spillane, Diamond, et al. (2002) could lead to the opposite result. Their research found principals needing to decide whether to adopt mandated accountability policy. Some principals considered that a possible consequence of adopting mandated policy would be resentment by educators, which they perceived as negative (outcome evaluation) and likely (likelihood of outcome). In this case, it is predicted that the attitude that developed would predispose principals to reject the policy as expected by the authority. This is precisely what happened in Spillane's study, with principals not adopting policies as expected. This application of behavioural beliefs to these two research studies demonstrates the usefulness of Ajzen's theory in understanding principals' evaluation outcomes about accountability and their influence on principals' behaviours.

6.2 Leaders' Accountabilities: The Determinant of Subjective Norms

Subjective norms relate to a person's perceptions of what they should and should not do in terms of the perceived expectations of others (social referents) (Ajzen & Fishbein, 1980). Subjective norms as a determinant of intention can be demonstrated in Shipps and White's (2009) study, in which the principals identified their stakeholders as state and district authorities (external) and teachers, students and parents (internal). Ajzen would call the external and internal individuals social referents (Ajzen, 2012). In Shipps and White's first wave of research (2004–2005), the principals were more likely to comply with the opinions of their internal social referents. In their second wave of research (2007–2008), the same principals were more likely to comply with the opinions of their external social referents. In these two studies, the principals' perceptions of the expectations of the social referents changed along with their intentions. These changes may have been attributed to the reported stakes at a higher level. School closures and staff deployments were some of the consequences in the jurisdictions where the later study occurred. These changes point to the possibility that principals are more likely to be influenced in their priorities (complying or not complying with particular social referents) according to the level of consequence. Ajzen's approach to subjective norms helps to clarify the dynamic that may have been at work in these principals' perceptions of their social referents and the value that they attached to different referents over time. In this way, the value they placed on complying with the particular referent influenced the behaviours of these principals.

6.3   Leaders' Accountabilities: Perceived Behavioural Control

Perceived behavioural control is described as the person's beliefs about whether they can perform the desired action and how these beliefs influence their behaviour to perform that action (Ajzen & Fishbein, 1980). This relates to a leader's self-efficacy. The kinds of considerations that can interfere with a person's control can concern a person's belief about their ability, such as an individual factor, or their beliefs about an opportunity or their beliefs about an organisational factor (Ajzen & Madden, 1986). Ajzen's understandings of perceived behavioural control can be applied to the existing research findings on principals' accountability. For instance, in high-stakes accountability regimes, Shipps (2012) found that ECPs believed that their own lack of ability (individual factor) hindered their enactments of mandated accountabilities. These same principals perceived that factors in the community (organisational factors) were an important influence for not attending to their accountability requirements (Shipps, 2012). Ajzen's understandings of perceived behavioural control can be applied directly to Shipps's (2012) study, where the principals' beliefs about their organisational factors influenced their behaviours by not attending to their accountability requirements.

This application of the TPB from the few available research studies on principals' accountability shows that a principal's attitude to the consequences of their behaviours while enacting accountabilities provide a useful way to investigate the ways principals might enact their accountability responsibilities.

7   Bringing the Re-namers Together

One conjecture in the ELM is that a school leader's sensemaking influences their sensegiving practices, at least observed in the phases Envisioning to Signalling. The second conjecture, using the TPB, is that under certain conditions, we can predict the likely nature of these sensegiving practices. Ajzen's most important proposition is that intentions precede behaviour. The determinants of intentional behaviour can be in line with the sensemaking properties. If we know the intentions of a school leader, we can predict the likely actions of the leader, their sensegiving acts.

Providing evidence about intentions and actions can be problematic, as the evidence relies on a leader's understandings of themselves, and a leader's behaviours being observed by themselves or others. Employing lenses that could be applied to situations, such as Weick's seven properties (Utz, Schultz, & Glocka, 2013; Weick, 1993), sensegiving phases (Gioia & Chittipeddi, 1991; Kraft et al., 2018) and the TPB can be applied to situations in education (Dadaczynski & Paulus, 2015; Underwood, 2012). Doing so offers descriptions, explanations, and indicators of school leaders' likely behaviours in similar school contexts. While Weick's sensemaking strategies and the sensegiving acts are useful in highlighting the possible cognitive processes that may be at play in leaders' interpretations, the TPB is concerned with the relationship between intentions and behaviours and the beliefs and attitudes for the leader's reasons (motivations) for acting in particular ways. As such the TPB is helpful, acting as explicit referral points for leaders themselves and those working with them.

Figure 7 represents an integration of Weick's sensemaking properties, sensegiving premises and the TPB. According to the TPB, three independent factors affect the pathway from intention to belief: attitudes, subjective norms, and perceived behavioural control. Attitude concerns the degree to which an individual favours a particular behaviour (Ajzen, 1991). Attitude can be aligned with Weick's *social context*, in which the social anchors can influence an individual's attitude towards a particular behaviour (Weick, 2001). Attitude can also be aligned with *retrospect*, whereby the individual's attitude is influenced by the noticing of past events and their mindfulness of the task at hand (Weick, 2001). From a sensegiving perspective leaders engage in the Energising action after teachers' Re-Vision through understanding, their cognitive processes (Gioia & Chittipeddi, 1991).

The subjective norm is the priority that an individual may give to a social referent in directing the engagement of certain behaviours over others (Ajzen, 1991). *Plausibility*, with individuals creating stories to explain the event (Weick, 2001), aligns with the subjective norm because the priorities of the social referent fit in with their story. *Salient cues*, using tiny indicators to elaborate full-blown stories (Weick, 2001), also align with Ajzen's subjective norm, with the *salient cues* about the social referent shoring up the story. *Ongoing projects* serve to place boundaries on the flow of events (Weick, 2001). This aligns

PROBLEM RE-NAMERS

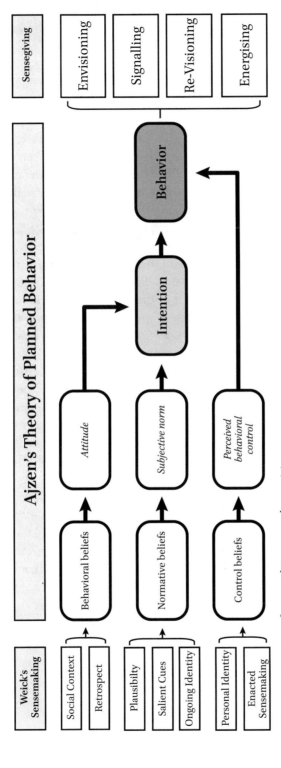

FIGURE 7 Integration of sensemaking, TPB and sensegiving

closely with the boundaries that the individual places on to whom they give preference (boundaries) regarding their social referents. In their sensegiving practices leaders aim to adjust their communicative acts (of credibility), in the Re-Visioning phase, to persuade particular referents about their priority decisions (communitive acts of credibility) (Maitlis, 2005).

Perceived behavioural control is the individual's perception regarding the ease or difficulty of engaging in the task (Ajzen, 1991). *Personal identity* involves the individual recognising the threats and enhancements that 'may be rendered efficacious' (Weick, 2001, p. 462) and aligns with perceived behavioural control whereby the individual interprets or evaluates their capacities to engage the behaviour. *Retrospect* parallels this norm because past experiences of the event may determine judgements about the likelihood of success or failure. Sensegiving practices are moderated by levels of credibility which are influenced by a leader's sense of their legitimate power (Kraft et al., 2015) completing the process of Energising, Phase 4 (Gioia & Chittipeddi, 1991).

The summary of this chapter is in the form of a table (Table 3). It demonstrates how Weick's sensemaking properties, sensegiving practices and the TPB contribute to an understanding of how school leaders may navigate their external demands with their teaching teams.

Table 3 demonstrates how Weick's sensemaking properties, sensegiving practices and the TPB contribute to an understanding of how educational leaders may navigate their external demands with their teaching teams.

The journey through these three theoretical foundations provides explanations which support the Model. But the reader is invited to go further. It may be worthwhile to think about the importance of a school leader's potential and legitimacy, to gain understanding of themselves and help others in their professional relationships. School leaders are called to their vocation because of their care, commitment to learning and teaching and, empowerment for others' humanity. Understandably, when faced with a problem as leaders, we could be tempted to jump in and solve the problem. However, as Thayer suggests, and with sensemaking and sensegiving skills, the school leader is 'not so much a problem-solver as a creative problem re-namer ...' (Thayer, 1988, p. 254).

The following chapter (Chapter 4) explores the context in which school leaders are working. The Principals' contexts need to be considered before the application in Chapters 6 and 7.

TABLE 3   Literature, sensemaking, sensegiving and the TPB

Examples from the literature	Sensemaking (Weick, 1995, 2001)	TPB (Ajzen, 2012)	Sensegiving (Gioia & Chittipeddi, 1991; Kraft et al., 2018; Maitlis, 2005)
Principals' decisions are influenced by stakeholders' likely responses (Shipps, 2012; Spillane, Diamond, et al., 2002)	Leaders seek support and validation with their school communities (social context)	Leaders weigh up the possible outcomes from their actions (behavioural belief—evaluating outcomes)	Leaders engage an Energising action after community members re-vision through understanding (Gioia & Chittipeddi, 1991)
Principals' decisions are based on how they relate one obligation to another (Shipps & White, 2009)	Leaders make sense of their expectations by placing boundaries (often referred to as constraints) on what and how they account (personal identity)	Leaders make decisions about their what is expected of them whereby they prioritise one social referent over another (normative belief—motivation to comply with referent)	Leaders aim to adjust their communicative acts in the Re-Visioning phase to persuade particular referents about their priority decisions (communitive acts of credibility) (Kraft et al., 2018)
Principals' decisions to act are influenced by a sense of their own ability (Shipps & White, 2009)	Judgements of relevance and sense emerge, which may be determined by the leader's sense of efficacy (personal identity)	Leaders' beliefs about the extent to which they meet the diverse expectations in their accountability of learning (perceived behavioural control—extent to which individuals are in control of their behaviours)	Levels of credibility in the Signalling phase (Gioia & Chittipeddi, 1991) are influenced by a leader's sense of their legitimate power (Kraft et al., 2015)

(cont.)

TABLE 3   Literature, sensemaking, sensegiving and the TPB *(cont.)*

Examples from the literature	Sensemaking (Weick, 1995, 2001)	TPB (Ajzen, 2012)	Sensegiving (Gioia & Chittipeddi, 1991; Kraft et al., 2018; Maitlis, 2005)
Principals' decisions are based on their professional beliefs (Shipps & White, 2009)	Leaders develop coherent narratives that hold levels of credibility and reason (plausibility)	Leaders give priority to their own values or beliefs about learning and accountability (Normative belief—motivation to prioritise own values)	A leader's legitimate power is high when they employ 'abstract, positive and normative language' (Kraft et al., 2015, p. 317), helpful for achieving a shared purpose in the Signalling and Energising phases
'Principals enact their accountability environments' (Shipps, 2012, p. 3), rather than react (Spillane, Diamond, et al., 2002)	Leaders act; they try negotiating gambits or make declarations for action (enacted sensemaking)	Leaders demonstrate their behaviours based on their intentions or self-efficacy (perceived behavioural control)	Leaders engage with confidence in the Signalling phase (Gioia & Chittipeddi, 1991), notably if their level of legitimate power is high (Kraft et al., 2015) is so they will employ direct, unilateral sensegiving strategies

CHAPTER 4

Context: Not Everything, But Something

> ... by placing the spotlight on leadership, researchers have unwittingly relegated the context of leadership to the shadows. Yet, until we highlight the interaction between context and leadership, we will remain handicapped in efforts to develop more satisfactory answers ...
>
> HALLINGER (2018, p. 6)

∴

This excerpt by Hallinger (2018) encourages the investigation of the interaction of context and leadership. Although I propose that the practices of school leaders are mainly determined in how they perceive the world, the way the world presents to the leader still needs to be considered. The context is not everything when we examine how a school leader manages their expectations, but it is something to be aware of when making theoretical claims, as this ELM does. The ELM is not in vacuum.

The contextual issues explored in this chapter tease out some of the interaction between the school leader and their contextual issues. It examines the impact of the purposes of education and precedencies on school leaders' work, along with the global, national, and state actors on educational jurisdictional expectations. The issues are complete with an overview of a secondary school sector as an example in context, including an explanation of the impacts of organisational, curriculum and leadership structures and career pathways on school leaders' work. These explanations are important as they provide the reasons for the way school leaders may prioritise certain tasks over others, or place boundaries around demands in the expectations of their role. While these contextual factors are situated in Australia, they hold commonalities with international jurisdictions, such as the United States and England.

1   Impact of Public Purpose on School Leaders' Work

The public purposes of education across the Western world are based on common ideologies of social justice, liberty and equity (Wiseman, 2010). However,

© KONINKLIJKE BRILL NV, LEIDEN, 2022 | DOI:10.1163/9789004517202_004

certain purposes gain dominance because of the political processes that reflect the climate of that time in history (Cranston, Reid, Mulford, & Keating, 2011; Lingard, Martino, & Rezai-Rashti, 2013). For example, there is evidence to support the failure of certain accountability arrangements, such as high-stakes testing in certain jurisdictions (Stobart, 2008), when accounting for student results (Siegel, 2004). At the same time there is evidence regarding the pursuit for ethical leadership responses to such high stakes accountability environments (Gunzenhauser, 2012). In Australia, the lack of alignment between the purposes of education and the federal and state arrangements of educational accountability has an effect on the ways school leaders are likely to perceive their accountability responsibilities (Cranston, Reid, Mulford, & Keating, 2011). Pertinent to their perceptions are school leaders' ideologies about the purposes of education and the ways their ideologies affect how they negotiate external demands, notably those which intersect with student learning.

1.1 *External Climate Influence Priorities*

The economic, political and social climate for any particular time in history informs the priority given to particular educational purposes (Gunzenhauser, 2003; Reid, Cranston, Keating, & Mulford, 2011). For instance, in England in 2006, the emphasis was on the challenge to reform education through improvement in performance outputs facilitated by the Education and Inspections Act, 2006. In the United States at the turn of the century, the emphasis was on improvement in learning, with particular attention to closing achievement gaps and minimising disadvantage, facilitated through the 'No Child Left Behind Act,' 2001. In South Korea and Singapore through 2008–2009, the emphasis was on social and economic regeneration. In Australia, by the turn of the century the emphasis was on promoting citizenship and economic responsibility (Lingard, 2010) as well as the individual purpose in educational goals (Cranston, Reid, Keating, & Mulford, 2011), with the move to an increased accountability for outputs in education (Rowe, 2005).

1.2 *Government Priorities*

Governments make choices regarding which public purposes take precedence (Biesta, 2004; Lingard, Martino, & Rezai-Rashti, 2013; Shipps & White, 2009). In most Western countries economic aims in education have been pushed to the foreground (Siegel, 2004). In England at the same time, for example, one of the economic aims involved a significant vocational aspect, such as individual employment and social well-being through economic prosperity (Wilkins, 2002). So too has the Australian Government made choices in determining which purposes of education should take precedence.

CONTEXT: NOT EVERYTHING, BUT SOMETHING

In the era of a federal Labor Government (2007–2012) in Australia, a priority on citizens being competent economic contributors increased the focus on performance results in education (Lingard, 2010) rather than inputs on resources (Rowe, 2005). This economic priority, combined with the priorities from the Howard era that promoted choice of schooling, found their expression in the dominant educational accountability measures in this country's landscape.

According to Reid et al. (2011), Australia's public purposes of education were dominated by three aspects: the *democratic purpose*, in which "society expects its schools to prepare young people to be active and competent participants in democratic life"; the *individual purpose*, which 'aims to advantage the individual in social and economic life'; and the *economic purpose*, which "aims to prepare young people as competent economic contributors" (p. 20, emphasis added). The point here is that the purposes that had precedence in Australia at the time of my study (Norris, 2017) with Principals were the *individual* and *economic purposes* (Cranston, Reid, Mulford, & Keating, 2011; Reid et al., 2011).

The individual and economic priorities of these educational purposes were reflected in elements such as the structures of schooling, the culture and processes of schooling and the assessment and reporting practices of the official curriculum (Reid et al., 2011). These priorities and the way they have shaped education policies in Australia are important in the expansion of educational accountabilities now impacting on teachers' and school leaders' work.

In the period of the Howard Liberal federal government (1996–2007) the *individual* purpose in education was a significant priority, with education policy aiming "to advantage the individual in social and economic life" (Reid et al., 2011, p. 20) and shaping policies that were premised on a view of education as a commodity (Bezzina, 2000). One priority, reflecting the individual purpose, was the emphasis on facilitating parents' and students' choices of schooling (Lingard, 2010; Reid et al., 2011). This emphasis, in turn, has influenced the accountability mechanisms being used to assess student success. For instance, in Australia, reflecting this individual purpose, the My School website was set up. It was initially designed to provide parents and students with public information on student performance results attached to their school, to help them choose a school (Australian Curriculum Assessment and Reporting Authority, 2009; Leslie, 2010). My School "is a resource website for parents, educators, and the community to find information about each of Australia's schools."[1] However, the My School website is now often employed to pit schools against each other, with the possible consequences of school cultures developing staff and student low morale (Ragusa & Bousfield, 2017). Whilst seen as a reasonable move, the emergence of the measurement of a 'year's growth' for each student from 2018–2020 continues to perpetuate the normalisation of student success being determined by and limited to a student's test score (Australian Government, 2018b).

1.3 Priorities: Consequences for School Leaders

At times, the demands of educational accountability systems, both in Australia and other jurisdictions such as the US, can pose difficulties and challenges for school leaders in achieving their commitments to these public purposes of education (Cranston, Reid, Mulford, & Keating, 2011; Shipps & White, 2009). In one jurisdiction in New York (Mitani, 2018; Shipps & White, 2009). Shipps and White (2009) found that principals faced moral and professional challenges in meeting their professional commitments when new accountability policy priorities were introduced. These studies suggest that principals experience tensions between their own understandings of what education should be and the pressure by policy makers to implement accountability mechanisms in particular ways. It is not just the local jurisdictional policy makers who pressurise school leaders and teachers to account for performance results, the tentacles of educational accountability are normalised, regularised, and are now globalised in school systems and schools.

2 Global Actors Impact on School Leaders' Work

The global stage is fraught with comparisons between countries. The Organisation for Economic Co-operation and Development (OECD), instrumental in providing public data about schools and leadership, fuels school systems' expectations which are passed on to school leaders. 79 school systems (2020) signed up to the OECD to test 15-year-olds' skills and knowledge. The OECD has built on past successes and continues to be given authority by leaders of school systems, as a key expert and resource for evidence-based education policies in member countries (Morgan & Shahjahan, 2014; Pons, 2017). Member countries pay for their membership for its resources. The OECD uses reports of data from the Program for International Student Assessment (PISA) to make recommendations to countries and jurisdictions, impacting on their policy directions (Breakspear, 2012), and at times with less scrutiny than should be warranted (Sachse & Haag, 2017).

2.1 OECD—Soft Power?

By 2020, more than 37 member countries are enlisted in the OECD, with 79 school systems taking part in the PISA survey (OECD, 2020), which allows the OECD to make recommendations in three areas: public policy issues in

CONTEXT: NOT EVERYTHING, BUT SOMETHING

preparing young people for life; literacy in the ways that students apply their knowledge and skills in key learning areas; and lifelong learning, with students measured not only in their reading, mathematics and science literacy but also asked about their self-beliefs.[2] There is a global trend "in which national policies are increasingly often debated through appeals to models and policy advice promulgated by international organisations" (Rautalin, Alasuutari, & Vento, 2019, p. 500), OECD being cited as one of them.

2.2 Data Don't Speak

To be fair the OECD simply provides data sets. The power rests with those who interpret data. On their own data sets do not speak for themselves. National governments analyse and make interpretations for their own purposes. Falling nation-wide results provide the impetus for countries to lever OECD data as an implement for change. Public discourse about the initiatives from such data has been evident in these member schools.

2.3 Unequal Playing Fields

Of import for school leaders is that Australian national and state policy makers are influenced by initiatives such as the OECD's PISA data to compare and contrast Australia with other countries (Lingard & Sellar, 2016). As is occurring across nations, these comparisons and contrasts influence the directions of school systems and jurisdictions. What is problematic is that member countries in the OECD are diverse and their base platforms are not equal. For example, a country such as Finland and a jurisdiction such as Shanghai are homogenous school communities. To compare their data with Canadian schools or metropolitan Australian schools with high levels of cultural diversity diminishes the validity of data to be employed to make informed evidence based educational directions.

The OECD operates through a soft power with 'cognitive' and 'normative' governance (Sellar & Lingard, 2013). Joseph Nye of Harvard University developed this concept to describe a way to 'attract and co-opt,' rather than use force (hard power) (Nye, 2012). Cognitive governance asserts its function through the agreed values of the member nations. While normative governance, described as peer pressure, is perceived as being vague (Woodward, 2009), this organic governance may hold the most influence because it "challenges and changes the mindsets" of the member people (Sellar & Lingard, 2013, p. 715).

2.4 Soft to Hard Power

One such example of policy makers and school system leaders being influenced by OECD data was the pedagogical leadership capabilities agenda for principals. An OECD 2013 publication on the evaluation of school leaders, advised the ways head teachers (principals) should be appraised in terms of fostering pedagogical leadership in schools (OECD, 2013). Not surprisingly what has followed are now the priorities that school system leaders give to certain areas of leadership. Notably in Australia, pedagogical leadership and evidence-based leadership have been privileged, with increasingly rigid appraisal processes. Principals are appraised on their instructional and evidence-based leadership knowledge and skills along with the outcomes such as their students' performance results. Possibly because of the OECD's soft power through data and recommendations, school systems are adopting new leadership roles to support principals, such as a reformed notion of the 'Instructional Leader' and 'Leaders of Pedagogy.'

2.5 *Instrument Confusion but Pressure Remains*

As National education reforms are drawn from OECD data, media sources are becoming highly skilled at tracking and presenting data with assertions from the OECD triennial cycle to the public. In Australia, these media assertions often disregard the incompatibility between the national NAPLAN test (skills—basic) and the PISA survey (applications of skills—higher order) (Baroutsis & Lingard, 2017; Lingard & Sellar, 2013) and other system impact factors on PISA data (Sellar & Lingard, 2013, p. 723). NAPLAN is the National Assessment Program—Literacy and Numeracy test As global studies increase both in number and in sectors, they will be employed more heavily by policy makers as benchmarks for comparative rankings and leverage. The main point here is that employing OECD data to make comparisons between countries and the Australian student performance data from cycle to cycle is questionable due to the diversity in member countries and Australia's current preponderance and drilling basic skills (NAPLAN) and not higher order applications skills (PISA).

2.6 *OECD Data Show Inequities*

However, as a counterpoint the data retrieved by OECD in their report on PISA results 2018 provides sobering news to leaders of school systems:

> ... in over half of the PISA-participating countries and economies, principals of disadvantaged schools were significantly more likely than those of advantaged schools to report that their school's capacity to provide instruction is hindered by a lack or inadequacy of educational material; and in 31 countries and economies, principals of disadvantaged schools were more likely than those of advantaged ones to report that a lack of teaching staff hinders instruction. In these systems, students face a double disadvantage: one that comes from their home background and

another that is created by the school system. There can be numerous reasons why some students perform better than others, but those performance differences should never be related to the social background of students and schools. (OECD, 2020)

This is a sobering finding. No umbrage can be taken about the source here (OECD) when the greater concern points to the inequitable actions by school leaders diminishing the life outcomes for children and young people.

3 National Actors Impact on School Leaders' Work

Public disclosure of student performance results at the Australian national level is a relatively recent phenomenon for Australian schools and school systems. Before 2008, states and territories had their own standardised test-based programs with various mechanisms used to account for learning. In 2009, the Australian Government reinforced and formalised the goals of education through the 'Melbourne Declaration' (Ministerial Council of Education, 2008) and entered into a National Education Agreement (NEA) with the states and territories through the Council of Australian Governments (COAG). Apart from that, the Alice Springs Declaration (2019) has few differences with the Melbourne Declaration (2008), despite 10 years of rapid educational change and widespread online consultations. The objectives of the NEA included specific statements about student performance: "performance indicators and performance benchmarks, which outline a number of outcomes-focused targets and progress measures towards the outcomes specified in this Agreement" (COAG, 2009, p. 4). In 2008, national standardised testing and reporting procedures were introduced with the aim of improving educational quality and equity. This aim was enacted through two policy tools: NAPLAN and My School (Australian Curriculum Assessment and Reporting Authority, 2009).

3.1 National Instruments
In Australia, there are several educational jurisdictions, including those of state and territory governments, as well as a variety of education systems such as faith-based schools. These different education systems vary in their accountability processes and often engage with the regulation of processes and/or outcomes. However, at the National level, performance based accountability occurs through the measurement of student performance results from NAPLAN testing and a number of process-type indicators reported through the My School website (Australian Curriculum Assessment and Reporting Authority, 2016).

NAPLAN has two main aims: "to help drive improvements in student outcomes and provide increased accountability for the community" (ACARA, 2013). As mentioned previously, the vehicle used to publicise data from students' performance results from NAPLAN testing, school by school, is the My School website (Australian Curriculum Assessment and Reporting Authority, 2013), with data colourfully displayed with pinks, greens and reds. These colours indicate where the school sits regarding the national benchmarks. Other facilities on My School website allow the public to compare schools' results with similar demographics (called 'like' schools).

In 2009, ACARA was formed to report on learning for all schools in Australia. ACARA's role currently was to provide information to the Government and to the public on each school annually (ACARA, 2013). By 2020 ACARA's stated purpose was "to be the authoritative source of advice on, and delivery of, national curriculum, assessment and reporting for all Australian education ministers, with international recognition" of their work (Council of Australian Government's (COAG) Education Council, 2020).

3.2 Consequences of National Testing

The national test on literacy and numeracy (NAPLAN), for Years 3, 5, 7 and 9 is the vehicle used by the Australian federal government to regulate outcomes. The public disclosure of these results, through the My School website, can rank the schools based on their student performance results. Up to a point, public disclosure, if employed to make judgements, results in a performance-based accountability regime. Public disclosure of performance results has consequences in terms of the public perception of a school and hence enrolments, which contributes to the affective components and economic viability of the school. My School, given its possible consequences such as morale or funding effects, is an accountability mechanism that some regard as high stakes (Lingard, 2010; Reid, 2011). However, as time has passed and with educators managing the public disclosure of student results, there appears to be less concern about such disclosures (Rogers, Barblett, & Robinson, 2016). With the emergence of these tests and now the consequential data-driven cultures, principals know their expectations. They are now normalised regarding accounting for outputs, as opposed to inputs—to a point.

ACARA, unlike the OECD's role, makes no judgment or recommendations leaving such evidence and implementation from NAPLAN data for education ministers in individual jurisdictions (Thompson, 2015). However, at times the Federal government will try and intercede on certain matters. The school restrictions resulting from the COVID-19 crises in 2020 in lockdowns demonstrated the pressure, yet with the Federal government having no real authority over government schools (ABC News, 2020). Such pressure from the Federal government resulted in a 'mixed messages' claim from parents, along with pressure on educators. Ultimately the operational decisions made by schools and school systems remain with the states and territories.

Compared with our global educational peers, it is reasonable to claim, from the point of view of the national authority (ACARA, 2013) and apart from the possible consequences of the public disclosure of performances from NAPLAN, accounting for performance results is a relatively low-stakes exercise for most educators. However, it is not low stakes if school system leaders in their jurisdictions impose stringent accountability expectations on principals, which they are free to do. In such cases, the stakes rapidly fly.

3.3   *A National Common Accountability for Australian School Leaders*

The key implication in the Australian education context for the Principals in the Theory in Practice examples that all Australian principals, irrespective of their state or territory accountabilities, were faced with is an added and common accountability mechanism for outputs from performance results. In 2021 the accountability continues to be regulated through the annual public disclosure of performance results from NAPLAN. Notably, the way states and school system leaders utilise this regulating accountability mechanism varies.

4   State and Jurisdictional Actors

4.1   *News South Wales—The Higher School Certificate*

Since the inception of NAPLAN in 2009, states and territories in Australia have chosen various paths to account for their 'outputs' regarding student learning. The state of New South Wales (NSW), where the Principals' experiences were recorded, no longer provides a separate state-based report on student results and utilises the national skill-based test data for literacy and numeracy. Previously, the state of NSW administered a Basic Skills Test (BST), beginning in 1989 and ceasing when NAPLAN testing started. Historically regarding the BST, educators in the non-government sector were resistant at the outset to participating in the BST yet moved to acceptance. The initial criticism by educators of the BST was like the continued criticisms of NAPLAN; that is, the tool is limited in its capacity to represent the broad aspects of a student's learning. However, the BST evolved to a diagnostic tool rather than a tool for measuring outputs. Political changes introduced by the Keating Labor Government (1991–1996) prompted the adoption of economic rationalism, which meant that educational policy makers shifted their accountabilities from services

60   CHAPTER 4

and programs (processes) to products, such as performance results (outputs). NAPLAN was conceived within this rationalist climate. Knowing about educators' initial resistance and the reasons for this resistance towards the BST is a pertinent contextual concern.

NSW has its own secondary school exit credential, the Higher School Certificate (HSC). Queensland, an Australian state to the north of NSW, introduced in 2020 a new exit credential for their Year 12 students based on NSW's HSC. The HSC is steeply aligned with curriculum outcomes:

> The HSC is a huge operation each year, and the NSW Education Standards Authority (NESA) oversees it ... highest award in secondary education ... students must complete Years 11 and 12, satisfy the HSC requirements and sit for the state-wide HSC examination ... The HSC mark is a 50:50 combination of a student's examination mark and school-based assessment marks for each course. Student performance in each HSC course is measured against defined standards. HSC marks for each course are divided into bands and each band aligns with a description of a typical performance by a student within that mark range. School students in New South Wales generally work towards the HSC in years 11 and 12. It is the highest level of attainment you can reach at school. (NSW Education Standards Authority, 2020)

4.2   *Curriculum Regulators*

The NSW Government uses the regulation of processes in their mechanisms through the NSW Education Standards Authority (NESA), with non-government school operations and curricula audited every five years. Schools are expected to meet standards of operation (in a process known as registration) and standards of curriculum delivery (in a process known as accreditation) (NESA). NSW government schools also use regulation of processes through the vehicle of school reviews to monitor and ensure adherence to the standards of the curriculum: "The main purpose of accreditation is to ensure that the requirements for the Record of School Achievement and/or the Higher School Certificate are being, or will be, met" (NESA, 2020).

4.3   *Accountability through the Market*

The regulation of outcomes by the NSW State Government is not accountability *per se*; however, the regulation of outcomes to hold educators to account for their students' learning may occur by default, through market forces. For example, aggregated HSC results are rank ordered by the media and are often used by schools for marketing purposes (Bishop & Limerick, 2006) and as a means by which parents also can make comparisons between schools. The disclosure of HSC results in the media and the options of post-school pathways are justifiably viewed by students, parents and educators as being a high-stakes experience (Ayres, Sawyer, & Dinham, 2004). Curriculum-based test results in a student's exit year (the HSC), are used to inform their entry into higher education. The publication of HSC data at the state level may be conceived by some as the same dynamics that are at play in the disclosure of literacy and numeracy results (My School) at the National level.

4.4   HSC: A High Stakes Event?

Whether results are public or not the HSC credential itself is viewed as a high stakes event. The various articles by Ayres, Dinham and Sawyer in the early 2000's demonstrate the elevation and scrutiny of teaching quality at the senior level: 'What makes a good HSC teacher'; 'Successful senior secondary teaching' and 'Effective Teaching and Student Independence at Grade 12.' This study investigated how five Australian teachers, who were considered to be exemplary in helping students develop independence, influenced and guided their students to extremely high grades in 12th grade (Ayres, Sawyer, & Dinham, 2001).

4.5   HSC Like Family

The HSC is like the family member that we are committed to yet need to endure. Keeping in mind, secondary school leaders in NSW have been accounting for HSC students' results in this environment since 1967 (NESA, 2020). The longevity of the consequences of the HSC public accountability, like the family Christmas, seems annually anticipated and seemingly accepted or 'lived with.' The amount of data available and the activity resulting from data analysis, particularly the data from the HSC results, have multiplied over the last 10 years. The implication here is that the Principals I report on in the following chapters were accustomed to a regulated and centralised curriculum, with annual public disclosure of their performance results of the HSC. While it is custom and practice it is likely that most secondary NSW principals would think, through their experience of the public disclosure of the results, that the HSC is a high-stakes accountability event. They would also be in two minds about the way the HSC now stands as being seen as an effective measure of students' successes.

5   Secondary Schools in Australia: Changing Times

Over the last two decades secondary schools in Australia have seen a massive change trajectory. Some of these changes have occurred with curriculum structures and programs, pedagogical processes, leadership structures and pathways and roles and functions for school leaders. The ways Australian secondary schools are organised have much in common with other developed countries, notably our counterparts such as US and UK jurisdictions. Most research from the consequences of NCLB and Ofsted echo the experiences of Australian educators in secondary school sectors. The goal for the secondary school sector is for the organisational structures of the school to be a support for teaching programs; to run smoothly and without undue hindrance or burden. There are Australian schools that are pursuing this goal more than not, along with many challenging the status quo of faculty silos. Schools are people, relationships and with the common purpose of student learning. When Australian schools are referred in this chapter this means the people in those school communities: students, parents, and staff.

5.1   *Closed Classrooms to Agile Learning Spaces*

The major change for the organisation of the secondary school over the last 20 years has been the transition from rigid and closed classrooms and faculties to flexible and open school wide approaches to pedagogy and cross pollination of knowledge generation. Leaders of secondary schools needed to manage this transition. Faculties had developed their own subcultures, particular ways of teaching and views about knowledge generation. Organising secondary schools into faculties of knowledge at times has resulted in leaders needing to manage entrenched behaviours by faculty staff. It was here that leaders faced many challenges in trying to be responsive in developing new school wide approaches to teaching and learning at the same time as managing external demands for high performances of student achievement, which were and are knowledge specific. The historical relationship between leaders and teachers in secondary schools was the leader was seen as the administrator, taking care of the 'business,' keeping parents at bay and be the key marketeer for the school. Teachers viewed themselves as the specialist, expecting autonomy wanting to be left to their own ways of teaching, subject specific.

5.2   *Rigid Knowledge Generation*

The late 20th century witnessed many leaders implementing changes to improve teaching and teachers' attributes. Devices such as smartboards, student tablets and online learning platforms were emerging in classrooms only to find them looking like 'dressed up' 19th century classrooms and mindsets. Teachers were still the font of all knowledge and skills, learning was still directed from the front; the smartboard replaced the white/backboard, tablets were used as books and internet and iPhone devices were used as the

CONTEXT: NOT EVERYTHING, BUT SOMETHING

encyclopedia, and with restricted access. How learning spaces were designed still resided with the teacher's decision. By the early 21st century the aim was to be more student-centred, such that learning could accommodate the student's own way of being in their world and their choices about their learning; open spaces and relaxed spaces for connecting with each other and the world in a global sense. How much change leaders could make in teachers adopting these more 'agile' pedagogies was challenging, and at times soul breaking for some in entrenched and rigid organisational structures. Often the privileged comfort and known ways of teaching, diminished the opportunities for vibrant learning which could mirror current everyday learning in the world (Robertson, Grady, Fluck, & Webb, 2006).

However, by the second decade of the 21st century students, parents and teachers have witnessed significant changes in the organisational structures of their school, especially the secondary school. Such structures mirror and support the changes made to learning and teaching programs (instructional walks, high yield and impact strategies, agile sprints, 'bring your own device') and their physical spaces such as open learning spaces and team teaching in these spaces (Whitby, 2013).

5.3   *COVID-19 Blessings*

Australian educators' adaptability to remote and online learning through the COVID-19 crises is testimonial to how diverse modes of teaching can be adopted. Such adaptability raises the question how teachers who often have been judged as rigid or conservative in their teaching practices could reach to a new way of teaching through COVID-19 restrictions, in such a short period of time (Ziebell, Acquaro, Tiong Seah, & Pearn, 2020). Dinham sheds light on this adaptability; his research found that teachers will change if they see a real benefit for their students (Dinham, 2008). Was this at play for teachers' adaptability and competence in moving to remote learning?

5.4   *Evidence Informed Practices*

The emergence of NAPLAN and the public disclosures through My School with increased accountability by school system leaders to school leaders has precipitated the widespread movement of using evidence to informed teaching practices. From 2012–2020 researchers such as Hattie, Sharratt and Breakspear have been resourceful in helping secondary school educators manage such changes. New structures in secondary schools enable the teaching and learning programs to be adaptable, accountable and to be supported by empirical research. No longer can a faculty within the secondary school be a silo or build walls to maintain their propriety about knowledge and skills. Nor can decisions about learning and teaching be based on intuition. The faculty walls are slowly coming down, across the country, with data informed evidence-based practices now the norm in those faculties.

5.5 *School Organisational and Curriculum Structures*

As the walls have come down, diversity in organisational and curriculum structures in secondary education has grown. This diversity has coincided with the growing interest and commitment by secondary school educators, often brought about by designated leaders in their schools and recruitment strategies, to broaden their understandings about learning in not only acknowledging their subject content but also to elevate the importance of knowing the young person as a learner (Goos, Stillman, & Vale, 2007). The high priority given to 'knowing your student' and their learning has occurred at the same time as national, state and territory governments have increased the priority of regulating accountability for student performance results. Tertiary programs with international study tours opening up leader-practitioners' experiences of curriculum structures (UNSW, 2016) prompted the emergence of diverse curriculum structures, notably the emergence of middle schooling (Dowden, 2007) and project and inquiry-based learning. The genesis of integrated curriculum and pastoral arrangements, in meeting the needs of the young person as a learner as distinct from teachers teaching their subject, has become widespread for junior secondary pedagogy in Australia (Connors, 2013). Moreover, teacher intuition has been downgraded in esteem replaced by data informed evidence-based practices, which is now a shared language within and across schools and jurisdictions.

Empirical research has influenced the school's physical designs, especially since the mid-1990s and with the injection of funds through Building Education Revolution (Australian Government Department of Education and Training, 2014), traditional classrooms of separate units of rigid bricks and mortar have evolved into learning spaces of blended amalgamations of flexible physical or digital arrangements (Burke & Grosvenor, 2015; Mulcahy, Cleveland, & Aberton, 2015). These changes impacted on the role expectations of the school leader in being innovative with teaching and influencing teachers and at the same time being accountable for student results.

An implication, given the changes to the organisational structures of NSW secondary schools, is that the Principals (see Chapters 6 and 7) were formed as teachers and leaders through this period of change. Leadership structures in NSW System Schools also changed to accommodate these organisational and curriculum structures.

CONTEXT: NOT EVERYTHING, BUT SOMETHING

Curriculum designs in secondary schools, such as the diverse learning spaces enabled by the Building Education Revolution (Lewis, Dollery, & Kortt, 2014), digital platforms and especially the changes in the mindset of secondary school educators from being focused not only on subject content to now include the student as a learner, certainly have also influenced the role expectations of leaders to be heading in this direction with their teachers. In the recruitment of principals in 2020, boards and school systems were looking for leaders of pedagogy, innovation, evidence informed practices, with a research base pointing to the latest empirical research in what teaching processes bring about best outcomes for students. Moreover, a leader's empirical research base was context specific to Australia's challenges. Gannicott reflects on the implementation of Gonski 2.0:

> ... for pupils from a low socio-economic background the difference between a good teacher and a bad teacher is a whole year's learning ... Australian students lose more than 2 years of learning due to the inadequate quality of schooling ... adaptive direct instruction rank near the top in their measured impact on educational effectiveness, inquiry based teaching ranks near the bottom. (Gannicott, 2019, pp. 23–27)

5.6 School Leadership Structures and Career Pathways

Leadership structures in Australian schools influence the career pathways that aspirant school leaders may follow. Some structures are tight and may mean that by default, an aspirant leader can miss opportunities to experience leadership positions in teaching and learning. Historically and traditionally secondary schools, depending on the student population, were organised with four tiers of leadership. The first tier was the teacher, who held two primary functions: subject and pastoral. The second tier was the faculty coordinator or the pastoral/year advisor. The third tier was the deputy principal or assistant principal, for discipline and welfare. The fourth tier was the principal. Hence, deputies or assistant principals could arrive at the doorstep of principalship without having experienced leading learning and teaching and of a larger school, nor any recent experience in teaching.

5.7 Pedagogical Leadership Is Privileged

For the Principals in the Norris (2017) study the effect of these school leadership structures was an important contextual issue. Secondary school principals employed, before the year 2000 and with a student population of 650 or more, were likely to have been distant from teaching and learning matters for a significant period, possibly between 4 and 10 years. However, by the beginning of the 21st century these traditional leadership structures were becoming less common. The role of assistant principals/deputy principals with teaching and learning portfolios was growing in popularity—for example in one large NSW School System, 'leaders of pedagogy' had been introduced (Conway & Andrews, 2015). Other systems were assigning one of their assistant principal's/deputy's roles to pedagogical leadership to the point where the curriculum administration function was removed, and in some schools downgraded to a coordinator's role, equivalent to a faculty coordinator. Such changes sent a message to educators in the secondary sector that leadership practices focussed on pedagogy were a priority, and no longer was teaching and learning an isolated activity for teachers. Moreover, the pedagogical leadership practices also had their own flavour; definitions varied between systems and the implementation of such pedagogical leadership styles was certainly unique. The definition of pedagogical leadership was common however the implementation held their own nuances for each school, understandably.

5.8   Enter Instructional Leadership

Within the pedagogical leadership style emerged instructional leadership again. It was known in a different form (Bridges, 1967; Brieve, 1972). It was revitalized with varying expressions and widespread influence across school systems in government and non-government sectors (Aas & Paulsen, 2019; Boyce & Bowers, 2018). Part of this influence is attributed to the emergence in the esteem of evidence-based practices (EBP). There was a direct cause in the rise of EBPS. EBPS in teachers' work arose shortly after the public disclosure of the school's results from NAPLAN testing. The subsequent competition between schools for their market share (Ragusa & Bousfield, 2017) also spurred school leaders at the school and system level to action.

5.9   Data to Evidence Informed Practices

The work of school systems' leaders and school leaders during the 2008–2018 period was ensconced in working with teachers in utilising data informed evidence for their teaching practices. Any change needed a reason, that reason needed to be based on data informed evidence. Intuition was obsolete and past practices were often viewed with suspicion. The work of Breakspear, Hattie, Sharrat, Timperely and Robinson played a significant role in reimagining leadership from conceptual understandings to practices. School systems employed their research and consultancy services to help teachers and leaders to manage the competition in driving for above benchmark results. Data walls, learning sprints, visible learning agile were a few of the teaching practices that arose during this time. Literacy and numeracy blocks in primary schools and literary devices across subjects in secondary schools where curriculum structural initiatives were designed for improving literacy and numeracy results. Literacy scaffolds for writing were popular and certainly improved secondary and primary students writing skills across subjects. Corporate student coaching clinics increased in magnitude with the purpose of gaining entry to selective schools. NAPLAN had become the pseudo curriculum.

5.10   *The Human Element Returns*

Yet by 2021 there were increasing signs of valuing the human element in the student relationship when utilising data to inform practice. One of the successes of data walls with students' photos was the acknowledgment and acceptance that teachers teach people, not numbers. The acknowledged relationship with the child or young person is valued as integral to their learning outcomes. Wellbeing and student achievement were no longer seen as discrete concepts but were interdependent of each other in terms of student success. From 2016–2020 the emergence of wellbeing frameworks with learning integrated through them were customary with the National Wellbeing Framework employed as the key referral platform for school systems (Australian Government Department of Education, 2018). For most of the 2020 school year, the COVID-19 disruption resulted in some school leaders eager to capture 'the best' in their leadership practices and those of their teachers, as they moved in and out of remote learning experiences. Some were seeking a 'new normal' for their schools. Opportunities abounded in the minds of some teachers and leaders resulting from COVID-19 and school lockdowns. However, these steps were measured with the consequential realisation that the wellbeing of students and their parents was first and foremost the highest priority to enable a healthy learning environment. Without 'well wellbeing' minimal learning engagement could occur.

During the 2008–2018 period Australian schools and school systems were becoming more responsive to empirical research and were adaptable and creative with their staffing. New positions according to their current contextual needs, their peer networks and moreover with relevant research, welcomed the emergence and acceptance of pedagogical leadership for all educational leaders. The Principals' experiences reported in Chapters 6 and 7 were part of such changes. Leadership restructuring had occurred in most of their schools over that period, privileging pedagogical leadership, as distinct from curriculum administration. School leaders and aspirants needed to know and understand teaching and learning processes, so they could guide and support others to do so. Role expectations hence changed for principals. They were no longer the 'administrator' or 'taking care of business.'

5.11 School Principals and Their Role in the Australian Accountability Environment

The role of the secondary school principal in Australian school systems not only reflects the local educational context of the pedagogical and accountability movement in these systems but also reflects the global trends regarding expectations of school leaders (Schleicher, 2012; Thessin & Louis, 2019). From the early 1990s to early 2020, the principal's function progressed from administration to a learning function (Brookhart & Moss, 2013) and explicitly, the principal's function became deeply embedded as a leader of learning (DuFour & Marzano, 2015). By 2020, instructional leadership was privileged, and in this mix being a leader of teaching practices informed by data informed evidence (see Figure 8): "Contrary to expectations during the 1980s, instructional leadership has demonstrated remarkable staying power, growing into one of the most powerful models guiding research, policy and practice in school leadership" (Hallinger, Gümüş, & Bellibaş, 2020, p. 1629).

5.12 Professional Standards for School Leaders

The introduction of Australian professional standards for principals, named 'Standard,' provides another level of accountability should school system advisors deem the Standard as an appropriate accountable measure. The Principal Standard, introduced in Australia in 2015 (Australian Institute for Teaching and School Leadership (AITSL), 2016) includes an expectation that principals 'manage high standards and accountability.' Managing high standards and accountability means principals will engage in professional practices which "use a range of data management methods and technologies to ensure that the school's resources and staff are efficiently organised" (Australian Institute for Teaching and School Leadership (AITSL), 2016, p. 18). Principals, including senior executive leaders, are expected to "review the effectiveness of processes and use of data to improve school performance' at the same time as embedding 'a culture of review, responsibility and shared accountability to achieve high standards for all" (AITSL, 2016, p. 18). 'Leadership Requirements' means that principals will "utilise their personal qualities and social and interpersonal skills by taking into account the social, political and local circumstances within which they work" (AITSL, 2016, p. 23). The implication of the Principal Standard on an educational leaders' work, and important for this book, is that some school systems adopt elements from the Principal Standard to guide the design of their appraisal processes for principals.

Tertiary institutions include the practices of the Principal Standard in their post graduate programs for leaders. Tertiary programs in post graduate studies for educational leaders also offer leading teaching and learning streams which target performativity and accountability in the context of their learning communities (Australian Catholic University, 2017; UNSW, 2016). These tertiary programs enable educational leaders and aspirant educational leaders to examine ways to integrate external accountability for performance results, such as the Year 12 exit assessment. One tool, found in the Principal Standard, named 360 degree Reflection Tool, is adopted by individuals and school systems as part of a principal's suite of professional learning experiences (Australian Institute for Teaching and School Leadership (AITSL), 2017). A new guide called the Evaluation of the Principals' Preparation guide released in November 2016 by AISTL (AITSL Australian Institute for Teaching and School Leadership, 2016) is a substantial practical guide for those preparing professional learning for principals, educational leaders and aspirant educational leaders. Such a guide indicates the high importance of the considerations that may be needed in preparing professional learning for principals, notably regulating for high standards and accountability of teachers and teaching.

By 2020 accountability cultures blanketed the work of Australian school educators. Teacher standards were well embedded across Australian educational jurisdictions, from teacher progressions to initial teacher education programs. Testing had become more prolific with literacy and numeracy expanding from pre-school testing to entry levels into the teaching profession with Literacy and Numeracy Testing for Initial Teacher Education (LANTITE). Leadership practices, privileging pedagogical and instructional leadership and teaching practices privileging evidence-based practices for improving student results had hallmarks which were understandably characteristic of performative cultures.

6 Faith-Based: Dual Bind or Single Resolve?

School leaders in faith-based schools/systemic schools across Australia have an additional responsibility to be leaders of faith; the custodian and care for the vitality of their identity and mission. This could be seen by some as a double bind and for others a source of release or strength. Their role includes holding a world view of their religious affiliation. Common to all faith-based school leaders, are the two functions of leadership, teaching and learning and faith. These could be in conflict requiring role negotiation by leaders. The shift to pedagogical and accountable leadership within a school system, the school system advisor-principal relationship along with the principal's faith leadership responsibilities are significant changes to a school leader's role.

Being accountable as a leader of teaching and learning not only includes performance results but improving pedagogies, establishing learning and teaching policies such as assessment, determining which courses are offered and when regarding timetabling and resourcing. In terms of the expectations of being a leader of teaching and learning some school principals in faith-based schools could possibly have seen this move in the priorities of the School System as an expansion of their role. Others may have been fortunate enough, depending on enrolments, to employ business or finance managers. Principals in most non-government systemic schools, like government school systems, are employed and report to a director of that school system, who in turn, in the faith-based school, is a head cleric and employing authority. Often the Head Cleric delegates the authority to a layperson who in turn, and in large systems, delegates their role to senior advisors, who support and supervise principals directly. These changes have meant a significant shift in expectations for principals themselves, the teachers with whom they work (Pettit, 2009) and changing expectations by their employers and advisors (see Figure 8). The changes hold several implications.

One implication about this structure concerns the school system advisor-principal relationship. The external accountabilities for performance results are made known to the principals by system advisors, with the expectation of the accountabilities being implemented by the principals and monitored by the advisors.

A further implication is that the principal's role in a faith based school is determined by the and "embodied in a particular set of values and ethics"

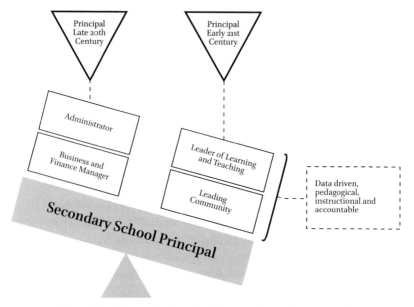

FIGURE 8   The shifting balance in the role of the secondary school principal

(Bezzina, 2008, p. 222). Such values and ethics may present certain determinations in the way principals view external assessments and ways principals enact their accountabilities.

The role of a faith-based school leader in Australia holds a dual function of leading teaching and learning and leading faith. It is reasonable to entertain the notion that the dual function of the role presents at times competing priorities for leaders in their interpretations and responses to accountability for student results. For example, school leaders' views of accountability for performance results (and the resultant competition between schools) may be misaligned with not only their beliefs about learning but also their religious beliefs. Comparably, Striepe, Clarke and O'Donoghue (2014) found that leaders' perspectives on leadership were enhanced by the ethos of the school's faith tradition.

6.1   *Leadership Styles*

School leaders' various commitment levels to their religious ethos (and embedded values and beliefs) may influence leaders' perspectives in their preference for a particular leadership style. Styles that are attractive to school leaders, yet not limited to, within faith based communities include servant (Greenleaf, 2002; Striepe & O'Donoghue, 2014), authentic (Duignan, 2008) and transformational leadership (Henson, 2020; Sosik, Zhu, & Blair, 2011). Other styles which may be expected from regulatory authorities, such as instructional leadership driving for student results, may conflict with the school leader's own choice of style. While this conflict is speculative there have been some research studies which supports this speculation (Schechter, Shaked, Ganon-Shilon, & Goldratt, 2018; Dulude, 2021; Shaked, 2018).

Yet, a leader's own values and skills in decision making may have more influence on such conflicts than religious beliefs (Chitpin & Jones, 2015). Religious and secular leadership perspectives may align closer than one may think. There is a secular shift in school leadership, moving from economic bureaucratic perspective to an ethical professional accountability perspective (Yan, 2019), albeit this shift is in a Canadian context.

Basically, in the application examples of the Principals, it was important to consider the degree that the Principals embedded their faith commitments into their role and the possible impact of this embodiment in their interpretations of and responses to their accountability for student performance results. The key point here is that it is not uncommon for principals working in faith-based schools being forced to reconcile secular expectations with their religious beliefs. That said, there is some comfort as principals in faith-based schools have professional networks within their school systems and are likely to share such tensions between themselves. And for another study, and although potentially contentious, investigating how religious and secular leadership perspectives align would be of interest.

This next section transitions to what is known about how school leaders manage competing priorities around accountability expectations for performance results. The section draws on specific empirical studies in this domain, demonstrating the challenges which mirror experiences of school leaders being accountable to a higher authority, and at the same time, leading their teaching teams to meet these authority expectations.

7 Principals' Interpretations of Their Accountability: Clashing Times

Government policies that mandate certain policies of accountability may not have the level of influence on principals that governments expect. It is inaccurate to assume that policy incentives are the only, or even the most important, influence on principals (Shipps & White, 2009). While Leithwood and Jantzi (2008) observed that district policies explained a large variation in how principals viewed their effectiveness in enacting accountability policy, the study by Shipps and White (2009) found that the variations stemmed from what principals decided they would attend to in their accountability environment and how they related one obligation to another (Shipps & White, 2009). Shipps's (2012) research into principals' enactments found similarities to Spillane et al.'s study (2002), concluding that "school leaders do not simply react to policy makers" expectations' (Shipps, 2012, p. 3). Similarly, Braun, Maguire, and Ball (2010) found that policy implementers engaged in a process of interpretation and translation of their understanding of the policy into the school environment, rather than simply implementing as the policy makers intended.

7.1 *Ignore or Adapt a Policy*

School leaders do not react to shifts in policies, they make strategic choices (Shipps & White, 2009). For instance, when a policy change is introduced, school leaders will deliberate about how they intend to respond. When faced with increasing accountability expectations, educational leaders make decisions about whether and how they will enact policy (Shipps, 2012; Spillane, Diamond, et al., 2002). Spillane, Diamond et al. (2002) found that principals in high-stakes accountability regimes could choose to ignore or adapt a policy, rather than adopt it *per se*. In their responses to government policies in these systems, principals translate policy then making considered decisions about how their schools are organised, what curriculum is taught, what counts for

CONTEXT: NOT EVERYTHING, BUT SOMETHING

high-quality instruction and how the needs of diverse learners can be met (Marks & Nance, 2007).

7.2 Blending Versus Forgoing

School leaders also engage in 'accountability talk.' Leaders' rhetorical sequences in their talk weave the external demands with the agreed morals and emotions of the community (Lowenhaupt, Spillane, & Hallett, 2016). Lowenhaupt et al. found that the principal's oral narrative was the main means in blending competing priorities. Integral to the blend were principals' own values and ethical commitments. On the other hand, leaders may choose not to align their professional and moral commitments with policy intentions. Shipps and White (2009) found that principals' values and commitments were 'decoupled from professional commitments' as they attended to 'less ethical precepts with their other responsibilities' (p. 370). Some principals no longer continued with certain learning platforms, such as social justice programs (Marks & Nance, 2007), reporting that they had foregone deeply held commitments and often experiencing a sense of loss (Shipps & White, 2009).

7.3 Lifelines: Competing Views Lead to Sensemaking

Clearly, principals need to make decisions and act when reconciling competing viewpoints. It is reasonable to propose that the ways principals reconcile competing viewpoints depends largely on how they make sense of them. Implementation of policy relies on getting a sense of the policy (Spillane, Diamond, et al., 2002). Sensemaking in accountability environments means first, examining what a policy means then working out how it may be implemented in context (Spillane, Diamond, et al., 2002).

Principals vary in their ways of making sense of external expectations, ranging from what appears to be confident in this respect, to growing in confidence over time. Principals who demonstrate confidence in managing the expectations engage multiple data sources, using bureaucratic guidelines (bureaucratic accountability) and competitive forces (market accountability) 'to create a coherent story about the school' (Shipps & White, 2009, p. 379). For others they frame accountability as a responsibility, privileging responsibility for students' learning and teachers' professional learning over performance results (Darling-Hammond, 2010). Others struggle with reconciling what is being asked of them and implementing policy in the ways they prefer. For example in one study, in an educational jurisdiction with external incentives (such as performance pay for principals) early-career principals (ECPs) were more likely to experience tensions between their interpretations of their expectations and their implementation phases than were mid to later career stage principals (Shipps & White, 2009).

7.4 Lifelines: Experience Helps

Some school leaders, irrespective of the stages in leadership, experienced changes in such tensions over time. In the same study by Shipps and White (2009), at least half of the principals reported that in their early exposure to high-stake accountability systems they were more likely to experience tensions between how they perceived the mandated policy and how they perceived the expectations of their school contexts. However, three years later, Shipps and White (2009) found that these principals' tensions had decreased; they seemed to have made sense of the policy expectations and felt more capable of implementing the policy in their contexts, in their own ways and without forgoing their personal ethical commitments.

7.5 Lifelines: Leader Networks

School leaders' professional experiences, values, and ethical commitments, and/or their world view are not the only influences on how they make sense of external policies, such as accountability demands. School leader peer networks are influential in the ways they make sense of policies (Jennings, 2010). The study by Jennings found Principal A employed in a small school system had some ties with other principals yet felt a lack of trust with their intentions. As a result, Principal A was making sense of the accountability demands in isolation. Principal B, also trying to manage accountability demands in a different school system, was put in touch with veteran peer principals. Principal B shared information with her current peer principals about what was safe to bend the rules and which policy demands could be ignored. Clearly Principal B was in a more supportive environment to make decisions according to their beliefs to the ones that the policy makers were expecting.

The literature sources reviewed here propose that school leaders' interpretations of the accountability expectations are not simply a matter of implementing what policy makers expect. Rather, leaders make sense of their expectations before they enact. It stands to reason that their sensemaking is predictive of their behaviours that follow. The Theory of Planned Behaviour (TPB) is prognostic and names likely outcomes when knowing an individual's beliefs, hence its pivotal inclusion in the ELM.

8 Policy to Practice Gap

While leaders, principals and CEOs need to firstly understand a policy themselves, they then need to know how to translate it to their constituents. Policy enactments is a process of understanding, interpreting and then translating these interpretations into acts (Braun, Maguire, & Ball, 2010). This process involves school leaders being able to understand and interpret before translating the accountability demands into acts which aim to influence teaching teams, in terms of their teaching practices. Hardy (2014) contends that policy enactment is a dynamic process; "putting policies into practice is a creative, sophisticated and complex process" (p. 549), where the practical enactments of policy are rarely a lived reality in a top-down approach. In other words the policy intention rarely reflects the lived reality (Ball, Maguire, Braun, & Hoskins, 2011). Disruptions occur. Assumptions in shared yet inexplicit decision making result in blame and confusion (Advertiser, 2020).

8.1   *A Paradox*

Enacted policies need to be monitored carefully at each step of the process (Hardy, 2014). As a result, the extent to which policies may hold influence, particularly upon teachers' classroom practices, is tenuous (Hardy, 2014), and at times a 'paradox of enactment' as Ball et al. (2011) found:

> The teachers and other adults here are not naïve actors, they are creative and sophisticated, and they manage, but they are also tired and overloaded much of the time. They are engaged, coping with the meaningful and the meaningless, often self-mobilised around patterns of focus and neglect and torn between discomfort and pragmatism, but most are also very firmly embedded in the prevailing policies discourses. (p. 625)

In Australia, some aspects of the impact for school leaders have been researched, such as principals' ways of viewing accountability and its possible impacts (Cranston, 2013); the importance of principals' understanding of the teaching and learning processes (Dufour & Marzano, 2011); the ways principals may integrate external and internal accountability processes; and the ways they buffer the impacts from the external expectations around external testing from teachers and students (Wenner & Settlage, 2015). Hardy and Lewis (2017) in their Queensland study found teachers' and school leaders' responses to data could be described as the 'doublethink of data'; teachers and school leaders engage with accountability processes but only for the purposes of compliance and 'not seeing any value in doing so' (p. 671).

8.2   *Increasing Expectations of Australian School Leaders*

There are increasing expectations that Australian school leaders, and principals, must be able to manage accountability expectations for student results and undertake these expectations as part of their professional responsibility. For some leaders they feel shackled with such responsibilities. Current studies into the well-being risks for Australian principals are of concern (Riley, 2017).

Emotional labour and regulation in managing multiple and complex demands in highly volatile environments for secondary school principals are pressing and an important research field (Hauseman, 2020; Maxwell & Riley, 2017). In contrast Cranston (2013), an Australian scholar in educational accountability discourses, argues that educational leaders need to examine their role critically and take control with a liberating professionalism, unshackling the potential chains of accountability.

8.3 Accountable for What?

Accountability responsibilities for Australian principals are broad: (a) enacting being leaders of learning (DuFour & Marzano, 2015); (b) meeting the non-negotiable expectations of employing data to inform their teaching and learning processes (Moss, 2013; Phillips, 2014; Shen, Ma, Cooley, & Burt, 2015); (c) demonstrating data use; (d) providing reasons for performance results to secure tenure (Drake et al., 2016); and (e) listening to the current mantra that the 'silver bullet' for these demands is instructional leadership (Rigby, 2016; Scott, 2016).

8.4 How Do School Leaders Manage Their Accountabilities?

Meeting these expectations requires school leaders to be adaptive and adept, not only with the task at hand but also with the plethora of advice that these researchers offer to system leaders and school leaders. For example, numerous evolutions of instructional leadership have been offered over the last 30 years (Bendikson, Robinson, & Hattie, 2012; Blase & Blase, 1999; Hallinger, 2003) with the latest instructional style promising a potential avenue to liberating professionalism and removing the chains of accountability (Thessin & Louis, 2019; Townsend, 2019; Wilkinson, Edwards-Groves, Grootenboer, & Kemmis, 2019).

Other empirical studies offer more strategic insights into the effective ways that school leaders may manage external demands for positive student results. They need to be more than simply leaders of learning but take responsibility for being proactive and committed to pedagogical reform (Simon, Heck, Christie, & Farragher, 2019); to personalise (Sharratt & Fullan, 2012) and understand data sources (Chen, 2019) rather than simply provide evidence of data use (Datnow & Hubbard, 2016; Kaufman, Graham, Picciano, Popham, & Wiley, 2014); to learn with staff in professional development experiences (Robinson, 2011); know the impact of collective teacher efficacy on student learning (Jenni Donohoo et al., 2018) and to seek current educational research.

8.5 The Perils in Driving for Results

Ineffective practices also provide pointers of how Australian school leaders are likely to manage the competing demands of innovative pedagogy with the drive for favourable results. Limiting the utility of data to inform performance targets can produce negative effects. Koretz (2008) found that in school systems with high stakes and where leaders used accountability processes to drive performance results, this drive gradually replaced the 'diagnosis of the strengths and weaknesses of individual students' learning' (p. 47). The student and their learning became obsolete. This study asserts the importance of integrating external demands with internal school commitments of teachers with their students and their learning relationships. The skills of managing external and internal accountability expectations are handled better by some school leaders in some contexts than others (Gonzalez & Firestone, 2013). The complexities of managing the external with the internal is a mastery (Thiel et al., 2012). Four skills of mastery in managing such complexities are: emotion regulation, self-reflection, forecasting and information integration. These skills enable leaders in navigating ethical competing priorities and conflicting dilemmas in organisations.

8.6 *Effective Management, Effective Integration*

It is important that the school's external pushes and internal pulls are managed effectively. School leaders who know how and do integrate external with internal accountability expectations minimise the possible negative impacts of the accountability expectations (Elmore, 2005). The findings by Seashore Louis, Knapp, and Feldman (2012) confirm that educational leaders, even though working in different environments, found similar strategising techniques, utilising resources from the array of external accountability demands (and supporting aids) to serve their own internal accountability goals. Both these studies demonstrated that school leaders internalise what is expected from external expectations and co-design accountable practices, such as leading through data and modelling learning and teaching processes in a fully accountable way. As they did this, these school leaders redesigned the scope of pedagogy and the instructional learning conversation and, at the same time made leading learning more overt (Seashore Louis et al., 2012).

8.7 *School Leaders' Influencing Teachers*

School leaders influence the ways teachers interpret and enact accountability expectations. If the percentages of in-school variance in student learning can be attributed to leadership (5–10% in Dinham, 2005 and 12% in Walker et al., 2014), then school leaders are likely to hold some level of influence about how teachers interpret and enact external expectations. For this reason, it is worthwhile to examine Australian teachers' and students' responses to accountability expectations for performance results, in this case NAPLAN. Knowing how teachers respond to the national testing regime of NAPLAN provides fodder for what school leaders need to consider in their professional practices.

Teachers' interpretations of NAPLAN results are negative when they are used to police and rank schools (Polesel et al., 2014). Teachers perceive that ranking undermines the school's reputation. In the publication of NAPLAN results on the My School website, the competitive pressures generated among teachers and even parents, and the use by systems of NAPLAN data, are interpreted by educators as blunt instruments for judging schools and teacher performances (Gorur, 2015; Polesel et al., 2014). The aims of My School were well intended; to "help drive improvement and provide increased accountability for the community" (ACARA, 2011) however using tests for accountability purposes are met with unintended consequences and certainly derail its original aim (Berliner, 2011; Stobart, 2008).

Teachers' practices potentially provide some indicators of how accountability expectations are being interpreted by leaders in the school. Student progression is another indicator. However, this indicator needs a word of caution. For example, the dramatic improvement in students' performance results that was attributed to Texas's processes of accountability was questionable. Approaches by school leaders enacting their prescribed accountability mechanisms failed the minority youth and their communities, as young Texan people had to repeat their courses of study if they failed to meet the benchmarks. This resulted in huge dropout rates (Valenzuela, 2005). However, these students did not appear in the Texan state's method of collecting data, which 'hid as much as it revealed' (Valenzuela, 2005, p. 1).

A study by Marsh, Farrell, and Bertrand (2014) found where accountability policies placed high expectations on teachers, they often enacted potentially demotivating, performance-oriented learning processes. They unwittingly involved students in data use with the aim of motivating the students. The data were disclosed publicly, with the results compared with other teachers and focusing on status, yet there was minimal support provided regarding ways of building knowledge. These contextual factors pressured teachers to focus on performance results. This research offers a cautionary tale of the 'trickle-down' effects of accountability policy on students. The point to be made from these studies is that principals or senior school leaders are likely to be influencing teachers' interpretations and their subsequent teaching practices (Donaldson, 2013; Supovitz, Sirinides, & May, 2009).

Alongside this empirical research of school leaders' responses to accountability demands there is an emerging research area on whether and/or how external demands such as accountability shape school leaders' professional identities.

CONTEXT: NOT EVERYTHING, BUT SOMETHING 79

9   School Leader Identity Formation

There is growing research interest about the impact of test based accountability in the identity formation of school leaders (Crow, Day, & Møller, 2017), and across international contexts (Johnson & Crow, 2017).

Providing opportunities for developing models, frames or schema are useful tools to improving, not only early career leaders, but all school leaders in their effectiveness in managing the tensions between external and internal pulls (Lakoff & Johnson, 2008). Moreover, in the school community, when school leaders have established, or ideally co-designed, effective internal accountability processes, which are agile and adaptable, they may easily align with external accountability systems whereby they easily reorder their goals and subsume the external expectations (Darling-Hammond, 2010b; Louis & Mintrop, 2012; Seashore Louis et al., 2012). As external demands increase, and school walls and doors diminish, an exciting area for future research is emerging, around the extent to which agile and flexible school structures and processes absorb and adapt to any external policy demands, or disruption (i.e., COVID-19, from school lockdowns to remote learning).

Moreover, the demands will require that school leaders themselves need to be agile and adaptable to these demands. Along with models, frames and schemata, to diminish leaders' tensions from the demands, they may to be skilled at values alignment, particularly in the early stages of their leadership formation (Darling-Hammond, Meyerson, LaPointe, & Orr, 2010; Seashore Louis & Mintrop, 2012). It is an increasing need for leaders to know themselves, their actual values (Branson, 2014) belief and attitudes (Ajzen, 1991) and akin to teacher identity formation this is crucial in the early years of their formation as leaders. The risk in not doing so becomes an attrition issue, for keeping not only teachers in the profession but attracting school leaders.

Chapter 5 deals with a particular external demand that school leaders face. This external demand is educational accountability. The chapter prepares the groundwork for the applications of the ELM in Chapters 6 and 7.

Notes

1   See https://www.acara.edu.au/reporting/my-school-website
2   See https://www.oecd.org/pisa/pisafaq/

CHAPTER 5

Educational Accountability

New Normal or Site of Struggle?

1 Introducing Educational Accountability

From highly regulated accountability environments with embedded data cultures (Lasater, Albiladi, Davis, & Bengtson, 2020) employing performative based mechanisms to the routine checklists, such as the audit, have the potential to create fear and distrust with educators (Lasater et al., 2020; Power, 2000; Shore & Wright, 2003). The aim therefore for school leaders is to trust their honest convictions and in this case not fear accountability expectations and help and encourage their communities to do so as well. Trust instead of fear mitigates these consequences where balanced leadership safeguards innovation (Schoen & Fusarelli, 2008). Ideally accountability is a catalyst for new possibilities and improvement for school communities.

Educators and scholars alike adopt preferential terms for accountability, the tell-tale signs of their world views. The term 'educational accountability' in school education can be derived by examining what regulators are asking of school leaders and how regulators monitor and evaluate the performances of leaders, teachers and students, and the consequences of such evaluation. The primary regulator sets out to make clear what is required of educators. The school leader needs to interpret such expectations, coach, instruct, or unfortunately in some circumstances, coerce their teachers around their practices to meet such expectations. As such the school leader is a mediating agent. In current school cultures regulators evaluate the performance of the mediating agents. This is a common pattern in the accountability cycle in school education in Australia.

In the theoretical ELM school leaders' sensemaking and sensegiving are triggered by external demands. This chapter situates educational accountability as that demand. The chapter does not aim to cover all aspects of education accountability, but to prepare the reader for Chapters 6 and 7. The Principals in these chapters report their experiences of educational accountability. This chapter (Chapter 5) presents the types of accountabilities facing school leaders, arrives at a definition for educational accountability, reviews the rationale for accountability, examines the accountability mechanisms, including their strengths and weaknesses employed by schools and finally evaluates the terms 'low and high stakes.'

© KONINKLIJKE BRILL NV, LEIDEN, 2022 | DOI:10.1163/9789004517202_005

EDUCATIONAL ACCOUNTABILITY   81

2   The New Normal: Site of Struggle?

> Education has always been a 'site of struggle.' Education is dangerous, because schools and colleges do not just reproduce culture, they shape the new society that is coming into existence all around us. (Connell, 2012, p. 681)

2.1   *New Normal*

Looking over the past decade (2010–2020), educators new to Australian education could easily assume that accountability as part of their school cultures were their norm. Teachers who entered the profession from 2010 would only have experienced school life with a school improvement plan (SIP). SIPs, for example, is a process that most Australian schools engage with, where the school community is at the beginning, middle or end of a cycle. By 2020 such plans included evidence-based practices (measurable and accountable) directing their work. Very few initiatives have any impetus in schools today unless they can demonstrate evidence, and that evidence needs to be measurable. There must be validated reasons for setting school goals, and moreover the nominated mechanism to measure the outputs from those goals needs articulating. Reasons for goals are also subject to accountability.

2.2   *Sites of Struggle*

For some teachers these evidence-based goals may mean their daily routine is slotted into instructional literacy and numeracy blocks of time with explicit and externally regulated instruction, resulting in formative or summative assessment. For some teachers and students their teaching and learning have been regulated to a point where the human elements of joy, happiness and self-fulfilment in learning and teaching are superseded by data driven and rubric centred institutions. Ironically these hard-driven performative, and at times hyper-competitive, cultures have seen the emergence of lifesaving and counterpoint instruments and practices such as wellbeing frameworks and programs (Australian Government, 2018a). Such programs are designed to support school leaders, teachers and students manage the perceived erosion of their professionalism (such as making their own decisions) and pressures of highly regulated accountabilities (Appel, 2020; Riley, 2017).

2.3   *Accountability an Eclectic Term*

Accountability in most spheres of life is a broad term. So too, in schools and school systems the term is wide-ranging and diverse in understanding. Some adjectives used to describe accountability for student performances include test-based accountability, assessment focussed accountability, performative accountability, or educational accountability. To be sure of what is being held to account, who is being held to account and the consequences of such accounts it is important to settle on and understand the types of accountabilities and what they mean. Educators may account for the inputs in education, which were commonly adopted in the mid-20th century. This accountability of inputs entailed annual accruals, for example how funds were spent, orchestrated often by the business managers of schools and systems. They also included justification of programs. The accountability for inputs remained. By the beginning of the 21st century educational accountability had and still is to be known in terms of outputs and restricted, yet not limited to, accountability for student performance results. However, two decades on and working with what and how educational outcomes are accounted, a more representative term of the reality is *performative accountability*. Students are held to account for their performances. Teachers are held to account for their students' performances. School leaders are held to account for their teachers' performances of their student performance results. If performing well it is a site of success, if poorly, a site of struggle. There is a plethora of literature regarding performativity in education (Ball, 2003; Hardy & Lewis, 2017; Perryman, 2009). Whilst performativity in education is important and influential scholarship it is not the purpose of this chapter to examine these literatures (Appel, 2020; Gobby et al., 2018; Hardy & Lewis, 2017). To avoid a vacuum by omitting a whole research stream regarding performativity, the broader term for accountability to be employed is *educational* accountability.

Performances for student results are not the only accountability in education. Educators and school leaders, face numerous accountabilities, where some of these intersect with students' performance results.

3   Typology of Accountability in Education

Numerous accountabilities face school leaders. The types of accountabilities are an important consideration for several reasons. First, they are referred to in several research studies in which educational leaders define to whom and for what they are accountable (Firestone & Shipps, 2005; Shipps & White, 2009), going well beyond the accountabilities set by governments (Adams & Kirst, 1999; Darling-Hammond, 1989). Second, the Principals in Chapter 6, like other school leaders often distinguish between the types of accountability facing them (Shipps, 2012) and in particular, notice the different pressures each type comes to bear on their work (Farrell, 2014). Third, other accountabilities

EDUCATIONAL ACCOUNTABILITY

intersect on school leaders in their accountability for student performance results, such as market or bureaucratic accountability.

The types of accountabilities described here that may dovetail into the work of school leaders are bureaucratic, market, professional, moral, and ethical accountabilities. These are by no means the full list however these are common types of accountabilities facing school leaders.

3.1   *To Market, to Market*

Market accountability in education emerges when educators are seen as competing in a marketplace to 'sell' more of their commodities (Grace, 1989). In these instances, a commodity may be students' performance results. The enrolment data may also serve as performance measures for school regulators (Harrison & Rouse, 2014). One rationale for educational market accountability stems from the intentions of governments to provide choice of schooling, with educators responding to parent and student preferences (Angus, 2015; Windle, 2009). Another rationale is that increasing the competition between schools improves school performance results (Jensen et al., 2013). The mechanism employed to achieve this is through a competitive vehicle (Firestone & Shipps, 2005). Market accountability in Australian education, for example, is the use of publicly disclosed student performance results. Parents and students make choices regarding schools from these results (Australian Curriculum Assessment and Reporting Authority, 2020; *My School and Beyond*, 2009). The consequences of market accountability are played out through possible loss of the market share reflected in decreased student enrolments along with the lived reality of competing with 'like schools' and between schools, resulting in possible low morale and secretive practices. In the early stages of the public disclosure of school results (MySchool), an Australian principal explains their competition in this way: "Why would I want to share all our successes with my colleagues down the road?" (McGuire, 2012, p. 46).

3.2   *Bureaucratic Accountability in Education*

In education, bureaucratic accountability involves educators being required to achieve targetted goals from an authority that is external to the school (Sleeter, 2007). The rationale for bureaucratic accountability is for the authority to expect adherence by the employee to the outcomes set by the targetted goals and to monitor the progress. For instance, bureaucratic accountability in Australian school systems may regulate processes between School systemic agendas, where school leaders with their community set school system learning goals which are monitored and evaluated by school system advisers. Each year, for example, school system leaders visit schools, where the school leadership team is required to present an evidence-based evaluation of their strategic plan. The plan is tracked to see if there is evidence that the school system goals are being met. The future 12 month plans also need to be aligned with the evidence of past performances. High priorities are given to tracking the publicly disclosed student performance results.

3.3 Professional Accountability in Education

Professional accountability occurs when educators are held answerable to the standards of the education profession (Jaafar & Anderson, 2007). Some researchers prefer to cast professional accountability as 'professional responsibility' (Cranston, 2013). Similarly, Darling-Hammond (2010) found that senior educational leaders prefer to coin accountability as a responsibility. The rationale for the emergence of professional accountability is a belief that monitoring a set of preferred practices (Firestone & Shipps, 2005) will improve the professional standards of educators (AITSL Australian Institute for Teaching and School Leadership, 2016; NSW Government, Department of Education and Communities, 2010). The mechanisms are through monitoring of and adherence to certain national and state standards and competencies. In Australia, these mechanisms occur nationally, with states and territories now being regulated to adhere to professional standards for entry to teaching and monitoring and adhering to early-career teacher milestones (ACT Parliamentary Counsel, 2015; AITSL Australian Institute for Teaching and School Leadership, 2016; Board of Studies Teaching and Educational Standards, 2016).

3.4 Moral and Ethical Accountability

Moral and ethical accountability are often described interchangeably in the literature (Firestone & Shipps, 2005). Educators are accountable for striving for their moral purpose (Begley, 2010), maintaining moral compass and acting as moral agents (Charles Burford & Pettit, 2011), facing fear and keeping with honest convictions; "an effort to use all knowledge for the good of all human beings" (Eleanor Roosevelt, as cited in Erikson, 1964, p. 801). Like the preferential term of 'responsibility' some scholars prefer to examine accountability from a moral or an ethical perspective. A moral or ethical perspective is a more intelligent form of accountability for educators (Sahlberg, 2010). The rationale for a moral and ethical accountability is the belief that internal morality of the collective beliefs (a set of standards) must be observed if the specific task of the institution is to be realised (Dorbeck-Jung, 1997). The mechanisms used in this type of accountability may be through internal evidence checks by community members. For instance, Begley's (2010) measuring stick of what 'is in the best interests of students' asserts the value commitment of educators in a

EDUCATIONAL ACCOUNTABILITY

particular school, with educators adhering to that value commitment of 'best interest' for the student, and measuring this through their internal school evidence processes. Keeping a balanced leadership approach is a key leadership task as cultures of performativity permeate the educational landscape. School leaders may find it helpful by employing self-reflection and self-reflexive exercises (Alvesson, 1996) to monitor their own actions, so that accountability is not 'done to them' but that they are guided by their own 'honest' convictions.

3.5   *Personal Accountability*

Personal accountability from a school leader's perspective is the sense of responsibility that the leader carries or exhibits through their actions, shaped by their ethical and moral convictions (Firestone & Shipps, 2005). As such personal accountability is likely to reflect both personal and normative reference points of the individual leader, which includes values, beliefs, ethics and morals (Gold & Simon, 2004). Noddings (2013) provides reasons in the education context of why a responsibility relationship is a preferred concept over accountability to educators. Noddings proposes that accountability has the likely potential to 'trigger a self-protective mechanism,' whereas responsibility places the emphasis on the individual's needs (p. 76). One other possible reason for responsibility being a preferred concept is its capacity to diminish individual blame. Responsibility may be viewed as "more inclusive and places the answerability for the success or failure of young people's learning on all of society—the public, legislators, parents, teachers, and administrators as well as the schools" (Shapiro & Stefkovich, 2016, p. 160). Responsibility is an acceptable term by decreasing individual blame and increasing collective ownership. Collective ownership has the potential for those in the accountability relationship to move away from the emotional triggers of accountability of individual blame. The term 'accountability relationship' is examined closely below.

In this way the accountability relationship in education asks everyone to place students at the centre and share the responsibility for the learning needs of the child or young person (Shapiro & Stefkovich, 2016), in a collective sense. When accountability is viewed in this way it is likely that the learning will encompass more than the results on a high stakes test but also "include evidence from broader and alternative types of assessment in determining what students have learned" (Shapiro & Stefkovich, 2016, p. 161). However, to equate accountability only with responsibility misses some of the nuances in its relational elements as identified in the definition proposed below. That said, for the purposes of this book the term responsibility needs serious consideration and whether the concept of responsibility is more palatable to school leaders. Table 4 acts as a summary for the narrative presented above.

TABLE 4   Typology of accountabilities in education

Type	Description	Rationale	Mechanism	Example
Market	Educators seen as competing in a marketplace to 'sell' more of their commodity (Grace, 1989)	To ensure that educators respond to parent and student preferences	Disclosure of information to stakeholders	Use of disclosed student performance results so parents and students can make choice regarding schools
Bureaucratic	Educators required to achieve targeted goals from an authority external to the school (Sleeter, 2007)	Educators to meet outcomes set by targeted goals	The regulation of processes and outcomes, with consequences (Firestone & Shipps, 2005)	Alignment of systemic learning goals and the school's learning goals
Professional	Educators held answerable to the standards or goals of the education profession (Jaafar & Anderson, 2007); viewed as a responsibility (Darling-Hammond, 2010)	To improve the professional standards of educators (NSW Government, Department of Education and Communities, 2010)	Preferred practices monitored (Firestone & Shipps, 2005) with the expectation of adherence and the consequences of ongoing employment	In Australia certain states have professional standards for entry to teaching. Early-career teacher milestones are monitored and adhered to (NSW Government, Department of Education and Communities, 2010)
Personal including Moral and Ethical	The judgements made about the realisation of an individual's (or school's) morality and ethics of their enactment from their espoused beliefs and value commitments (Firestone & Shipps, 2005). Responsibility is a significant dimension of personal accountability	To ensure that the specific task of the institution is realised (Dorbeck-Jung, 1997) and sharing collective responsibility in meeting the individual's needs (Shapiro & Stefkovich, 2016)	Internal evidence checks by stakeholders: individual self-audit	Educators monitor and adhere to a value commitment of 'in the best interests of students' through internal school evidence guides; leaders engage with their own self-reflection to monitor behaviours and beliefs (Branson, 2009)

EDUCATIONAL ACCOUNTABILITY

4 Defining Educational Accountability

Definitions of accountability are sparse in educational literature (Garn & Cobb, 2001; Stobart, 2008); other spheres are worth examining to establish a substantial and meaningful definition. Ironically, the mechanisms employed in the economic sector regarding accountability, and their impacts for leaders, have already found their way into education in Australia (Connell, 2015). The next section begins by reviewing a sample of definitions from different contexts, to form a definition of accountability that is suitable for the educational context.

4.1 *Grouping Definitions of Accountability*

Several definitions of accountability are synthesised into five key concepts. The word 'accountability' can have varying emphases, depending on the context. The economic sector defines accountability as the *obligation to provide information* so that people can make informed *judgements* about the performance and financial position of an organisation (Halligan, 2007). In a corporate governance context, Huse (2005) defines accountability as *defending one's reasons* for actions and *supplying* normative grounds by which they may *be justified.* Within a legal context, Bovens (2007) describes accountability as a 'relationship between the actor and a forum, in which the actor has an *obligation to explain and to justify* his or her conduct, the forum can pose questions and *pass judgement* and the actor may *face consequences*' (Bovens, 2007, p. 450).

Gray's (2002) definition in a social context, similar to that of Bovens (2007), is clear about the persons involved and the consequences that are to be faced. Accountability is explained in terms of individuals and organisations presenting *an account* of the actions for which society *holds them responsible* (Gray, 2002). Kuchapski's (2001) definition, from a political context, specifically identifies consequences as *'redress,'* defining accountability as those in office *providing information, justifying, and explaining* and providing redress to the people. Coghill et al. (2006), in the economic context, similar to Gray (2002), include the notion of a relationship in the sense of 'direct authority'; defining accountability as the "direct *authority relationship* within which one party accounts to a person or body for the performance of tasks or functions conferred, or able to be conferred, by that person or body" (Coghill et al., 2006, p. 457). Note that Coghill et al. (2006) and Gray (2002) are explicit about the term relationship in their conceptualisations. Historically in the educational context, the definitions have been less specific, explaining accountability as the processes involved in *meeting goals* (Leithwood & Earl, 2000) or as regulations for *measuring* educational outputs (Rowe, 2005).

4.2 Drilling Down to 5 Key Concepts of Accountability

Five key concepts from this initial sample of definitions for accountability deemed useful are drawn from Bovens (2007) and Kuchapski (2001): (a) *disclosure*, making information known (Kuchapski, 2001); (b) *transparency*, providing clarity about the disclosed information and ensuring that this information makes sense and is accessible to those receiving the information (Kuchapski, 2001); (c) *consequences* from the information disclosed, with some form of *redress or appropriate action* able to be taken from the disclosed information (Bovens, 2007; Kuchapski, 2001); (d) being obliged to *explain and justify* the information (Bovens, 2007); and (e) the notion of *relationship between the person being held accountable and their constituency* (Bovens, 2007).

4.3 Defining Accountability in Education

In defining accountability, it is often confused with responsibility and defined in terms of each other (McGrath & Whitty, 2015). While this alignment may be the experience for educators, at the outset it is important to define and describe it without any preconceived conceptual understandings attached to it. The reason for this detachment will become clearer in Chapter 6 reading the ways the Principals conceptualise accountability.

In the school education sector, Stobart (2008) posits that "we are so familiar with accountability in many spheres of life that it is hardly defined" (p. 117). His notes reviewed Herman and Haertel's findings, *Uses and misuse of data for educational accountability and improvement* (2005), resulting in no single formal definition of accountability, therefore 'assuming we know what it is' (Stobart, 2008, p. 193). The following definition draws on the 5 key concepts sourced above, and in doing so contributes to the literatures surrounding definitions of accountability in education.

The five key concepts, coined now as elements, that form the substance in the definition include: (1) *disclosure* (Kuchapski, 2001); (2) *transparency* (Kuchapski, 2001); (3) *consequences* in the form of *redress* or *appropriate action* (Bovens, 2007; Kuchapski, 2001); being obliged to (4) *explain and justify* the information (Bovens, 2007); and (5) *relationship between the person being held accountable and their constituency* (Bovens, 2007). These elements are integrated to form the definition for this book:

> Educational accountability is a relationship between the school leader who is held responsible for the delivery of favourable performance results in external assessment programs and the regulatory authority from whom they receive their mandate. This relationship requires that the school leader behaves transparently and discloses, explains, and justifies their ways of accounting for the performance results around the

EDUCATIONAL ACCOUNTABILITY 89

TABLE 5   School leaders enacting educational accountability

Element	School leaders
Behaves *transparently*	– analyse data from performance results clearly and understandably with an accurate representation
Discloses	– reveal and make accessible student performance results
Explains	– describe the student performance results
Justifies	– defend the reasons for the outcomes of student performance results
Redresses	– demonstrate how they resolve or rectify issues or outcomes arising from student performance results

mandate, with the expectation that there will be consequences (*redress*) contingent on these.

Adopting this definition, the school leader is the person who acts with responsibility to another. The 'another' includes their regulatory authority, state and federal, or parents, students and at times could be teachers. The school leader's role in the accountability relationship is obliged to be transparent, to disclose, explain and justify their performance results to their communities and demonstrate redress when appropriate (parents, students, and school system, state, and federal authorities). In preparation for the following chapters, these key elements need further defining in the Australian context. Table 5 contextualises the elements in the accountability relationship from the Australian school leader's perspective with their community and the school systems.

In their accountability relationship, educational leaders are accounting in different directions: to the government or school system, to parents and students, and to teachers. All too often it is taken for granted that accountability matters. However, such assumptions are problematic and gloss over the reasons for the need of accountability in education. The next section provides an overview of these reasons.

5   Rationale for Accountability in Australian Schools

5.1   *Economic Purposes*

It is understandable that government policy makers and politicians seek to apply similar metrics to education as those in the economic, political, and social sectors to hold educators to account for student learning. It is what they know. Moreover, the economic downfalls in companies, misuse of corporate funds, loose governance arrangements have forced political leaders to demonstrate some responsibility for shareholders' protections. Being responsible to constituents and shareholders have made their way to being responsible to parents in Australian education. The 'bang for buck' and measuring such, is alive and well, particularly in non-government schools.

5.2   *School Choice: Marketable Accountable Enterprise*

Providing school choice introduces by default market accountability. School choice, introduced by policy makers, increases competition between schools. Expectations of educators to deliver the goods for service, with the elevated expectations of higher fees means commitment to supply favourable performance results, better than the rival school in the neighbourhood. Increasing levels of competition between schools have made some education communities commodified performative cultures. This competition is problematic. Such commodification is often misaligned with school communities' beliefs about learning and children and young people, and the precise nature of the accountability mechanisms in this cultivation depends to some extent on the particular outcomes being pursued.

5.3   *Pervading Myth: Accountability Improves Learning*

The rationale for Australia's national accountability regime is that accountability mechanisms are viewed as significant way to improve learning (Council of Australian Governments, 2012). Similar positions were adopted in England (Education and Inspections Act, 2006) and the US ("No Child Left Behind Act of 2001," 2002). However, improvement through accounting for performance results has been shown to be an assumption that is not always borne out in practice (Perryman, 2006; Stobart, 2008). Moreover, continuing with this assumption holds implications. The time and commitment required for school leaders to meet such expectations, with possibly little return, could be of concern for them and for those articulating such expectations (Anderson & Macri, 2009). This anomaly and lack of alignment between the rationale and the practice of an accountability regime raises the question of the appropriateness of certain mechanisms.

Terms such as 'regulating systems' and 'regulating results' help explain the mechanisms used in education to account for student learning outcomes. For this book's purposes, these have been called the regulation of processes (systems) and the regulation of outcomes (results).

EDUCATIONAL ACCOUNTABILITY 91

6   The Mechanisms

Governments often employ both processes and results to regulate educators' work in their account for learning outcomes (Rothstein, Jacobsen, & Wilder, 2009). For example, England uses regulating processes and regulating results in their inspectorial accountability regime (Ofsted, 2011; Perryman, 2006). The British Office for Standards in Education (Ofsted, 2011) uses the vehicle of auditing school plans, along with their implementation (regulating processes). They can do this through the vehicle of 'the inspecting' to measure student performance results (regulating outcomes) (Perryman, 2006). The inspectorial methods also 'inspected' teacher practices.

6.1   *Regulation of Processes*

In the context of schools, an accountability system that focuses on the regulation of processes is described as a process-based regulation. Those who adhere to the process-based approach argue that goals can be regulated by instituting the appropriate systems for monitoring the implementation of an acceptable plan (May, 2007). Educational systems that regulate processes use mechanisms that are designed to assess long-term plans and the success of their implementation, such as quality teaching and teacher education programs (Collin, 2017; Sahlberg, 2007). A significant number of school systems in Australia use the vehicle of a 'school review' in their regulation of processes (AIS NSW, 2020; Catholic Education Office Wollongong, 2016; Queensland Government, 2021; Victorian Government, 2021).

Ensuring that professional development and the general school operations are aligned with the school's learning goals is another mechanism that is used in regulating processes (Darling-Hammond, 2010a). Accountability regimes using the regulation of processes have shown positive outcomes for student learning as measured through the OECD scales (Darling-Hammond, 2010). Korea, Singapore, and Hong Kong, with a determination for long-term reform, evaluate their education practices (Darling-Hammond, 2010) through regulating processes. In her précis of countries that were achieving well in OECD scales in the PISA performances, Darling-Hammond (2010) found that countries using mechanisms that regulate processes perform consistently better than those regimes using outcomes as their regulator. However, in more recent times there has been little associating between the accountability mechanisms and test results in PISA (Högberg & Lindgren, 2021).

England currently encourages internal accountability processes, which has received more widespread acceptance by school leaders than previous inspectorial processes. Moreover, there has been significant improvement in student performances (Matthews & Ehren, 2021). OECD reports suggest that accountability and autonomy are a healthy union. Within a culture of account-ability, and when autonomy is given to schools regarding curricula, assessment and resourcing, they appear to be associated with improved student perfor-mance (OECD, 2016).

6.2 *Regulation of Outcomes*

To regulate outcomes or outputs the 'regulator' employs performance-based mechanisms (PBMs). PBMs in education, defined here as vehicles to account for the performance of students or subjects, provide measures of the outputs (Lingard, 2010). England, the Netherlands, New Zealand, the US, and Australia all place a degree of emphasis on regulating student performance results as a mechanism to account for learning (Lingard, 2010; Perryman, 2006).

School systems across the globe centre around three main policy principles: standards, accountability and decentralisation (Verger, Parcerisa, & Fontdevila, 2019). National large-scale assessments are a core component of these systems and are increasingly employed for accountability purposes along with moni-toring and regulating, that in the end, schools "achieve and promote centrally defined and evaluable learning standards'"(Verger et al., 2019, p. 5). As standard reforms have expanded, so has the list of countries that use PBMs in education.

Accountability regimes using PBMs with large-scale assessment and report-ing instruments make use of standards and benchmarks in tests that are based on a state or national curriculum (Lingard et al., 2015; Perryman, 2006; Stobart, 2008). PBMs in educational accountability systems focus on the output of 'quality' (Lingard, 2010). These include students' test results, teachers' perfor-mances as indicated by their students' test results, schools' overall ratings of test results, or students' grade promotions and graduations based on their test results (Fuhrman & Elmore, 2003). Measuring these outputs are now universal practices for school leaders in Australia (Heffernan, 2018).

Given the significance of test-based mechanisms in Australian school sys-tems across jurisdictions, it is important to understand their relative merits as vehicles of accountability.

6.3 *Strengths of Test-Based Mechanisms*

The focus of this book is about school leaders' interpretations of, and agency in managing, such mechanisms. As such the strengths of test-based mecha-nisms are identified from two perspectives in a school leader's accountability relationships; the first is from the perspective of the authority and the second is from that of the school community.

6.3.1 From the Perspective of the Authority

Test-based mechanisms provide to the government or education system visible, rapid and quantifiable results (Lingard et al., 2015). PBMs such as testing and assessment are relatively inexpensive, can be externally mandated, can be changed rapidly and notably have visible results (Fuhrman & Elmore, 2003). This fits an economist's need to see whether investments are paying off and further, it is seen as an efficient way for the government to exercise control over school funding, especially if the performance results fall short of expectations (Stobart, 2008).

Two strengths have been identified from the perspective of the Australian federal government regarding test-based mechanisms. The first strength is that test-based mechanisms are seen as an efficient way to track student growth in literacy and numeracy (Council of Australian Governments, 2012) where non-performing schools can be benchmarked, ideally to provide more resourcing and support. For instance, programs in the past have seen injection of funds between federal and state authorities. The injection has served in this assistance (National Partnerships: Literacy and Numeracy, 2009), with targeted professional learning for teachers. The second strength of test-based mechanisms is that they allow the results to be made available publicly. Both the parents and the federal government perceive this positively, as parents can then make an informed choice of school for their children through their access of student performance results across all Australian schools (Gillard, 2008).

6.3.2 From the Perspective of the Community

Four strengths for the school community are identified in the literature in relation to test-based accountability regimes. First, the use of test-based mechanisms sends a signal to the community that improvement is expected (Stobart, 2008). Second, the data provided by national, state or system-mandated mechanisms give essential information to educators regarding required improvements in practice (Pettit, 2010). Accountability frameworks linked to large-scale test-based assessments have had a positive influence on teaching and learning. For example, principals and teachers involve themselves in test item writing and marking return to their schools with training and experience that they can apply to their classrooms and leadership (Cizek, 2001; Reinertsen, 2020). The third strength is for the school itself. In some schools, when test-based mechanisms are incorporated into school cultures with existing strong evidence-based systems, they add value (Elmore, 2005). There also is evidence that some schools in some jurisdictions embrace standards and are thriving (Roche, 2004). Being mindful the success is owing to the collective responsibility for students' academic success by teachers (O'Day, 2004). Fourth, test-based accountability regimes which also facilitate public disclosure provide additional information about the performance results (ACARA, 2009; NCLB, 2002), enabling correlative data to be analysed. For example, information on expenditure and demographics may be used for research into those systems or schools that achieve well. The OECD data from PISA is one such example of how school systems look to what high performing countries/jurisdictions are doing or not doing to achieve well in PISA.

The strengths identified in test-based accountability systems apply to those educational accountability systems exercising both low and high-stakes. However, there are concerning limitations of test-based accountability regimes which also exercise high stakes (see the explanation of low/high stakes in Section 7 of this chapter).

6.4 *Limitations of Test-Based Mechanisms Exercising High Stakes*

For the purposes of improving learning, test-based accountability systems in high-stakes environments are less effective than those exercising low-stakes (Stobart, 2008; Taubman, 2009). Undoubtedly, there are unanticipated and undesirable consequences in high-stakes testing regimes (Diamond, 2007; Perryman, 2006; Stobart, 2008; Taubman, 2009), such as educators displaying resistance (McNeil, 2000) or experiencing discomfort (Pettit, 2009; Wronowski & Urick, 2019) or engaging in unethical practices, such as gaming the system (Dee, Dobbie, Jacob, & Rockoff, 2019; Oplatka, 2016). The limitations found internationally are examined here, followed by those within the Australian context.

One key limitation of using a test as an accountability mechanism in high-stakes testing systems is that there is an overemphasis on the results from the test (Au, 2009; Goldschmidt et al., 2005). The test may become a form of pseudo-curriculum (O'Connor & McTaggart, 2017; Sloan, 2008), as the curriculum evolves to replicate the subject goals of the test. Moreover, an overemphasis on the test means that educators are likely to resist the test-based accountability mechanism. This resistance is more common for educators when the performance results of students are used to compare schools (McNeil, 2000; Pettit, 2009). In accountability environments where there is an over-reliance on test results, with minimal formative assessments, there are negative consequences.

6.5 *Prioritising Results*

Five consequences are identified here when schools or school systems over-rely on, emphasise, or prioritise test results. The first consequence is that when the stakes are high there is an overemphasis by schools and school systems on the number of students who score above a benchmark (Hanushek, 2011).

Many schools and jurisdictions use 'above' and 'below' benchmarks to gauge how they are faring, with schools pressured to use the performance scores as a marketing tool (Bishop & Limerick, 2006; Fullan, 2011; Shipps, 2012; Wilkins, 2012). Within high-stakes testing regimes there is an over-interpretation of data (Cook, 2006), with the risk that educators will narrow the curriculum by judging all learning and teaching from the lens of the test score (Sloan, 2008).

The second consequence from an over-reliance on test results is that comparisons are made about the overall school performance from a single test—another form of narrowing and oversimplification. If public choice is a priority of the present-day government, then the consequences may influence enrolments and therefore funding (either positively or negatively). As the single test only assesses those outcomes for that particular time, it has limited value in providing all contingencies (Linn, 2000), especially for overall student learning growth. Goldschmidt et al. (2005) found that "unadjusted single-year cohort information (status measure) is an imprecise indicator of true school performance" (p. 18).

The third consequence is that the test results can limit both students and teachers when students are reduced to test scores (Au, 2009). Student learning is narrowed by students engaging only in pedagogical activities which lead to better performances in test results (Au, 2009; Comber, 2012). For example, large prescribed and explicit instructional blocks of literacy and numeracy have emerged in Australian early years and primary programs. Professional learning for teachers is targetted for these times only, appearing robotic, and diminishing teacher professional judgement and autonomy. Teachers may over-rely on content, as opposed to pedagogy, using more didactic forms of instruction rather than interactive forms (Diamond, 2012).

The fourth consequence of high-stakes testing regimes is that the focus on test scores provides little explanation of what needs to be changed (Kuchapski, 2001). A test measure does not track the growth in student learning; it tracks the performance measure on an arbitrary rating (Goldschmidt et al., 2005). Tracking individual student growth from tests alone and implementing an individualised program continue to challenge educational leaders and teaching teams. While educators agree on the merits of data sets to inform practice, the complexities of the tracking, setting goals and implementation, results in an out-of-reach frustrating unattainable goal, or a difficult one.

The fifth consequence is that teachers working with such prescribed programs may not be focused on improving learning outside of the outcomes expected on the test (Stobart, 2008), resulting in a narrow focus on certain curriculum areas (Hanushek, 2011; Polesel et al., 2014; Sloan, 2008).

Consequences also are precipitated by what is at stake when student performance results are central to the accountability in a school or school system.

7 Accountability Stakes Drive into the Hearts of Educators

A term that is rarely left out of accountability discussions is the subject of stakes. The term is relative and is dependent on those reporting on the stake. That is, what is 'at stake' says more about the person's judgment of the context than the stake itself. The year 12 results (exit) Australia hold significant consequences for students' career trajectories and arguably fodder for a school's marketing opportunities. However, discourses in the literatures are scarce about such consequences being a high stakes exercise. In Australia, external tests cloak some school systems like old cardigans (the NSW HSC exam is close to a 40 year history), with high-stakes tests being the cloth that is worn as a symbol of a normalised culture (Ayres, Sawyer & Dinham, 2004). That is, the stakes associated with the HSC have become normalised to a point where little has been referred to in the literatures as suggesting high stakes. HSC designers and implementers (educators) espouse its credibility as a rigorous and almost the superior instrument over other exit credentials from other jurisdictions and programs in Australia (i.e., the Diploma of the International Baccalaureate). On the other hand, NAPLAN has been tarnished with destroying schools, cheating, teaching to the test and developing a 'naplanish pseudo curriculum.'

Since the introduction of NAPLAN testing and its public disclosure of results, there are multiple references in the Australian literature claiming that NAPLAN testing and the consequence of its disclosure is now a high-stakes accountability exercise (Klenowski & Wyatt-Smith, 2012; Lewis & Hardy, 2015; Lingard et al., 2015; Smeed et al., 2009). It is an irony as the Year 12 exit credentials, across Australia, have more at stake for the individual student than the disclosure of NAPLAN results—which is limited to the amalgamation of student results telling a certain story about the school, not the student. The research studies arising from NAPLAN and the disclosure of results through MySchool is a hundred-fold compared to one or two sources about year 12 exit exams. One possible reason is that the school reputation is more important, or 'higher stake' than an individual student's post school options. Another reason could be that policy makers continue to be steadfast in their views if schools are publicly held to account (inevitably high stakes) that this will drive school improvement.

While there are few definitions for the terms low or high stakes in the research literature, where they are mentioned, the term stake is interchangeable with the term 'consequence' (Jacob, 2005; Stobart, 2008). If we apply this understanding of a stake to this study's definition of educational accountability, then the consequence (stake) would be the outcome about the levels of favourability of the performance results from the external test. While consequences in accountability regimes are often described in terms of low or high stakes, the determination of the stake, like performance results, is often relative and subjective. However, in low-stakes environments it stands to reason that there are few or no consequences from the regulation of performance results (Klinger & Rogers, 2011). One such low stake is accounting to the school community in general terms regarding annual learning goals, in the form of the Annual Report (NSW Government, 2020). Whereas in other contexts, the consequences are classified as high (or extremely high) stakes (Stobart, 2008).

Some Australian educational scholars, such as Klenowski and Wyatt-Smith (2011), Smeed et al. (2009), Reid (2011) and Hardy (2015), describe the consequences of public disclosure of student performance results from NAPLAN testing as high stakes with detrimental consequences. For Australian education, the consequences such as low staff and student morale and loss of enrolments would suggest high stakes. However, some US jurisdictions have experienced greater consequences than this from public disclosures of students' performances, such as loss of enrolments (funding), school closures and loss of employment (Perryman, 2006; Shipps & White, 2009; Stobart, 2008). Hence, the review of the interpretation of stakes in the literatures appears relative to the experiences of those reporting them. To date in Australia, there have been no high-stakes consequences compared to our global peers involving performance pay, school closures or loss of employment resulting from the nation-wide test results.

At the beginning of NAPLAN testing in Australia (2010), distinct differences were observed in the reactions from various school sectors to educators' descriptions of NAPLAN testing and its consequences. These differences were marked in the first inquiry into NAPLAN testing (Senate References Committee on Education, 2010), with primary school principals by far the most disaffected group as a result of the initial testing and subsequent public disclosures of results. Secondary school principals featured less in the initial research (Klenowski & Wyatt-Smith, 2012), but they were included in the research from an ethical leadership perspective by Ehrich, Harris, Klenowski, Smeed, and Spina (2015). It is reasonable to propose that secondary school principals were normalised with external testing and disclosure of results. NAPLAN results itself hold fewer consequences in their minds about enrolments and the greater stake appears to be the results from the year 12 results. The public disclosure of these year 12 results are high stakes for both the students and the school: the students post school options and the school's marketing opportunities, externally and internally. Of importance here is the influence that an external test has in the minds of educational leaders and their actions. Notably the higher stake the greater the need to resolve some of the ensuing issues.

Irrespective of the relativity of the stakes, the evidence is strong that high-stakes consequences are likely to present complications for school communities. International studies have shown that educational accountability systems that regulate outcomes through performance-based mechanisms (PBMs) with high-stakes consequences have undesirable outcomes for students, teachers, and leaders.

8 Effects of Educational Accountability on School Leaders

> ... a society that increasingly seeks to minimise risk, and to avoid blame, swings the pendulum away from trust towards reporting. Whereas a culture combining trust and reporting would ideally encourage good practice, an over emphasis on reporting discourages action and encourages avoidance. (Ieraci, 2007, p. 63)

Here, Ieraci suggests balance in the context of accountability cultures, between trust and reporting. This is adding another dimension to the balanced leadership idea discussed at the beginning of this chapter. Australian principals, as the delegated authority to account for performance results, are likely not only to be challenged by implementing these test-based mechanisms, but also the time spent on reporting on the outcomes of the mechanisms. Up until the late 20th century principals would have experienced a culture of trust. The effects of performative accountability twinned with the datafication of teaching, notably the early years (Bradbury & Robert-Holmes, 2018; Neumann, 2019), has swung the pendulum away from trust with the risk of inaction, as Ieraci proposes. However, Australian school leaders, as the Principals in this book demonstrate, seek to make accountability policies and the reporting processes less toxic, through ethical mediation of policy and like their global peers to protect staff from the stress and the work as much as they can (Comber, 2012; LeChasseur, Donaldson, Fernandez, & Femc-Bagwell, 2018).

However, the 'emotional labour in sustaining a positive school ethos and a unified teaching team (Comber, 2012, p. 128) under these conditions, is arduous. Performative cultures bind the professional identities of school leaders, as well as their moral pursuits and professional identities, to the ostensibly neutral and cogent measures of outputs, translated as 'achievement' of their schools and students (Ball, 2003). Part of their identity formation is caught in the performative world of data, evidence informed practices and accountabilities of such (Ball, 2016).

There is a clear empirical picture of the impacts on school leaders in high stakes testing systems in jurisdictions inside and outside Australia. Initial surveys in Australia of educators with the first iterations of NAPLAN testing (Senate Submissions) and studies by Comber (2012), Cranston, Reid, Mulford, and Keating (2011), McGuire (2012) and Gobby et al. (2018), along with continued discourses (Wilkinson, Niesche, & Eacott, 2018) about school contexts illustrate concerns about high stake testing, notably for school leaders (Keddie et al., 2020) all pointing to tensions. International studies by Crow, Shipps (2012), White (2006), Firestone and Shipps (2005) and Spillane, Diamond et al. (2002) are trusted sources regarding the impacts of regimes on principals. Of concern is the growing empiricism about irresponsible leadership or the dark side of leadership and the impetus for such leadership in education (Oplatka, 2016; Sam, 2020).

We need to support our school leaders when performative and rigid regimes continue to threaten their moral and ethical commitments:

> My greatest fear has always been that I would be afraid—afraid physically or mentally or morally and allow myself to be influenced by fear instead of by my honest convictions. (Eleanor Roosevelt, 1942)

The Australian Principals' views of their accountability regimes in Chapter 6 are easily seen as a reasonable sample of what school leaders may experience given their school contexts in their school systems, ranging from low to high stakes accountability regimes.

CHAPTER 6

'... Somehow Frame Accountability to Make Sense of It'

This chapter is about taking the Eucalypt Leadership Model (ELM) and situating it into practice. It demonstrates how school leaders' interpretations of their external demands, in this case accountabilities, can be applied to the theoretical ELM's sensemaking and sensegiving. It shows how the Principals in context understood, interpreted and conceptualised their expectations of accountability. Strikingly, one principal made it clear how he conceptualised his accountability in school context through framing: "... somehow frame accountability to make sense of it" (see p. 189). Chapter 7 extends the application and describes how the Principals reported their enactments of responsibility.

The pseudonym names of the Principals have a special meaning. First, the pseudonyms given are metaphorical. They stem from my interpretations of some comments they made. Two, they tell a story. Their stories demonstrate both consistencies and anomalies. The Principals' names with their comments are as follows:

Barry, the Buffer:	'I suppose I do see it as ... a buffering system'; 'I am the human shield between the [School System and the teachers]—the buffer'; '... my job is to be the human shield, which protects the teachers from the excesses of [the accountability regime].'
Bianca, the Balancer:	'The most important accountability is that the kids are happy.'
Brian, Broadview:	'We're digging deep to ensure that our students at this school in this context are working towards achieving their potential .... We understand where we were and where we're going .... But now we're actually moving whole cohorts into far higher and greater levels.
Charmaine, the Cheerleader:	'So I know at times you feel like you're the cheerleader ... like to work with them when they have professional opportunities .... Bringing them, walking slowly with them.'

© KONINKLIJKE BRILL NV, LEIDEN, 2022 | DOI:10.1163/9789004517202_006

Julie, the Juggler:	'I see myself as a juggler. Here you are one minute—and my day will be one minute ... I will go from you to a meeting with a parent who has booted his daughter out of home and wants me to boot her out of school at the same time.'
Larry, the Learner:	'I don't know much about teaching and learning. When I first came into the job, I was told I needed to improve in this area. I've no idea. Do you know of a course where I could learn about learning?'
Leonie, the Light:	'I am the lady of the light, whatever, the torch or the little flame or whatever ... need to hold the lantern up to see how we are going.'
Levi, the Leveller:	'Most conversations with peers turn to the HSC ... need to keep the vision on learning .... I'm at my best when I have the ability to articulate a vision for learning.'
Malcom, the Moralist:	I will never market our results. It's immoral. Keep the results out of the conversation. I only look and talk about learning.'
Owen, the Opportunist:	'... [accountable] to my teachers to ensure that what I can do in my role maximises their learning environment, maximises the opportunities for them to engage kids.'
Ralph, the Rationalist:	'So somewhere, if we've gone along a grades journey there has to be a sort of upper limit to that journey .... Yes. I want the learning growth, I want the improvement, but I've also got to accept there's got to be some sort of plateau ....'
Steve Savvy:	'Look it's (accountability) a leverage really. I welcome it.'
Terence, the Target-Setter:	'... I teach to the test. If that's your measure, you are not going to fire a 100-metre sprinter at the Olympics doing 800-metre training. They'd be doing 100-metre sprints. You need to drive it though.'

Throughout Chapters 6 and 7 bold font is applied to emphasise the salient points made by the Principals. There is a consistent use of the memoing technique, to draw out the theoretical understandings which underpin the ELM.

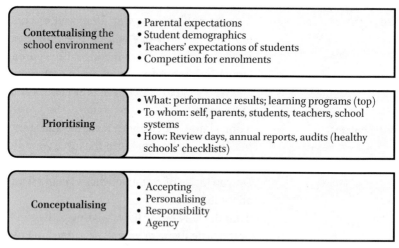

FIGURE 9   Principals' interpretations of their accountability expectations

The Principals' interpretations of their accountability expectations fall into three themes: 1) Contextualising their accountability environments; 2) Prioritising their accountability expectations the 'What, to Whom and How'; and 3) Conceptualising their accountability expectations. Figure 9 illustrates the sequence of the main content.

Certain contextual factors from the Principals' school environments, such as the demographic characteristics of the students and parents, were important considerations when meeting their accountability expectations. These considerations, along with Principals' beliefs about what represents learning and their own levels of self-efficacies about influencing teachers, impact on what the Principals perceive they should be accountable for, to whom they should be accountable and how they should be held to account for student results. That is, the 'what, whom and how' of their accountability arrangements. For these Principals their philosophical viewpoints are cemented into comfortable and workable conceptualisations of their accountability expectations. However, there are anomalies in each of the themes. These anomalies showcase some of the complexities about accountability in education and even more so, the complexities of the individual Principals in how and why they may view this specific accountability the way they do.

1   Contextualising

Without prompts Principals refer to factors in their school environment as being influential when being held to account for test results. Owen advocated the importance of knowing his students and their families: '... big families, poor families, many migrant families, many first-generation migrant families ... **our cultural mix** in the school is pretty much the United Nations.' Owen's view of his school environment influences the way he makes sense of his accountability: 'When it comes to assessment-focused accountability, my personal view of it is in this community it's about **taking kids from a wide range of backgrounds and capabilities** [*cultural mix*], enrolling them, giving them the opportunity here and just **having them as part of the culture** [*success culture*] and systems and protecting the teaching time to ensure **that these kids get the opportunity to be successful** [*high achievement in learning*].' The school environmental factors that Principals report as being important included parental expectations, demographic characteristics of the students, teachers' expectations of students and competition for enrolments.

1.1 *Expectations*

The Principals' comments about the parents' expectations in their school's mix demonstrated that their accountability environments were perceived to be unique, deserving serious consideration. Compare the views of Julie and Charmaine regarding their parents' expectations:

> Julie the Juggler: Parents ask, 'Tell me about what percentage of your kids go into universities' ... accountabilities in the eyes of the parents are **very, very, tricky.** Very important. (emphasis added)

> Charmaine the Cheerleader: So, we have a very articulate, as you can imagine, parent group. Socio-economically, the school is **quite interesting** because almost everybody here is very wealthy. (emphasis added)

Julie interprets her parents' expectations as wanting the option of a university education for their child. Thus, accountability for performance results is challenging ('tricky') for her and possibly needs a strategic approach in response to the parents' expectations. In contrast, Charmaine's explanation suggests a curiosity ('interesting') when parents articulate their expectations:

> We **have a student structure** where our tutors may not teach the [students] in their tutor groups ... a couple of parents last year expressed a bit of frustration with it because they wanted to know how is [student] doing in maths and you're not her maths teacher, what can you tell me ... **the biggest difficulty with that is your parents.** (Charmaine)

Charmaine's challenge around the parents' expectations is not the performance results *per se* but persuading her parents about the merits of a new learning structure.

The profile of the two school sites mentioned in these examples, such as the gender of students, historical data of students' performance results and ICSEA, are not dissimilar. However, the main difference between the two Principals is their career stage and pathway (see Memo 3).

> **Memo 3: Julie, the Juggler and Charmaine, the Cheerleader: Differences. Why?**

I am puzzled about the reasons for these differences between Julie the Juggler and Charmaine the Cheerleader, which clearly show differences in their emotions and thinking about their parents' expectations. At the outset, their differences could simply be their school contexts; however, there are too many similarities here. The second possibility could be their stage of career. This is a distinct possibility. Julie the Juggler shows some anxiety and sees the expectations as challenging, whereas Charmaine seems to be calm, with a sense of curiosity. The third possibility for their differences may be in their career formation. Julie has been 'formed' (my term) through a pastoral pathway and Charmaine through a curriculum pathway—could these pathways have an influence over how they see learning and ultimately, how they lead learning? I'll hold these ideas until I come to their leadership descriptions—another possible access point for insight.

 This difference raises the question whether mid-career Principals can manage expectations more effectively and whether a principal's career trajectory pursuing a curriculum pathway (versus pastoral pathway) is more effective in managing performative expectations.

1.2   The Characteristics of Students

Several Principals revealed that the characteristics of their students, such as their students' capabilities to perform at particular levels, were important factors when being held to account for their performances. Larry the Learner reasoned, '… **in terms of graduate outcomes, good, solid kids, but not necessarily academic … all of the indicators** say that we're **below state average**' (Larry).

Ralph, the Rationalist and Barry, the Buffer make compensatory remarks, indicating that their students are performing as well as they can: 'When they [results] are made public, the various circumstances running in each of the schools is not made public, so sometimes you can't do as well as other schools but **given the clientele** that you've got, they've actually achieved marvellous results (Ralph).

Barry the Buffer evaluates the capabilities of his clientele's performance results: 'Now how is it fair or just to make a judgement about the quality of a teacher's performance, or indeed any principal's performance against top 200 schools when you've got **a clientele that's below average?**' (Barry).

These Principals' beliefs about their students' capabilities are an important point in their attitudes of their expectations of students and attitudes to their performative accountability expectations.

The choice of language is important here. Employing the term 'clientele' sets a conceptual boundary. A boundary that minimises the human relationship and reducing the principal and student relationship to an economic transactional relationship. The choice of words, suggesting an oral distancing, may continue to support Barry's schema in holding low expectations of students performing well.

 Would Principals' low expectations of students' performance results influence teachers in their expectations of students?

1.3   Teachers' Expectations of Students

The Principals' perspectives about their teachers' abilities regarding their students' performance capabilities influenced their view and responses to the accountability expectations. For Charmaine she describes the teachers' behaviours as loving them but to the possible detriment of student progression:

Charmaine: I suppose what's dawned on me over the last six months or so, because when you come in new to a school you peel back layers of what you're seeing, is that although our [student gender] **do well in the HSC, they could probably be doing better** and that **we love them all.**
Researcher: You love them?
Charmaine: Yes, we **love them—a bit too much.**

Loving the students too much suggests the teachers are overprotecting their students or lowering the expectations of what the student can do.

Similarly, Leonie, the Light reveals that her teachers' expectations of students could be detrimental to student progression. In one faculty, these expectations are perceived by Leonie as influencing the outcomes of students' performance results. Leonie provides reasons why few of her students are choosing to study mathematics: 'we don't have a lot of our [students] choosing maths. **We don't** have a lot of teachers who feel confident that our [students] can do maths. Our **maths teachers have said our kids can't do maths.**'

Part of the Principals' perspectives stem from these Principals' own self beliefs in being able to influence their teaching teams to implement performative expectations. Both Charmaine and Leonie judge that their teachers need to raise their expectations of what their students can do. However, Larry, the Learner has felt little confidence in understanding the data around results and being able to influence his teaching teams in their practices resulting from data analysis: 'I am new at this, and I know we need to improve results **but there are others who are better at this than me.**' Larry leaves the work of implementing change for better results to others.

1.4   *Competition for Enrolments*

School enrolments were perceived by some Principals as being tied to their school ranking from the public disclosure of results. Julie copes with high levels of competition for enrolments yet exhibits elevated levels of anxiety about how enrolments are dependent upon the students' performance results: '... but **your enrolments are very much determined by your results** ... there's that **level of accountability in terms of your results** ... big thing here is enrolments ... **you've got to keep your enrolments going.**'

Leonie the Light is aware, and with some frustration, that her success of a reasonable market share for enrolments, is dependent upon her results: '**They look at the pinks and greens** [NAPLAN] and **then they make their choices.**' At the point of this interview Leonie did not view her results in favourable terms, nor did her system advisor. At her initial appointment as principal, she was asked to '**fix**' them.

Competition for enrolments and its dependence on favourable performances are important contextual factors that influence the ways these Australian Principals thought and felt about performances in external tests being used for accountability purposes. Thoughts such as injustices and unfairness and feelings of frustration, anxiety and in some instances, despair are disclosed.

In summary, these Principals' perceptions that the school context is important suggests that socialising these performative expectations with their communities, notably their teaching teams, is an important leadership task. For some, their thoughts, and feelings about their accountability for student performance results are either eased or aggravated by their self-beliefs in their capabilities of influencing their teaching teams to carry out certain implementations in managing the expectations. The environmental factors between some schools appear similar, as in the case of Charmaine and Julie, however it was what they themselves understand the factors to be. Their perceptions of their contexts are unique to them.

These differences in perceptions of their environments raise the possibility of other influences, such as participants' stage of career and/or their previous leadership experiences. Those in their second principalship and with several years at the school, along with previous leadership positions in a curriculum pathway (hence strong curriculum knowledge), perceive their school environments in meeting their accountability demands with more at ease than principals with less experience and curriculum knowledge. Principals' contextualising may reveal more about them rather than what the context is.

1.5 *Emerging Proposition*

Principals interpret their accountability demands considering their school contexts. However, Principals who perceive a strong knowledge base about teaching and learning perceive they can manage these demands irrespective of their school contexts. Those Principals who perceive they hold this strong knowledge base along with 5 years' experience or more as a principal, report less concern about the demands than those who do not have the knowledge base or years of experience.

2 Prioritising Referents: Account for What, to Whom and How

Principals were asked to describe their referents—what and to whom they accounted for. Within these questions they were also asked how the accountability was carried out. Not many regarded the students' performance results as their key referent. Moreover, they reported that while they are ultimately accountable to the school system advisor for performance results, they give priority in terms of their accountability to the students, parents, or themselves. In other words, the Principals create priorities regarding what and to whom they are accountable to, and these priorities are not aligned with school system expectations.

2.1 *Prioritising What Is Accountable (Objects of Account)*

Principals report that they should be accountable for performance results from the external tests; however, the value that they gave to test results was lower than other priorities. Table 6 provides the examples of the range of these priorities. Charmaine explained, '**I'm more concerned that the [students] do**

108 CHAPTER 6

TABLE 6   Representing the objects of account

Object of accounting	Examples (emphasis added)
Learning programs and initiatives	'Your role as a leader of learning is **to seek improvement in authentic learning** (Leonie the Light); 'They [KLA coordinators] **go to other schools who are doing well in that area** [learning from them] (Malcolm, the Moralist)
Post-school options	'... the number of students who are getting into **the courses post school and the pathways post school that they want to go to.**' (Levi, the Leveller)
Growth in performance results	'... review of HSC data more so from a learning gain point of view, a DeCourcy **learning gain far more.**' (Steve Savvy)
Teacher professional learning and recruitment	'... to **my teachers** to ensure that what I can do in my role maximises their learning environment, maximises the opportunities for them to engage kids.' (Owen, the Opportunist)
Working with data; responding to data	'... **how we respond to that data, what implementation of programs** have been done. (Steve Savvy) 'We had **accountabilities for the National Partnerships program**—not onerous.' (Ralph the Rationalist)
Student and school well-being, faith, excluding assessment	'Ultimately I am responsible ... for his [**Bishop's**] **mandate**' (Brian Broadview) 'I'm more concerned that the [**students**] **do as well as they can as individuals.**' (Charmaine, the Cheerleader) '**Student happiness is pretty important;** it's not just about the marks.' (Bianca the Balancer)
School organisation	'... my role **maximises their learning environment.**' (Owen, the Opportunist)
Performance results (Anomaly)	'So **how many Band 6s** ... We've got to give these kids the best possible chance .... Every **child achieves beyond their capacity.**' (Terence, the Target Setter)

as well as they can as individuals rather than ... which probably puts me out of kilter a little bit with the system, **the push for [results].**' In this excerpt, Charmaine identified the School System expectations, which had an emotional edge—a 'push' for favourable results. Charmaine places importance on individual students doing their best. Describing students as individuals emphasises Charmaine's esteem for the student as human (referent) rather than an inanimate object of a result score (non-referent). In this example, Charmaine makes it known (comfortably) that her priority is not the same as the School System's priority ('out of kilter'). Her experience, in this instance, is that her personal accountability expectations and those of the School System are misaligned.

2.2   *Student Learning More Than a Number*

The participating Principals describe that their accountability for their students' learning means more than a numerical score on a test. Their perspectives on 'learning' determine their views about their performative accountability. One perspective is the kind of learning experiences that the student has while at school (the 'present state' of learning) and the other is the learning experiences which prepares for their after-school pathways (the 'future state' of learning). Charmaine embraces the present state of learning view. She is accountable for 'all the other opportunities that they get to learn and to grow and get experience in a variety of things.' Bianca the Balancer signalled several times throughout the interview that performance results were not her key focus:

> ... student happiness is pretty important; it's not just about the marks. Whilst performance results are important, I think **having happy classrooms with happy kids who want to come to school, who want to engage with what learning** they want to engage in and be part of what they want to be part of in the school community is just as important. If you get that, as they get older, that relationship is so solid that a lot of kids do engage more, I think. That's when you get the performance.

These two accountabilities of diversity and happiness are situated in the present moment experience of learning as distinct from learning for a student's future state. Their beliefs about learning criss-cross with their beliefs about the purpose of schooling and in turn, influences what they believe they should be accountable for.

Holding a broader perspective about learning is highlighted in Sammy's excerpt. Sammy's self-talk also reveals the boundaries he sets when being held to account for test results:

> It's an expectation and a requirement of a principal to be accountable and take it on board. You do what you can with it, but don't lose sight of the bigger picture, which is about learning .... But there are a lot of unheralded heroes of past HSCs of students who never made it to auditoriums

to receive prizes, who have achieved results that are extremely satisfying from our perspective and that's because we treated them with the same dignity and respect that the highfliers received and Catholic schools do so well, where we look out for those students who struggle the most.

Sammy's self-talk reveals his conceptualisations of learning, which are more than a test result. Sammy extends. He provides reasons for keeping his vision on learning so that the students who do not gain high performance results are treated with the 'same dignity and respect.' Sammy reasons that there is a mission of taking care of students who may struggle and equipping them of skills for future: 'I don't take much notice of the results ... It's not just about getting a great ATAR in Year 12, it's about the skills that will sustain them to lead a happy and satisfying and joy-filled life.'

How the Principal views their accountability for performance results is a reflection on how they view student success. This link raises the question as to whether their views are situated in their ideas about the purposes of schooling. For Charmaine and Bianca learning is for the present, creating diverse and happy student experiences. Sammy Savvy's view is about the future in the individual student leading a happy, satisfying and joy filled life—with or without favourable results.

3 Anomaly: Terence Prioritises Performance Results

Terence the Target Setter reveals quite different views about what he prioritises in his accountability compared to the other Principals. His main referent is the external test results: '... **it's [performance is] their ticket to the future. They only have one chance** ... call it **my moral imperative**.' Interestingly, and unlike other principals in the Norris study (2017), is that Terence rationalises his decisions, albeit performance driven, from a moral position. This reflects the sense-making property of social context; seeking support and consensual validation and here drawing on 'moral imperatives' to make sense of the accountabilities.

Terence also reports that considerable time is spent in preparation for tests and examinations. This anomaly supports the previous point about how Sammy views student success and purpose of schooling. These views of success and purpose influence how Sammy conceptualises learning, which in turn impacts on the ways he perceives performative accountability expectations. Memo 4 teases out this relationship further.

'... SOMEHOW FRAME ACCOUNTABILITY TO MAKE SENSE OF IT'

Memo 4: Beliefs about learning, post school and accountability

It seems as if the Principals' views of what they prioritise and what they account for is influenced by their views about learning. Charmaine, for example, explained in detail her whole-school wide-learning program, yet provided little explanation about performances in external assessments. She also expressed the belief that: '... if authentic learning was happening, results would take care of themselves.' Charmaine also emphasised that she was accountable for students having enjoyable learning experiences. 'Post-school options' for Charmaine was missing. Was this important? In contrast, Terence was clear about what learning was for—the performance results. He instead emphasised the importance of post-school options. These links are important to the central research questions regarding the impact question of Principals' views in the ways they lead learning. I need to map this.

The Principals' experiences point to an intersection between the Principals' conceptualisations of learning and how they prioritise what they believe they are accountable for. In turn, these views about learning influence the Principals' beliefs about the purpose of schooling, especially the way they reconstitute their expectations, making performance results a lower priority than other aspects of learning because privileging performance results misrepresents their views about learning (see Figure 10).

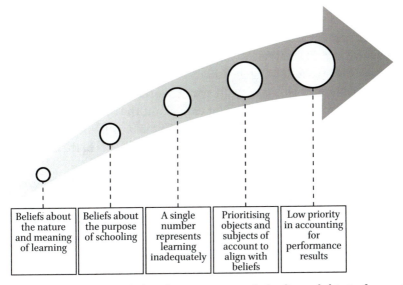

FIGURE 10   Linking views: Beliefs about learning, purpose of schooling and objects of account

3.1 *Emerging Proposition*

Principals' beliefs about their representations of learning align with the priorities they set in response to the external demands. Principals who hold expansive views about student learning, such as joy about the learning experience, hold a low priority for themselves in being accountable for performance results.

3.2 *Prioritising to Whom (i.e., the Subject or Referents of the Accounting)*

The principals disclosed in a cursory manner that they, of course, were accountable to their School Systems; however, they emphasised their priorities to other referents such as students, parents, teachers, and themselves. Table 7 represents each referent and the frequency of occurrence, along with a display of text data.

The Principals who held themselves to account (i.e., self-accountability) is a point of interest. This self-accountability is often interchanged with responsibility and indicates substantial respect for their relationships with their school communities. For example, Barry the Buffer explains explicitly to whom his teachers are accountable: 'So ... talking now about accountabilities again ... the accountabilities of the teachers are **to the students ... it's not to the [School System]**.' Conversely, Sammy Savvy explains accountability as '**... a responsibility to the teachers** ... to ensure that we are being professional.' The School System was a necessary 'body' to report to; however, the Principals consistently note that their accountability priorities are to the people in their schools; the students, parents, or teachers.

The subjects of account represented in Table 5 do not adequately reveal the feelings of the participating Principals. There is a sense of dogmatic resolve and commitment to ensuring that they themselves would keep their relationships— with students and at times, with parents—central to their accountability commitments. Charmaine does '**not care about the** *Sydney Morning Herald* **ranking**'; Graham '**quite frankly**' did **not take too 'much notice of the results'** and emphasises that he is **more accountable 'to students in their learning.'**

3.3 *Prioritising the Methods of Educational Accountability (Mechanisms of the Accounting)*

The Principals' views regarding the mechanisms used for accountability are expressed in negative terms. This unfavourable view stemmed from the distasteful consequences of certain mechanisms. Yet one mechanism that is viewed favourably is the DeCourcy instrument of analysis. Figure 11 provides an overview for the reasons of the criticisms.

'... SOMEHOW FRAME ACCOUNTABILITY TO MAKE SENSE OF IT' 113

TABLE 7   Subjects of the account: Frequency and excerpts

Referent	Examples (emphasis added)
Self	'Holding **myself accountable**.' (Steve Savvy)
	'[Accountability is] It's **who you are** and who you really are, isn't it?' (Charmaine, the Cheerleader)
	'Key accountability for me **is to lead that [Australian Curriculum]** strategically.' (Owen the Opportunist)
School System	'Accountable **to the School System.**' (Bianca the Balancer)
	'**I answer to the system far more than I do to government.**' (Steve Savvy)
Students	'So, in that sense ... talking now about accountabilities again ... the accountabilities of the teachers are to the students ... it's not to the [School System].' (Barry the Buffer)
	'I think we're **accountable to the students.**' (Charmaine)
	'**I'm accountable to those kids; to each of those students.**' (Larry the Learner)
Parents	'What sort of results are you going to get for my daughter?' (Julie the Juggler)
	'Next accountability is to **the parent community**, working in partnership with them.' (Owen the Opportunist)
Public	'... but your enrolments are very much determined by your results ... there's that level of [public] **accountability in terms of your results.**' (Julie the Juggler)
Government— National Partnerships	'We had accountabilities for the **National Partnerships program.**' (Ralph the Rationalist)
Teachers	'**Third accountability would be to my teachers**, to ensure that what I can do in my role [for them].' (Owen the Opportunist)
	'You know I have a **responsibility to the teachers** ... to this community to ensure that we are being professional.' (Steve Savvy)

3.4   *Assessing Learning through Inadequate Measures*

Principals disclosed a tension between their philosophical beliefs about learning and the measure that was used to account for students' performance results. There is alignment between the School Systems and Principals that the outcomes for results should be accountable, however most Principals report

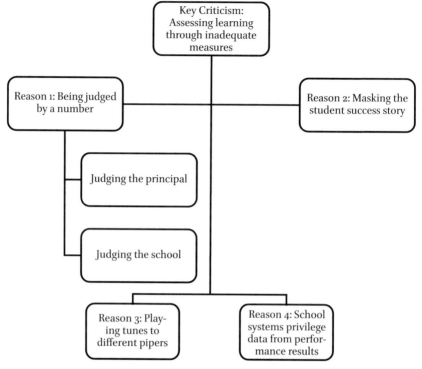

FIGURE 11 Principals' criticisms of their accountability mechanisms

disagreements and negative emotions about the measures employed for such accountability.

The measure used to account for performance results, notably the NAPLAN instrument, is not esteemed by Principals when its diagnostic dimensions are overlooked, and when the students' performance results are elevated in the public arena. Barry derides the NAPLAN test itself: '**We use blunt instruments.**' Charmaine reveals a conflict between the test assessing a small part of learning and not the development of the whole person: 'There's **tension there and a conflict … you're saying the development of the whole person is important and yet you're only testing this little bit.**'

Performative processes which the School Systems employ are reported to be gruelling and result in fear. Bianca, a mid-career stage principal, describes her emotions and thoughts during the regular review day: '**I was fearful; I felt grilled.**' Julie, an ECP, emphasises the numbers of people who participated in the review day and implied challenge: 'You might have three or four people in that meeting, as well your leadership team, and **they ask challenging questions.**'

'... SOMEHOW FRAME ACCOUNTABILITY TO MAKE SENSE OF IT' 115

While the Principals express heightened emotions about the ways that that they are held to account by the school systems' performative processes, these are minimal challenges. There are other challenges that were reported to be the consequences from these accountability processes employed by the System.

3.5 *Judged by Numbers*

The Principals report that students' performance results are used to make judgements regarding the quality of the school and the success of the principal and teachers. They reveal feelings of frustration and anxiety when raw results are used to inform these judgements. Some report a sense of injustice and pressure to perform because of them. Barry becomes indignant when he experiences judgements about the success of the school according to the performance results: 'The degree to which **the number of Band 6s drives the thinking about what success is** incredible ... **irresistible for the advisors at the [System] to look at results** and ... **make judgements about the principal and teachers.**'

There are risks when being judged on results. Principals suggest that the judgement may mask the student success, damage the school image and the principal's identity.

3.6 *Masking Student Success*

The public disclosure of performances from the external tests do not tell the human story behind the results. While Julie reports that the performances are about her leadership of the community, she reveals the limiting nature of public disclosures of results:

> Whether you were above or below state average in the various components of NAPLAN ... **it doesn't actually tell the story of your community and the great things that you've done with that community.** Because I honestly believe that **that aspect of growth doesn't come through at all,** in that website [My School] ... People need to know something about your story as well and the sorts of kids that you're dealing with.

Barry also reports that the judgement as unfair, as it does not take into account the students at each of the schools: '**Saying this school is underperforming now and its results are inferior to, say, [school] up the road is I think radically unfair because it's not comparing apples with apples.**' Steve recalls certain students at graduation and what they have achieved given their starting place, 'their success is more than a number. Some achieve incredible outcomes which cannot be measured in a number.'

3.7   *Judging the School*

Principals experience pressure when the school's performance results are used by families to make decisions about their choice of school: 'I knew when I applied for this job that those two areas were going to be massive and they were intertwined, essentially '... So, the big thing here is enrolments. You've got to keep your enrolments going. **But your enrolments are also determined very much by your results**' (Julie).

3.8   *Judging the Principal*

There is a sense of unfairness when the performance results influence the outcomes of Principals' or teachers' appraisal processes. Julie discloses her anxiety when coming up against her appraisal processes for the first time: 'We generally set goals as well, as part of that are **the results. That's also linked into the [principal] appraisal processes.'**

Terence justifies his reasons for targeting performance results: 'I'm very acutely aware that **they're the measures that we are going to be judged by and therefore we have to perform**.' Terence and the teachers were going to be judged professionally from the performance results. Barry registers his sense of disgust in teachers, or any principals being benchmarked against the publicly displayed 'top' schools: 'Now how is it **fair or just to make a judgement about the quality of a teacher's performance, or indeed a principal's performance, against the top 200 schools when you've got a clientele that's below average?'**

Being judged according to performance results is reported as the source of the greatest internal conflict by participating Principals. The internal conflict is brought about by their perception that student results in external tests fall short about what is important. Malcom places a higher value on maximising opportunities, intertwined with well-being, than students' performance results. Other Principals echo this frustration regarding students' performance results being given a higher priority than other aspects of learning. Bianca values student happiness: 'Student happiness is more important than any results.' Owen emphasises student well-being and learning in providing opportunities for students as holding a higher priority for him than just performance: 'You **don't separate learning and well-being and ... there is no measure of what we do for kids just to maximise their opportunity in life and that's measured by more than just learning gain.'**

3.9   *Tunes from Different Pipers*

Barry describes the 'layers and actors' of accountability as 'tunes and pipers': 'The reality that we live in day by day is that we've got **huge external accountabilities to a whole lot of different pipers trying to play the tune and those** from the [Local Office] to the [Central Office] yet the state government almost seem to be a non-player.'

The sheer content, such as the numerous domains of schooling of what needs to be accounted for, is conveyed as being hard and scrutiny reigns. Julie reveals the challenges in the enormity of the School System's expectations and its impact on her: 'It's **damn hard. It's so big .... Everyone is watching to see whether you've got any credibility.**' She discloses that the levels of accountability are confronting: 'Coming in as a principal, **the level of accountability was quite ... yeah, it sort of hits you in the face a little bit.**' The 'pipers' are a challenge for later-career principals (LCPs) as well. Charmaine, in her second principal's appointment, explains how the expectations are still foreign to her: 'I have been **here [jurisdiction] for four years now and I am still not used to it [accountability].**'

Along with review days, both school systems mandated learning programs to redress any shortfalls in students' performances in their external tests.

3.10 *School Systems: Performance Data Count*

School System advisors are perceived to place a greater emphasis on results than Principals themselves. Principals experience this mismatch of priorities as demanding, unfair, and confusing. This is combined with the drive by school systems to demonstrate that they use data as leverage for improvement. This is reported as another pressured layer.

At the time of the Norris investigation (2017) data driven practices were emerging with schools employing the 'Faces on Data' technique (Sharratt & Fullan, 2012) to entice teachers to take data seriously, and use them to inform their practices. Memo 5 poses a question about the possible link between this technique of Faces on Data and the drive for favourable performance results.

 Memo 5: Numbers on a page: Faces on results link with faces on data?

I wonder if educators switch off a light when the numbers 'on the page' (*Charmaine*) are associated with students' learning? In their minds, does the presence of numbers signal a depersonalising which causes a possible ethical dilemma when comparing students? I must look up the research about Faces on Data as to why this initiative was introduced. 'Numbers on a page' certainly is a flag for other possible research. I am also seeing links with the research on Maths's anxiety—my colleagues conduct research in this space.

Owen, the Opportunist in his appraisal of the School System and their over-attention to results and their data, reasons that when more attention is paid to school-wide learning it is a liberating experience for everyone: 'There's **not the same amount of attention given to them** [well-being programs and school-wide learning] ... and in reflecting with colleagues around some of the results from the conversations which can take place, it seems to me that **if we take a broader perspective on what we think are the critical outcomes from our schools, ultimately that liberates everyone.**' Owen's colleagues, being his peer principals in his cluster, are seen as important referents in making sense of the decisions taken with his teachers regarding results. This collegial thinking about results is widespread amongst the Principals. Memo 6 picks up on this finding.

Memo 6: Peer relationships

I have noticed several times that Principals refer to their peer principals about what they think and their attitudes to performance results. None of the Principals reported that they were out of step with their peers; however, some did report how some principals in their system network 'drive home the results,' and practise and drill for tests. In some ways the peer principals are their referents and a compass in helping them make sense of their accountabilities.

All Principals specify the importance of NAPLAN as a tool for providing information for diagnostic purposes yet dismiss its utility as a device for holding people to account: '... yes, NAPLAN can diagnostically [be used] as a tool, to provide us with information, but **I don't think it should be used to hold [us to account]. I think we've gone nuts** .... I wish we should **focus less on data and more on create.**' (Leonie)

Owen suggests that the School System advisors would serve schools better if they could '**get away from a blaming and shaming perception.**' The changing nature of accountabilities set by system advisors is unsettling for Principals. Ralph the Rationalist notes: '... from time to time the ... I'll call it the measures ... have moved ... **the accountabilities do tend to move.** They're **not as clear-cut.** You can't just look them up.' The 'fluid' accountabilities are the results from the NAPLAN program rather than the results from the HSC course.

The Year 7 NAPLAN results are not the only area of accountability that some Principals think lacks clarity; another area is the way the Principals use their data. Malcolm the Moralist wishes that 'there was less emphasis on data,' revealing: '... **we are [even] measured on the ways we use data.**' Malcolm's phrase for being held to account as 'measured' is interesting. Possibly, Malcolm means 'being sized up,' inferring that they are feeling as if they themselves are animated objects to be measured.

There are also contradicting narratives about performance results. The Principals report contradictory messages from senior school system leaders, with the public narrative by the senior system leaders contradicting their private narrative addressed to schools. The public narrative, found in brochures to parents and system websites, is used to market the HSC results to the broader community: 'Look, when meet with a consultant and **when the Director rings up and congratulates us ... it's always about learning growth** and they understand that narrative. But when it comes to **what's said publicly, it's always about state averages and about number of Band 6s** (Barry). The author notes that in one School System's newsletter there are four pages devoted to the results achieved in the HSC. Similarly, Ralph's report emphasises such contradictions: '**Rhetoric does not always match their [School System's] actions with regard to what they are really interested in**' (Ralph).

Levi's experience of the senior leaders not examining the vocational education accountabilities implies a narrow view of learning. Malcolm argues that the concentrated focus by school systems and the public on raw performance results in the HSC diminishes not only learning in particular areas but also the significance of teachers' and students' work together. Malcolm further contextualises the way prioritising performance results diminishes access to the curriculum and does not reflect their religious ethos of learning: '**It can be measured, but it's not advertised because it doesn't sound as exciting. But in terms of the Catholic model of learning and teaching and increasing access to curriculum for all, some of the best work happens down with those kids.**'

To sum up Principals reveal their frustration and annoyance when performances from external assessment programs are elevated as the only form used to account for student learning. The Principals purport that this accounting under-represents student learning; the numbers inadequately represent the full student experience, diminishes students' and teachers' meaningful work and, in setting targets in the form of performance results, appears short-sighted.

One mechanism which both school systems employed was the DeCourcy instrument of analysis. It is an anomaly regarding the Principals' views of it. Most enjoyed the data, the analysis, and the leverage the tool gave them with teachers.

4 Anomaly: Prioritising the DeCourcy Instrument of Analysis

The majority of Principals employed tools of analysis to respond to the data from their external assessments. These tools, such as DeCourcy and SMART data are esteemed by both cohorts of Principals because results could be analysed longitudinally over a two- to five-year period. Internally growth in results over several years was of greater importance to Principals than the single year results. The DeCourcy tool has an added facility for predicting what could be expected of students' results, given their past results in junior years. School Systems' advisors expected Principals to employ these tools to analyse the results of external testing programs and to use the analysis to develop their implementation plans. Brian Broadview explains the importance of using the data provided by DeCourcy:

> We're digging deep to ensure that our students at this school in this context are working towards achieving their potential. It will be **reflected on the cross [the DeCourcy cross chart] and we have shifted. We understand where we were and where we're going to** ... So, **on that yardstick,** we're ... which is what [School System] ask us to look at ... we know we've shifted a lot, so at this school, we're always **quite high in learning gain** between Year 10 and Year 12 .... But now we're actually moving whole cohorts into far higher and greater levels.

The Principals revealed that they employed these devices for their own accountability purposes more than for benchmarking bands of scores or to meet the School Systems' expectations. Overall, these devices are judged as more favourable than being held to account for raw performance results, because growth is esteemed more than a single cohort of raw scores. Sammy conveys his esteem of the DeCourcy tool: '**We do spend a lot of time, we do exhaustive review of** HSC **data, more so from a learning gain point of view,** a DeCourcy **learning gain far more.**' Moreover, prioritising accountability in growth performances is reported as being respectful of the learner. Sammy explains further: 'It's **about treating everyone with respect, it's about learning gain, it really is, and I love the DeCourcy data, I love it for that reason, you know.**'

The Principals who use the DeCourcy tool also esteem its value in improving performances: 'I would suggest that our results over the last couple of years are actually results of efforts that started four and five years ago, where we were examining DeCourcy data.' (Bianca) Bianca professed that '**DeCourcy actually gives us a better acknowledgment of that overall learning growth.**'

From a long-term view of performance results gained over several years, devices such as the DeCourcy tool are viewed as useful for also addressing possible teacher performance problems: '**I don't need to say much; they [teachers] look at those results and draw their own conclusions**' (Sammy).

Overall, the Principals' reports suggest that they adopt practices that are beneficial to them, rather than integrating school system expectations into their own practices. Yet some could. They reported a win-win for meeting their own internal school purposes and meeting the School System's expectations.

Considering the two School Systems' explicit expectations, this surprise regarding the Principals' priorities in their responses to the accountability expectations provides support for naming this group of findings prioritising. Yet looking at prioritising from a sensemaking lens it is more like constraining. That is, Principals place constraints over what they pay attention to and what they do not. Prioritising to constraining as an idea, is developed further in the Grounded Theory Model in the final chapter.

Given the Principals' assortment in views about 'what and to whom and how' they were accountable, the School System advisors were sought to see if they were clear about their expectations of the Principals' accountabilities.

5 Anomaly: The School System Expectations

The School System advisor from the Penola School System reports: 'When it comes down to it, **performance results are the most important measure.**' Likewise, the advisor from the Mackillop School System maintains that students' performance results compared against state performances matters more:

> So, I've certainly been strong on HSC **data is not the be-all and end-all, but it is a measure and it's a snapshot of the health of the school,** particularly in terms of trends in relationship to state performance and whether there's a learning gain [growth in performance results] happening at that school. If you're analysing HSC results and over time you can't see any improvement ... **principals can't deny that that's a reflection of their leadership of learning in the school.**

These Schools Systems' advisors are explicit about their expectations of their Principals.

Researcher: Would Principals be clear about these expectations?
Penola advisor: Yes, I'm pretty sure they would.

School System advisors are clear that their Principals would know their expectations. This finding is surprising given that the Principals all hold different views about their priorities regarding their performative accountability, particularly the contradictions of what advisors say privately (growth) and what they publish publicly (scores).

First, Principals' priorities are not aligned with School System expectations. Second, each principal holds their unique stance on what, to whom and how they are held to account. Schools Systems are not only the Principals' key authority for monitoring and regulating accountability processes, but they are also the Principals' employing authority. Therefore, it is surprising that the Principals did not prioritise School System expectations more highly. Chapter 8 explores some possible reasons and their implications from this finding.

A key finding in the Principals' preferences regarding the methods of performative accountability is that all Principals reason that a number is an inadequate measure for assessing their students' learning. The Principals accept that they are accountable to their school systems; however, they prioritise being accountable to themselves more often than to any other referent, following being accountable to students, parents and then teachers. The Principals hold common views about the mechanisms that are used to hold them to account. Mechanisms which are used to judge, and blame create negative emotions. They report unfavourable views of system review days and public disclosure of performance results and yet favourable views towards imposed tools such as DeCourcy, because of the usefulness of the tool to analyse their data from a growth perspective and its facility to hold low level accountable conversations.

Figure 12 demonstrates the Principals' reported self-efficacy levels in meeting the dual expectations of meeting the accountability demands and the role function of the leader of learning identity.

Principals who demonstrated *high* levels of self-efficacy in meeting their dual expectations and *often* mentioned learning and teaching as their reference point had:

– Acknowledged the importance of knowing about learning and teaching
– Been active in their pursuit of learning more about learning and teaching processes
– Identified and embedded the Leader of Learning role in their function as principal
– Worked with teachers closely
– Impressed on the need of articulating a vision for learning
– Developed mentors such as lantern, cheerleader, facilitator, and images such as perspective taking
– Reflected on their previous career pathway as enabling their role as Leaders of Learning

'... SOMEHOW FRAME ACCOUNTABILITY TO MAKE SENSE OF IT'

TABLE 8   Summary of principals' educational accountability: To whom, what and how

To whom	What	How
Self	Student learning; joy in the school; performance results; growth in performance results; performance results measured against state averages; ways of working with data; comparing school's performance, using DeCourcy data, with other schools in the system	Utilising members of the leadership team to present documentation to School System
School System	Performance results; HSC results; numbers on a page; growth in performance results in NAPLAN and HSC; learning programs; school plans; School System priority areas; number of students in top bands in HSC	Meetings, review days with supporting documentation, i.e., school plans in response to results, appraisal processes with DeCourcy, SMART data tools
Students	Performance results—best chances; HSC results; post-school options; responding to data; authentic learning; responding to students' needs; learning; professional; recruiting the best staff; elements of school life that lead to more authentic learning; using results to find out what is wrong and then implementing solutions	Exit surveys; learning surveys
Parents	Performance results; HSC results; post-school options; responding to data; professional; elements of school life that lead to more authentic learning	Public ranking of top 200 schools; My School; parent meetings
Teachers	Protecting, honouring teaching time; professional reputation; staff learning; professional; responding to data to initiate for teamwork in the professional community	DeCourcy data
Government—National Partnerships	Specific learning outcomes from school goals	Written plans displaying outcomes
Bishop	Students' spiritual development	None identified
Public	Performance results; displaying performance results favourably; number of students in top bands in HSC	Enrolments; marketing materials; media; My School; ranking in top 200 schools
Priest	Performance results	Conversation with expectation of improvement

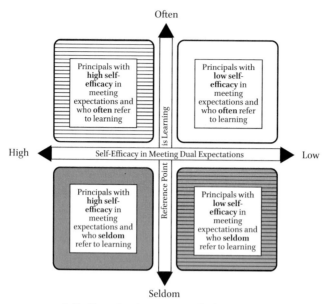
FIGURE 12   Self-efficacy levels in meeting dual expectations

Principals who demonstrated *low* levels of self-efficacy in meeting their dual expectations and *often* mentioned learning and teaching as their reference point had:
– Acknowledged the important role learning had to play in their role
– Been active in their pursuit about teaching and learning
– Realised that their career pathway hindered their current understandings of teaching practices
– Acknowledged the importance of building credibility with teachers which took time and skill
– Explained that they were employed to improve performance results to build enrolments
– Used metaphors such as juggler and facilitator

Principals who demonstrated *high* levels of self-efficacy in meeting their dual expectations and *yet seldom* mentioned learning and teaching as their reference point had:
– Made comparisons and developed competitive thinking in the form of student performance scores from and with other schools
– Seemed agitated with being held to account for performance results
– Set performance results as targets for teachers and students
– Reported teaching to and drilling for 'the test' rather than improving teaching practices to improve results

- Acknowledged and resigned that teaching to the test was not quality education
- Used metaphors such as salesman and conjured images of bulldozing to influence teaching practices

Principals who demonstrated *low* levels of self-efficacy in meeting their dual expectations and *yet seldom* mentioned learning and teaching as their reference point had:
- Believed improvement in performance results occurred only through attracting high performing students
- Believed the only reference points were performance results, competing for the best students, through enrolment strategies
- Held low expectations for teachers to improve performance results
- Set grade targets for students
- Seemed agitated in being held to account performance results notably, with the public and the School System, placing constraints on School System interventions
- Experienced their previous career pathway hindered their beliefs in improving teaching practices
- Used metaphors such as buffer, human shield

Principals who had unfavourable student performance scores or declining enrolments and yet valued 'authentic' learning, may have been tempted to drive for performance targets. To the contrary, three Principals who reported the school's history of scoring unfavourable results, with consequences of poor school image, declining enrolments and/or staff redeployment, did not report the need to drive for results. They emphasise the importance of evaluating their progress according to the learning journey and their leadership of this with the staff. While one ECP reported some minor anxiety, the others pursued their learning goals and revealed that 'the results would take care of themselves.' In contrast, the Principals who reported negative feelings (of being unfairly judged and frustration in being unable to change public views) with greater magnitude and frequency than the others, refer more often to the compelling need to improve their students' grades and bands. The Principals who disclose a relentless pursuit in their commitment to know and understand teaching and learning (notably Malcolm, Sammy, and Charmaine) report fewer concerns about being held to account for student performance results. Their need is deeply aligned, in a cognitive sense, with their identity and their School Systems' expectations of being a leader of learning.

5.1 *Emerging Propositions*

1. Principals who demonstrate commitment and capability in their pursuit of knowledge and skill regarding learning and teaching report with less frequency and magnitude about the demands of the accountability expectations.

2. Principals who seem to show indifference or lack of importance about the function of the leader of learning identity often report feelings of frustration and resignation about the accountability demands.

3. Principals' levels of self-efficacy in influencing the teaching and learning cycle impact their views about performative accountability. Principals with high levels of self-efficacy to influence teaching practices seldom report their accountability demands in negative terms.

4. Principals drive for performance results through setting score targets and drilling for tests when they report that they would find it difficult to influence teaching practices and/or remain silent about influencing teaching practices to improve results. These Principals also report strong negative emotions about their School System expectations, mechanisms, and consequences such as public disclosures and marketing performance results.

6 Conceptualising

> ... somehow frame accountability to make sense of it. (Owen)

The findings so far show that some Principals are reflective about accountability expectations, internalising their own understandings of accountability in a general sense. One such indicator is the reference to self-accountability and responsibility. Owen, for example, points to the self as being the key agent in making sense of accountability expectations. He reveals that his accountability is personal; he needs to understand himself and at the same time, expected others to have their own views about accountability: 'I think **it's a personal thing how you see accountability**. I really do .... It's an understanding of our mission in education ... **what our purpose is** .... I think if you **have an understanding of what you're about yourself as a principal, and what's your agenda, then you can somehow frame accountability to make sense of it.**' Part of Owen's personalising is embedded in his shared purpose within his religious tradition, with both his employing authority and his spiritual counsel. Owen's use of the term 'frame accountability' portrays a sense of constructing a cognitive schema of accountability.

6.1 Accepting Accountability

'Accepting' involves Principals readily accommodating their accountability expectations for students' performance results. For example, the way that Sammy positions his accountability shows accommodation, resolve and alignment: '... if a principal can **understand and accept and understand that ... accountability is something that I sense is a positive part of our landscape.**' Sammy advocates 'a place for accountability in the overall broader greater objective of learning ... **ignoring the political point scoring.**' Sammy also professes the necessity of accountability: 'I'm sounding like an advocate for accountability and I'm not—and **in one sense it's necessary.**' Terence also accepts accountability as necessary: '... **it's important and it's necessary and really there's nothing I can do about it.** I have to do it.'

While accepting their accountability for students' performance results, most of the Principals held qualifiers: 'Ignoring political point scoring'; 'I'm not necessarily into ... league tables'; and 'I'm sounding like an advocate for accountability and I'm not.' These qualifiers raise questions about the internal cognitive tasks that are required for Principals to accept what is being asked of them.

6.2 Personalising Accountability

Principals 'personalising' their accountability expectations occurred when Principals reported the importance of their own views about accountability, were reconciled with these views, aware that others would hold differing views and act upon the expectations differently to them. When Owen explains that **'it's a personal thing how you see accountability,'** he suggests that he knew of other Principals' views about accountability and how they act upon the demands: 'Look, **I know others teach to the test.'**

Brian Broadview's idea of personalising is about owning the accountability: 'Yeah, it's probably **owning it in myself** and that [the accountability] sitting **not as an uneasy tension.'** Brian's thinking about owning the accountability also conveys a sense of needing to understand it as a cognitive process. The benefit of owning his accountability helps Brian soothe the feelings about his tensions with the expectations.

In contrast, Terence reports that his philosophical views of education do not align with being held to account by external testing:

> I have some philosophical positions on this. Firstly, NAPLAN, School Certificate, HSC, and any other measure you want—the RE test, whatever—**I don't believe [it] measures [the] quality of a school.** I think

it's an indicator of what's happening, but **not a measure of [learning] ... because education is significantly broader than a number on tests.**

Personalising their accountability meant that the Principals take time to reflect on what accountability means for them in an intrapersonal sense. Intrapersonal knowledge can be described as a means of coming to know self and of coming to know the self as a leader (Dinham, Collarbone, Evans, & Mackay, 2013; Gardner, 2011). Their views also indicate that being held to account is not an action that is being 'done to them.'

6.3 *Accountability as a Moral Responsibility*

Principals described accountability as a responsibility, with some being explicit in their differentiation between responsibility and accountability, along with responsibility intertwined with their moral purpose.

Charmaine aligns her responsibility with people and aligns accountability with answering to her School System:

> **I feel responsible for the [students]. The people I answer to in terms of accountability are definitely your system leaders**, your consultant, your directors, those people and, of course, to the parents .... You're responsible to do your best for them [students] in all ways.

Barry argues his case for accountability being a responsibility through research: **'We're not really interested in accountability. We're interested in responsibility.** It's interesting Pasi Sahlberg talking about The Finnish Way, the book out now about his work there in Finland. He says in Finland, there's not even a word for accountability.'

Charmaine also engages reflective practices in resolving where accountability and responsibility fit together for her:

> When they [students] **are doing well, I think that's part of both accountability and responsibility.** Because I think you should always want to sit back in a school like this and say, well, we've got 80—what did we get this year—83% of the courses above state average in the Higher School Certificate.

Charmaine almost suggests when numbers are being counted, such as the students' performance scores, she uses the term accountable. When she is speaking about students' broad learning experiences, she describes it as a responsibility.

In a similar way Ralph differentiates between responsibility and accountability:

> In ... a numbers system it [accountability] would be to my employer, which is the [School System]. So, I am very responsible to the [supervisor in my School System]—that would be the person that I would have to account to for learning. I would say [Name] is the one. It's their team—we would be accountable to the learning team at the [School System office] ... I think **I have a responsibility to every mum and dad out there to try and get the best results for their kids. I suppose that's what I believe .... That's more a philosophy** ... I feel **part responsible to try to get them, to get the best they can** ... Straight-out accountability—I think it's more to the [School System], but I see a **moral purpose to the families.** (Ralph the Rationalist)

Ralph perceives that accountability is about the results ('numbers') to the School System ('employer') and yet responsibility is to the parents ('every mum and dad out there'). He ends with an interesting twist here, describing responsibility to the families as a moral purpose. Charmaine also introduces morality in her interview when she explains her responsibility:

> Suppose **I would say morally, I feel responsibility for the [students] to ensure that we're doing the best that we can for the [students]** ... make a difference out there in the world .... That we're talking about the whole person and so I would see that that's my moral imperative if you like. (Charmaine)

Both Charmaine and Ralph make the distinction that accountability is *for* the number and responsibility is *to* the person.

'Personalising accountability' and 'Accountability as a responsibility' may explain the importance attributed to school leaders placing 'faces on data,' which was a popular practice during 2015–2020. Memo 7 elaborates on this point.

Memo 7: Faces on data: Faces on results

As I analysed Ralph the Rationalist's text data, I reread some of my observations from the school visit after interview. Ralph was so keen to show me his learning hub; a place where all leading 'learning' staff was located. Within the learning hub, a space was paved for other teachers to come and learn new skills and to tackle new areas of curriculum. However, the most important visual in the hub was a feature wall with the faces of students with data attached to their names. At the time of interviews, these 'faces on the data' were popular among the leaders of learning. Studies at the time demonstrated that teachers were more likely to use data for improvement if the data were personalised. However, my point here is not the data walls but the process of personalising the data—I wonder if Charmaine and Ralph both explicitly differentiate responsibility and accountability so that they make distinctions between one that is personal and the other that answers back to the School system (seen as an impersonal body and interested only in the number). I wonder how much the 'Faces on Data' practice has found its way into principals' thinking about personalising the whole student body's performance results—or for that matter, vice versa. Is this personalising a psycho-social process or a way to make sense of their accountabilities?

While Norris's research (2017) demonstrates that Principals construct cognitive schemas of accountability as a responsibility, others construct their accountability as a self-responsibility. Leonie the Light argues that she would hold herself to account regardless of whether the system or society was holding her to account:

> Irrespective of whether there was a system asking me to do that or not, irrespective of what society or what the system was asking of me; **my accountability factor would be high enough anyway, to be asking those questions of myself anyway.**

Levi also emphasises that 'If leader **requirements and learning accountabilities are not going well, it is my responsibility to take action.**' Both Leonie's and Levi's excerpts demonstrate that their constructing schemata is a disciplined self-responsibility.

Principals' views that accountability is linked with responsibility signals complex cognitive schemata on the part of Principals, who are endeavouring to make accountability more palatable to themselves and at the same time making sense of their expectations.

6.4   Accountability as Agency

At times, accountability was referred to as a source of energy, a leverage for action and as Sammy describes, 'a positive part of the educational landscape.' He also points out that others do not necessarily view accountability in such positive terms: 'So certainly you know accountability can sometimes be interpreted as a dirty word, but **if it's used for the purposes of responding to a** learning need, it's actually a very good thing to be—I wouldn't say subjected to, but to be a part of.' Sammy's views here suggest that accountability is an agent or catalyst for action, 'responding to a learning need.' Sammy also clarifies that he is *not subject to* accountability but rather, is *part of it*. This correction of being an agent—that is, 'part of'—suggests the need for Principals to be in control of and establish their autonomy from the effects of accountability.

Accountability is viewed as an obligation to act; that is, certain conditions necessitated action. For example, Levi the Leveller resolves, '... I have accountabilities. I have compliance requirements, leader requirements and learning accountability there and **if it's not going well—yeah, there's accountability on me and I think, do something about it**.' Levi recognises that when certain elements such as learning are at stake, he is obliged to act. Leonie aligns accountability with action and consequences: 'They [staff] know that **if there's no accountability and they know if there's no action, we could lose staff as a result of declining** [enrolment] numbers.'

It is important to note at this point that these findings refer to those Principals who reported the importance of conceptualising the whole notion of accountability as an entity. Some did not. There were Principals who did not speak about accountability itself as an entity at all. Those who were silent about accountability as an entity were Principals who targetted for scores and drilled for tests and were highly critical of their School System's expectations.

These findings taken together indicate that certain Principals develop schemata about their expectations and particularly the whole notion of accountability. Once acceptance of the accountabilities is realised, they personalise it. Part of their acceptance is that performative accountability can work to their advantage. They conceptualise their accountability as an authorising agency, perceiving expectations as a positive force for purposes that are meaningful for them, such as a learning need. The specific imagery Principals employ points to the importance of wanting to be in control of their expectations—'*to drive it*' (Sammy), '*not be subject to it*.' The Principals' imagery made their views clear that being an agent in carrying out their expectations meant they were likely to make sense of accountability. The Principals' sensemaking was constructing cognitive schemata that ensured that they enacted, rather than reacted to the accountability expectations (see Memo 8).

Memo 8: Constructing cognitive schemata

This is an interesting development in the interviews. Principals' constructions of personalising through to their enabling their agency to indicate to me that these principals in the study possibly engaged in psychological processes in their interaction with the accountability expectations. Yet, their interaction was not limited to psychological processes. Social processes also occurred where the participating principals were making sense of their account by comparing their experiences with their peer principals, where there was similar thinking because principals had worked together previously. To that end, the participating principals' interactions and constructions of accountability could be identified as a psycho-social process—a Glaser and Strauss term.

Their cognitive schemata demonstrated that they were reconfiguring their expectations of performative accountability, framing it in a way that was acceptable and meaningful for them. Hence, the theme 'conceptualising' is described as Principals framing their understandings of educational accountability (see Figure 13). This group of findings is re-named 'Framing.'

6.5 *Emerging Propositions*
1. Principals develop cognitive schemata to manage their accountability expectations for performance results.
2. Principals who personalise, accept and view accountability as a responsibility and a lever for agency are more likely to manage their dual role function as leaders of learning and meeting their accountability expectations for performance results.

FIGURE 13   Framing educational accountability

The examples of the Principals' understandings have presented the ways in which they contextualised, prioritised, and framed their responses to the accountability expectations (see Figure 14).

It is clear from the Principals' comments about their priorities suggest that they are engaged in complex processes in making sense of their performative accountability expectations. These understandings are influenced considerably by their own philosophical beliefs about learning. The Principals' understandings of their expectations are like acts of sensemaking and are represented in the themes of contextualising, constraining and framing accountability.

The process of constraining is influenced by the Principals' perceptions of their school environment factors and their representational beliefs about learning. The Principals' beliefs about learning appear to influence their priorities more than their views about their school environment factors (refer to Memo 3).

Principals' self-beliefs about their capabilities in mobilising their teaching teams to analyse data to implement new processes, also dominate their views about their performative accountability. Those Principals confident about their capabilities, combined with their longer years of principalship, are less concerned about, to the extent they are even welcome the external accountability from the public and their School Systems.

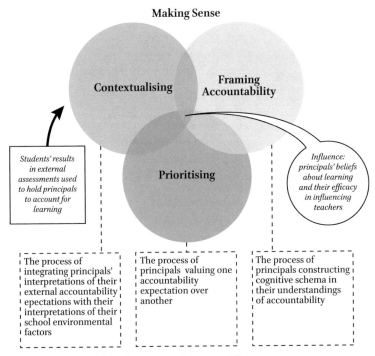

FIGURE 14   Principals making sense of accountability

Although the School System is the employer and chief regulator, surprisingly, the principals do not necessarily prioritise their expectations according to their system regulators. Principals' interpretations of their school environment are represented in this as a process of contextualising, defined as the way the principals create integrative meaning of their interpretations of the external accountability expectations with their interpretations of their school environment factors. The principals' rich philosophical notions about performative accountability suggest that they may have reflected on their expectations over a sustained period. This group of findings is described as a process of framing accountability, described here as the way the principals construct cognitive schema to make sense of performative accountability.

CHAPTER 7

The Lady of Light

Principals describe how they were 'at their best' in managing their expectations. Their descriptions range from sensemaking through mantras and narratives and enacting their Leader of Learning identity to ensuring their school communities had a sense of coherence between external demands and internal commitments. 'At her best' Leonie explains she needs to keep the vision in the faces of her community: 'I am the Lady of Light ... the torch or little flame ... I need to hold the little lantern up.'

The relationship between Principals' sensemaking, as shown in the previous chapter, and their reported enactments is a key interest point in this book. This relationship is teased out through four case examples in the final section of this chapter.

The practices the Principals employed to guide their teaching teams were intended to be 'meaning making' for their communities. The practices, as a whole, suggest sensegiving acts. These acts were created through metaphors, mantras, oral and written narratives, enacting their leader identity and building school cultures of coherence.

Figure 15 provides an overview of Principals' descriptions of when 'they are leading at their best' through external accountability constraints. The scaffold in Figure 15 provides the structure for the chapter.

The metaphor, the mantra and the oral and written narratives were used by the participating Principals to make meaning for and give sense to their communities. Such examples of their sensegiving acts were *articulating a vision for learning; 'languaging' learning; telling the good news story;* and *ignoring naysayers*.

1   Sensegiving Acts: Persuading Teachers

1.1   *Metaphors, Mantras and Narratives*
There were conflicting views between the Principals' ideas of a learning target and what was measured and reported. When Principals described their ways of navigating these conflicts, some spontaneously created metaphors, narratives, and mantras. This is quite surprising when further probing took place in the second round of interviews. All participants could easily provide a metaphor. Barry for example described himself as a 'human shield' to guard and protect

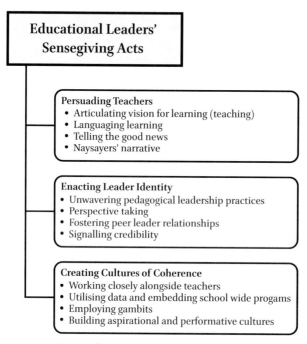

FIGURE 15   Principals' agency in managing accountability

the teachers from their School System expectations. This line of inquiry was pursued with the following question: *What kind of metaphor describes how you manage being the leader of learning and at the same time being accountable for performance results?* Table 9 summarises the types of metaphors and narratives that the Principals reported they adopt to manage the dual expectations.

Aligning Principals' metaphors with their other data provided several insights. For instance, the teachers in Owen's college are inclined to be overfocused on the number of high-performance bands they can attain in the HSC. Owen created mages of sense-making several times during the interview. Owen explained that he needs to help teachers see that using results for improving for the next year is good enough and that the results need to be made sense of, rather than be used as targets.

Charmaine works with her teachers closely in their professional learning programs, with no indications that she monitors or holds teachers to account. She champions their successes and 'walking with them,' slowly when needed—her metaphor is cheerleader.

Terence, who uses performance results as targets, described is behaviours as bulldozing at times because he experiences resistance by some leaders in middle management positions in using data to inform practices. These metaphors,

THE LADY OF LIGHT

TABLE 9   Leaders' metaphors, mantras and narratives

Metaphor	Narrative	Text example
Perspective taker	Building balance	'Facilitator of perspective taking'; 'I **don't think our balance is too bad here**'; 'Need to build it'; 'I think I'm comfortable that **we've got the balance right**'
Filter	Sifting what comes into the school	'I see the role of **principal as a filter** ... what is a priority and what isn't a priority .... The filter part is about basically **saying yes and no to certain things**'
Buffer, human shield	Protecting teachers	'I suppose I do see it as ... **a buffering system**'; 'I am **the human shield** between the [School System and the teachers]—the buffer'; 'He said, my job is to be the human shield, **which protects the teachers** from the excesses of [the accountability regime]'
Coach	Preparing for a race	'... teaching to the test. If that's your measure, you are not going to fire a 100-metre **sprinter** at the Olympics doing 800-metre training. They'd be **doing 100-metre sprints**'
Protector	Honouring	'So it's about saying no to a lot of that **to protect what's going on here**'
Cheerleader	Part of the team, on a journey	'So I know at times you feel like **you're the cheerleader**'; 'I like to work with them when they have professional opportunities'; 'Bringing them, walking slowly with them'
Juggler	Diverse and many experiences in the day of a principal	'... **a juggler** ...'; '... So here you are one minute— and my day will be one minute ... I will go from you to a meeting with a parent who has booted his daughter out of home and wants me to boot her out of school at the same time'
Bulldozer	School is the vehicle, need to drive	'I **never bulldoze**. Or maybe I **do sometimes**'; 'Just **need to drive for the results**'
Sense-maker	Making sense of results and building on them	'... we will improve [results] for the next year and **build on that** ...'; '... there is a need to **make sense of it** [performance results] ...'
Salesperson	School offers the best chance	'It's like the old story where **the encyclopaedia salesman used to knock on the door and say to mum, do you want to give your son and your daughter the best chance possible in life?**'
Lantern	Torch—Lady of the Light	'I am the [lady of the light], whatever, **the torch or the little flame** or whatever'; 'Need to **hold the lantern up** ...'

while showing diversity in the Principals' narratives of themselves, provided a window of some of their motivations when dealing with the dual expectations.

The Principals also develop mantras to align their private voice with their public voice. Sammy, by integrating instructional leadership for results and students being responsible citizens, explained his approach with his mantra: 'We are **pushing that mantra here.**' Terence revealed the importance of a mantra for his role: 'So I think when you sort of articulate those things really clearly ... **learning as a mantra** all the way along and you've just got **to chip, chip your way at it.**'

1.2 *Articulating a Vision for Learning*

Principals argue not only the importance of a vision for learning but also articulating that vision. Charmaine, the Cheer Leader explained the importance of having a vision for learning and sharing it:

> ... [need] **a vision for learning** ... [and] **sharing that** so we, having a school-wide pedagogy, having a **school-wide vision for learning** and being able to say to parents and I suppose the community as a whole—this is the way that we see learning here and what we consider to be important. (Charmaine)

Holding a vision enables Principals to articulate to the community the elements of learning that they value. Notably the vision of learning was broader than a performance result.

Levi, the Leveller reflected 'When you've **got the ability to clearly articulate a vision for learning ... you articulate the vision for learning.**' Owen was at his best in leading learning and emphasised the necessity of articulating the vision: 'I'm at my best ... **when I've got the ability to clearly articulate a vision for learning.**' Alongside holding and articulating a vision, enacting the vision was reported as important. Enacting the vision was also viewed to build credibility with teaching teams.

1.3 *'Languaging' Learning*

Principals explained they were at their best in leading learning when most conversations centred on learning. Malcolm was relentless in his push for the learning to be the 'only' conversation worthwhile having, hence the title 'languaging of learning.'

> ... the conversation is **always primed around learning.** That **quickly gets around.** When **you talk to parents, it's about learning.** That's when **I'm at**

THE LADY OF LIGHT

my best, when I just do that. You've just got to find the time to make sure you're doing it .... That's the first point you push—that in this school, **we want more of our conversations to be around learning.**

Malcolm revealed his sense of confidence in carrying out his core work in leading learning, placing constraints on his own conversations with teachers, students, and parents, to be centred on learning. As an aside, Malcolm views marketing results as immoral and pays little attention to the raw performance scores. Similarly, Bianca, the Balancer explained that she is at her best when she is having conversations about learning: '... and there is always a **segment in the staff meeting where you're having a conversation about learning.**'

Malcolm emphasised that '... in every classroom we have got **a learning conversation,** not a managing conversation' along with Bianca's comment suggests that the 'languaging learning' acts as a change agent for creating norms in the community, maintaining that learning is broad and the common core purpose for teachers, students, and parents.

1.4   *Telling the Good News Story*

The 'good news' is framed by one principal as public storytelling. Barry described it elaborately when he communicates to the community the students' performance results in favourable terms:

> So, in **the public story telling** that we have to share from this place, it's got to **be telling that story about hospitable, welcoming** ... I can point to that in the data, in our great NAPLAN learning growth in School Certificate before it was abolished. In the Higher School Certificate, we have got the fastest growing number of subjects above state average .... This is about **finding the statistics that tell that story, which is real,** ... **it's not dishonest.** It's not in any way dishonest but it's what [previous mentor principal] taught me. You have **got to find the good news story** and having established that, here is high-quality education, but it's open to your [child] even though your [child] is not an absolute brain box. **Then tell the story, here's how we do it.**

Like Barry's narrative of the "Good News Story," Brian Broadview positions Basilicata's results favourably. When Brian knows that Basilicata's results are compared publicly, he ensures that their results are given an equal and esteemed voice to the public: 'Publicly ... well, **the local paper gets in quick and so we make sure that we push our results in the best light** we can and **the results for the last few years have shown continual improvement.**' What may seem ironical is that Brian prioritises student happiness and holistic learning over performance results yet is willing to play in this competitive contest of favourable results in the public arena.

Some Principals warn that the public story telling needs data that are not based on folklore: 'So that's been a big effort in trying to ... increase the enrolments. Along with that, then you have to **maintain good academic results. But you've got to tell the good story. You can't just build enrolments on folklore.** You've **got to have** some **data back it up**.'

Together, these findings provide insights into the various ways that Principals managed their dual expectations of being accountable publicly and being the leaders of learning seamlessly. They adopt roles such as public story tellers to describe the best that their students can be, which in their reports are much more than reporting the students' performance results. They reward improvement such as growth in results. They use other criteria to draw out important growth points, such as the number of subjects with above-average achievement and continual improvement in overall school performances over several years.

1.5   *Ignoring Naysayer*
Keeping learning as their consistent referral point results in Principals ignoring teachers who attempt to derail the learning focus of the school:

> You **waste no energy. I don't waste one jot of time worrying about** *naysayers*. I just **work with those people with the capability and the inclination to have a go. I just don't listen** to the others. You have to be **a little bit thick-skinned.** (Malcolm)

Malcolm's learning focus—and his languaging of learning—assists by warding off worrying feelings, resulting in him remaining steadfast and committed to the broader learning goals. An interesting point here is the way Malcolm described how he needs a 'thick skin,' suggesting that the naysayers are confronting for him. His cognitive schema helps him internally manage their criticisms.

Keeping learning as a reference point ensures that the tensions of being held to account are eased. On leaving the focus group, Brian Broadview whispered 'Just want to tell you ... **tensions of leadership are eased when there is an understanding of learning ... or clarity about learning**.' Ignoring naysayers, deflecting and diverting (to learning) are important management strategies that enabled Principals to hold learning as their reference point when the pressure of performative accountability jeopardises them realising their school's goals.

1.6 *Emerging Proposition*

Principals who seamlessly manage the dual function of the leader of learning and being accountable for results do this by positioning their reference points around learning, as opposed to performance results.

Two anomalies regarding Principals being 'at their best' when leading involved the selection of students and the other setting targets.

2 Anomaly: Principals Manage Demands by 'Cherry Picking'

One principal reported that the reasons students from other schools achieve better results than their school is because of the type of student they attracted or marketed for. The consequence of this principal's belief was a minimal expectation that a teacher could improve results. The principal explains:

> When **you have got the numbers, you can then set a cut-off quota** and then **you cherry-pick the best students. That's how schools improve** and every [Catholic] school that you could quote to me ... in **this district that has improved its results** in recent years, has [done so] **because they have got better-quality cattle than this school and that's how they have improved, they cherry-pick.**

The inference from this principal is that the demographic of the student improves results not the teaching practices. The consequence of this principal's belief is that teachers' expectations to improve student learning are likely to be lowered.

3 Anomaly: Principals Manage Demands through Target Setting

As an internal mechanism of accountability, some Principals set targets in the form of students' performance results in HSC. The teachers at Ralph's school are completing the end of their implementation phase of a target-setting program. Ralph notes that once the targets had been met, there was confusion in terms of what the next goal would be. His particular concern is situated in the hard work that teachers had undertaken to reach particular performance results:

> So somewhere, if we've **gone along a grades journey** there has to be a sort of **upper limit** to that journey ... Yes. I want the learning growth, I want

the improvement, but I've also got to accept **there's got to be some sort of plateau ....** I've got to come to terms with how we celebrate that, because that's just as good.

In contrast to Ralph is the frustration some Principals felt when they themselves were focused on improving the raw performance results but the teachers and those in middle management positions are not. Terence feels frustrated when performance results are not improving, and he has attempted to solve the problem: 'We've tried [for] two or three years now to address what I could see was a **problem and it's not improving.**'

Several points need to be made here. First, 'cherry-picking' students to improve results is linked with this particular principal's levels of confidence in leading the teaching teams '... now, **how to do it** [leading teaching] is **another matter,**' suggesting that 'another matter' is the difficult one. This principal consistently refers to the School System's expectations and public judgements with disdain and a sense powerlessness about the students' performances, comparing these with other schools in the region. These references are perceived as unjust. The principal perceives that other schools' results are more favourable because those Principals can select their students. As a response, this principal's school sets up their own internal target setting in the form of grades. This finding confirms other findings from the Norris study (2017), where Principals develop quite sophisticated (yet possibly unconscious) cognitive schemata to justify their actions or inactions in their responses to accounting for student performance results.

Second, this principal's level of confidence appears to be high from the outcomes of the target grade-setting initiative: '**I challenge anybody to tell me that's not [expletive] brilliant.**' The principal's sense of confidence may stem from their greater control over the process of target setting for results than from their confidence in influencing the teaching and learning processes. Target setting for grades is reported to occur through the pastoral groups and as such, these Principals would be able to influence and carry out this initiative relatively easily, possibly with minor resistance from faculties.

The third point contributing to the target setting anomaly is the principal's leadership history, which are predominantly pastoral, and as such, possibly more influential with pastoral/year advisors than with curriculum/faculty coordinators. It follows that implementing such an initiative at a practical level could occur more easily than the principal facilitating teaching and learning processes. This case illustrates that initiatives need to be within the principal's perceived capabilities, both in practicalities and in skills.

THE LADY OF LIGHT

To sum up, the Principals report that they are at their best leading learning when they can see indicators that they were influencing the teaching processes: 'Then **the light comes on. It's not so hard. I can do that**' (Charmaine). Within the influencing process, the Principals advocate the importance of working closely with teachers, bringing them along, circling and going around, using data for leverage, and holding teachers to account, developmentally or punitively. In a minority of cases, they try to influence teachers to strive for performance results. These cases are silent about the level of success they have influencing the teaching and learning process.

The findings here demonstrate two divergent views. Malcolm is seen to show high levels of confidence in being able to influence teacher thinking. Simultaneously he ignores public judgements about the results of external testing and regards marketing via performance results as 'immoral.'

3.1 *Emerging Propositions*

The Principals who emphasise the importance of building credibility with their teaching teams are the same Principals who emphasise the importance of conceptualising learning in broad terms and are confident fulfilling the leader of learning function.

Whereas the other view, held by two Principals, is silent about teaching strategies or influencing their teaching teams revealing the overpowering impact of system and public judgments in leading at their best with performative accountability.

Enactments of cherry-picking students and performance target setting indicate these Principals' key referents are competition for enrolments and their comparison of their results by the public and system. Conclusions drawn about the school image and themselves as principals are overwhelming.

Table 10 illustrates this summary.

4 Sensegiving Acts: Enacting the Leader Learner Identity

4.1 *Unwavering in their Pedagogical Leadership Practices*

Deflecting other distractions to ensure that they enact their core purpose of their leadership (leading learning and teaching) is viewed as an effective management strategy. Malcolm while comparing himself with his peers, stated the importance of leading the community around learning and teaching:

> Those **principals who have to micromanage every element** of their complex organisation can't possibly do their key job, which is to **lead the**

144 CHAPTER 7

TABLE 10   Diverging views: Building credibility with teams

Element: Credibility		Elements of influence	Leadership practices	Reported levels of confidence in ways of leading	Points of reference
Participants	*Majority view*	Getting teachers to focus on learning and working in teams	All foci and conversations on learning	High	Learning is broad Leading learning through empirical research
	Minority view	Judgements made based on students' results in external testing	Silent about positioning learning in the centre and influencing teachers	Low	Injustice of being judged via students' performance results Cherry-picking students

> community around learning and teaching. You can't be at your best if
> you're being drawn into these [other] areas ... so you know you should
> be spending time on this ... but at times you know you have to spend time
> on this if you can let it go a little bit in the future.

Here, Malcolm stresses the importance of his focus on the leadership of
learning, yet he also reveals how he is constructing his professional identity—
by comparing his practices with other Principals' practices.

A common view among the Principals is to remain steadfast in pursuing
their visions for learning, not chasing numbers. As such, Principals report that
they themselves are best placed to make decisions about learning, not their
School System. In response to school expectations for achieving favourable
student performance results, Charmaine reasoned that learning is her moral
imperative, not numbers on a page:

> I mean, we've got our vision and we're sending them out to be who we
> say they're going to be and to make a difference out there in the world.

THE LADY OF LIGHT   145

> Then **that's not achieved just by excellent numbers on the page** ....
> We're talking about the whole person and so I would see that that's my
> moral imperative if you like.

Leonie noted that her role is to be centred on teaching and learning, irrespective of what the School System expects: 'I love pedagogy and **I consider
myself a leader of learning** .... So **irrespective of whether there was a system asking me to do that or not** ... my accountability factor would be high
enough anyway.' These findings, taken together, suggest that the School Systems' expectation of Principals carrying out the 'leader of learning' function is
reasonably well aligned with the majority of the Principals' thinking about this
function. This is important research. Principals readily embedded the leader
of learning identity into their role, supported by the School System, yet did not
readily adopt the expectations (by the School System) to drive for performance
results. The Leader of Learning identity is uniquely embedded and witnessed
in Principals' metaphors, such as lantern, cheerleader, and perspective taker.

4.2   *Taking Perspective*

Principals position themselves deliberately as being responsible for providing
leadership in making sense of the accountability expectations. Owen explained
that he wants the teachers to focus on improvement and in this way, they needed
to make sense of the expectations, rather than focus on the measure: '**My language is deliberate about how we can improve it, not how can we get them
above a state average** .... I'm not putting the pressure on that we want that, **that
is a measure there** .... Mine is about improvement ... **improve for the next year
and build that** ... There is a need to **make sense of it**' (Owen). Others describe
their position as keeping the expectations in the right perspective: '... Yeah, so
you're trying in some ways to inspire them to want to continue the authentic
learning and you want them to see the relevance to some extent of the testing
that's happening that's external but to keep it in the **right perspective** .... To **not
give in to just ... teach to the test in** NAPLAN.' Ralph the Rationalist proudly
acknowledged his school's practices as making sense and keeping results in a balanced perspective: 'Here there are really good processes and systems and a culture that **makes sense of it**—keeps it on the agenda but **keeps it in perspective.**'

4.3   *Leader Identity: Comparing*

Principals explore their positions as leaders carrying out their performative
accountability in and through their collegial relationships with other peer
principals. Comparing and reconstructing their professional identities help
them to manage the challenges associated with a range of impacts of being
held to account.

146 CHAPTER 7

Malcolm explained the processes of arriving to common understandings in his system, through his peer principal relationships:

> ... **Working with** [a principal in the region] and then myself and [another principal in the region] **you find an ally**, or **similar-thinking person** who probably blocks you from looking to see [another viewpoint] ... **next is the team** [secondary principals' cluster] **that work together**, share data. If that happens, I imagine that **those views of principals in this little team would become more similar.**

Four of the participants had worked together as assistant principal and principal, in each of the cohorts. They all hold similar beliefs about the position of student performance results in their representation of learning.

These findings indicate that Principals compare their own beliefs with others and in this way are co-constructing and settling their beliefs about themselves, either through agreement or disagreement.

The Principals who report this importance of learning, such as remaining contemporary to be leaders of learning, are also confident in their leadership. Malcolm, for example, who holds this view, also reports high levels of confidence in being able to influence teacher thinking. Conversely, a minority of participants report working towards target setting in the form of grades and number of bands on the HSC. These Principals promoted practising and at times drilling for tests, with one principal suggesting that they need to 'bulldoze' teachers for better performance results at times. One possible reason for this minority view could be their own confidence about leading learning—'How to go about it, well that's a different matter'—which raises the question of the impact of their own self belief in influencing their teaching teams from through a pedagogical approach.

An interesting finding is the way the Principals create metaphors and images to build their own sense of coherence around their professional identities. These metaphors and images provide a rich lens on where they want to be in their roles as leaders of learning within their accountability expectations. These findings indicate that while this process is internal, it is active and seemingly requires Principals to enact sensemaking strategies to gain self-coherence.

4.4 *Leader Credibility Essential*

Principals describe some qualifiers in their leadership practices when in the signalling phase of the accountability cycle. Charmaine for example wanted to signal to a teaching faculty the importance of using the DeCourcy data:

THE LADY OF LIGHT

My science coordinator will say, 'Sorry, I don't think much of DeCourcy data; I don't think that's valid.' 'What do you think is valid then? We do have to measure growth and value add.' I've had **to do a bit of relationship building in those things** … before you do those things. But I think we're **now ready to take on some of those**, to **sit down and look at the things that DeCourcy** talks about, asking the hard questions. (Charmaine)

Charmaine qualified that before signalling the value of data analysis, relationships of trust need to be built first.

Charmaine is a MCP with several successful principal appointments. She displayed confidence in managing School System demands at the same time as gaining solid results, along with esteem by her teaching teams. As well as indicating that relationships need to be developed before conversations about utilising data can be had, Charmaine's excerpt also points to the challenges in holding conversations about the teachers' performances based on students' external test results. It seems to be a difficult conversation for the Principals. Sammy prefers the data to speak for themselves with teachers. To some extent this is the appeal for Principals of the DeCourcy data. They spoke favourably about the 4 questions devised by DeCourcy and their helpfulness to 'hold the conversation' about performance results without blaming and shaming.

5 Sensegiving Acts: Creating Cultures of Coherence

Principals guided their school communities to adapt to the performative demands by creating cultures of coherence.

5.1 *Working Alongside Teachers*

Participating and engaging with teachers' professional learning was one way to influence teaching practices. Charmaine, the Cheer Leader explained:

Yes, it's about getting people on board. **Bringing them, walking slowly with them at times to get them to understand new** things. Helping them to understand, to learn about it and I suppose you try to give them the tools so that they can understand what you're trying to achieve and so that they can have the capacity to get on board with it and **feel that it's something that …, I suppose, adds value to their own repertoire as a teacher.**

Charmaine's strategy suggests she understands Vygotsky's Zone of Proximity (the importance to the learner, in this case the teacher), thinking that they are in reach of being able to understand and carry out the practice, combined with the importance of understanding the teacher's knowledge base and skill sets.

5.2   *Utilising Data, Designing and Embedding School Wide Programs*

The Principals' School Systems expect principals to use data from the external instruments—HSC and NAPLAN results. In most cases, the Principals consider that the data are helpful for evidence to inform practice; however, they hold a variety of views on the ways they use data.

5.2.1   Utilising Data for Guiding Decisions

A minority of cases mention that using data sets is at times onerous, yet most agree that data analyses *inform practice* to *help with making decisions*. Bianca explained that she uses data 'to **make decisions**, it's about **using data to inform**. You don't use [your gut]—the gut's gone out long ago. You go and **look for the data, look for the evidence** that say **either this is working, or this isn't working**' (Bianca). Leonie revealed that 'it's important that you **use data to guide your decisions**.' Leaders of school systems no longer accept that educational leaders can make decisions according to feelings or intuition.

5.2.2   Responding to a Learning Need

Data are reported as helpful in making decisions about needs: '... **if it's used for the purposes of responding to a learning need, it's actually a very good thing to be**—I wouldn't say subjected to, but to be a part of ...' (Sammy). Sammy's qualifier is that he does not want to be 'subjected to' the data suggests a desire to have control of data for his and the teachers' analyses.

> Is autonomy a better word than control? It makes sense that educators would want to 'own' their data, have some sense of autonomy in the analyses of their data, given the data are the consequences of their teaching practices.

5.2.3   Leveraging

Some Principals indicate that being judged through the public disclosure of test results creates fear and uncertainty. This public accountability threatens enrolments and precipitates the possibilities of staff losses and low staff and student morale. However, some Principals disclose that these public judgements about school image are leverage for engaging teachers in change. One Principal explained:

THE LADY OF LIGHT   149

> So, I have been **fortunate on one level** to walk into a school where we've got declining **enrolments.** So, my **staff members have a natural curiosity about how they can improve** what they're doing, because they understand things are slipping and their results are not great … They **know that if there's no accountability and … no action, we could lose staff as a result of declining numbers.**

Before teachers can become curious about or willing to improve results, it needs to be made clear to staff that poor results could hold negative consequences not just for students but the entire community. How Principals frame their perspectives on such results is likely to be a determinant on how teachers accept or own a collective responsibility to improve results.

5.2.4   Holding Teachers to Account without Blame

The strategy of holding onto the control of the data (as in Sammy's case) is important for other Principals as well. Some warn that data should not be used to judge schools. Most strategise that if data are used as part of professional conversations, they are useful: 'If **it's** [data] **used** and DeCourcy **uses this** and **I'm trying to use it all the time … if data are used for conversation rather than judgement there will always be growth**' (Sammy).

The Principals explain that they are not only expected to use data to inform teaching practices but also must demonstrate the outcomes of such practices. For one cohort this demonstration is the evidence they must provide as part of their performance appraisal processes. Some Principals welcome this expectation and adopt this as a management strategy, to meet the School System's and their own school goals. Sammy convincingly reported 'But I find that in **engaging in the accountability there is a lot of useful data and information and evidence that comes from that …'** (Sammy, Veneto College). Charmaine described they (leadership team) are at their best when data are analysed and employed for making improvements: '**That would be us at our best.** Whether that's engaged in **some things that we've done, looking at … our data and saying these are our students, how do we improve this?'**

A minority of cases report a strategy of adopting the DeCourcy tool to encourage teachers to self-evaluate from their own students' performances. Sammy impresses on the importance of teachers making their own judgements about their students' performances in external testing and choose their own consequences for themselves: 'But **in the end, the teachers bring themselves to their own judgements far quicker than what I can do and it's better that they do it than I do it'** (Sammy). Influencing teaching in this way suggests Sammy encourages teachers of adopting their own self-accountability. Having

150   CHAPTER 7

a structure such as the DeCourcy tool which promotes responsibility was deemed advantageous and positive for all Principals in the Norris study (2017).

5.2.5   Privileging Inputs over Outputs

> ... they're other aspects of learning that I think have been important without being measurable. (Levi, the Leveller)

The majority of Principals privilege process inputs, rather than performance outputs. This is understandable as most of the Principals adapt or ignore the School System and public expectations in the drive for results. One process input mentioned by Principals is embedding learning through the implementation of school-wide pedagogies. The Principals reported a sense of accomplishment when these programs improve the overall learning and teaching. They also believe that programs such as project-based learning promotes other areas of student learning that are not necessarily measurable. That said, the Principals also emphasise that if the school-wide programs are authentic, performances on external tests would also be favourable.

Charmaine revealed that she encourages the continuation of project-based learning with several year groups:

> So, when I look at **project-based learning** ... [it] should be developing ... our girls' **thinking skills, ability to work cooperatively, collaboratively, to think globally,** to do all those sorts of things, then if they've learned that in [Years] 9 and 10, **they're already thinking critically ... if you're doing the right things, that should reflect in their results.**

Charmaine also revealed 'One of the best things we've done, both in terms of our e-learning and our project-based learning, is to have **some sessions for the parents ...**' and emphasised that success in these programs should bring about the desired performance results in external assessment tools, such as NAPLAN.

Malcolm advocated picking a certain number of areas of learning that would influence teaching practices and enact these:

> ... when I've walked into a new setting ... I would **pick the three most important** things that I **believe are central to the way we run** schools now and I **would just push them.** They are our **formative approach to assessment** and the **expert teacher rather than the experienced teacher**

.... I would **encourage every team to have a project**, to have an **improvement project that's based on informed understanding of a particular need.**

Ralph explained with pride that their school-wide learning scaffold is implemented to improve writing across all subject areas. At the same time, he proudly revealed the establishment of a staff learning hub in which teachers meet, but not according to subject areas: '... curriculum led ... for the [subjects] and the [specialist leaders] **is all one.** So, **they're not in separate spots.'** Ralph's College participates in a government funded partnerships program yet downplays how the students meet their targets. Rather, he emphasises the school-wide pedagogies being implemented and the sense of success their students experience. He said, '... they're **other aspects of learning that I think have been important without being measurable.'** Ralph with pride offers a guided tour to the staff hub. There is a demonstrable hum in the space. Along with a data wall that the teachers explain with pride is enthusiasm for these cross faculty common goals. In this way, Ralph's accountability enactments are expressed in term of inputs, not outputs in performances.

Some Principals note that focusing on performance results narrows the learning experiences for students. Owen, the Opportunist explained

> The only contradiction there is **when accountability is weighted so heavily that you're unable then to engage with learning** on the broad spectrum of things; engagement of kids on pastoral issues, discipline issues are all opportunities for learning there. If you're so focused on the HSC results and NAPLAN, you're driven to see the learning as fairly narrow.

Measuring only performances from external tests could threaten building expansive curricula. Leonie warned:

> I really believe that we are losing a lot of valuable education because a number of schools know accountability's so important and it's focused on this **very narrow [part] of the school curriculum**, but **we'll make sure we get that right and a lot of the other stuff is going out the window.**

Alongside School System mechanisms, Principals such as Sammy Savvy and Terence, the Target Setter, reveal that they design or build on existing mechanisms to develop their own internal accountability systems. Building on DeCourcy data, Sammy holds professional conversations with teachers as

152   CHAPTER 7

a matter of course after results are released. Terence designs exit and learning surveys as a form of internal accountability.

5.3 *Employing Gambits*

Principals reveal the importance of being able to persuade teachers' thinking and actions. Their strategies vary. Bianca, the Balancer talked about throwing an idea out there to teachers, which is like a gambit to see if an idea is acceptable:

> I don't even know if it's a challenge and **sometimes I find you've got to go around people** to **come back** and **throw an idea around.** Have you thought about where you are at? What are you doing to get a bit of change? **Then the light comes on. It's not so hard. I can do that** and some people would say I don't challenge people. They say, **I don't tell people .... I don't go and say ... this isn't good enough.** That **doesn't honour the person.** It does not honour a human being in any way, shape, or form; ... you've got to value the work that people are doing, no matter who they are.

This gambit technique could be termed a 'form of circling,' which Bianca believes is her preferred way of influencing teaching teams rather than berating them.

The Principals also use gambits as a means of 'testing the waters' to see if teachers would come around to their way of thinking (e.g., Malcolm). This sense of confidence about learning appears important in being able to persuade teachers' practices. Malcolm's method is to keep his attention on his languaging of learning, which in turn gives him the confidence to convince others:

> It's **simple but hard.** You **need to remember to do** it [all language is about learning]. When they know it's going to be all about learning, they relax but they also get excited .... **I've got the confidence. I have not got overconfidence.** Just that I have **got the language to convince.** So that helps and [if] I've got enough understanding ... eventually they will come round—they do.'

A standout phrase which also demonstrates positive levels of self-efficacy from the text data is from Charmaine: '**If rich, authentic learning is occurring, the results will follow.**' This phrase signals confidence the principal knowing what conditions lead to favourable performance results. Phrases by Sammy, Charmaine, Malcolm and Brian all point to their beliefs that learning is broad, and not limited to a number: 'Ultimately they [**results**] **look after themselves**

THE LADY OF LIGHT 153

as the conditions for learning are in place at the school ... if you **get the conditions right,** the **results will look after themselves'** (Sammy Savvy); 'I suppose **deep down inside I believe if there's rich, authentic learning the results will follow** and I think as long as you're monitoring so that that's not in fairy land, ... it is actually happening' (Charmaine, the Cheer Leader); 'It's **a fair bet that if the results were in decline,** then the **conversation hasn't been about learning,** or it **hasn't been a productive one'** (Malcom, the Moralist); 'Getting to **understand how we teach, why we teach it, just understanding learning is going to give us the results that they're [School System] saying you will get'** (Brian Broadview).

Likewise, Terence shows confidence in being able to persuade the teaching teams, albeit for different reasons. His gambit is:

> 'I am trying to get **my staff to understand the reasons why we need to do** this. We could do this because the [School System] says so or we could do it because we want to improve our enrolments. We could do it because we want to be seen as better than other schools or whatever .... But I don't think they are very good reasons ... so **we have a duty for these kids** to ensure that that's what we are doing for them .... **I call it a moral imperative** ... I think that you stand to **gain a lot more long-term support ...** But **no-one is going to argue with you over a moral imperative** ... if we are coming from that.'

He constructs an internal story, with reasons as a strategy of pushing for performance results. He then wraps these reasons around a moral imperative in the form of a gambit, that he articulates to the staff. Terence's use of the word 'argue' suggests some tension between himself and teachers in changing their thinking about teaching for the sake of performance results.

Performance setting through a grade or number raises the question about the level of confidence that Principals reported in their perceived power to influence teachers, and how much their self-belief plays a role in managing the accountability demands, at the same time as holding onto their professional commitments or moral purpose.

It was a surprise the confidence issue being raised by several Principals. The surprise led to further questioning. The level of confidence to persuade teachers is teased out further with Malcolm:

Researcher: So, you have a reasonable level of confidence in your capacity to persuade teachers?

Malcolm: ... [Yes] Only because ... I will do the work to find out what the experts are saying, and I will take the time to find a setting where it has worked. That whole notion of let's just sit around and plan something here based on looking at this site for the last 10 years—no.

Memo 9: The power of influence for the right reasons

Both Malcolm the Moralist, early career principal (ECP), and Terence the Target Setter, middle career principal (MCP), seemed determined to influence teachers' thinking. My gut says that Malcolm the Moralist would be more influential than Terence the Target Setter. I questioned my thinking around this because my judgement has the potential to influence my thinking about many other aspects of this thesis, namely that being centred in holistic learning rather than performance results is the 'better' way to handle the tensions/challenges of accountability. Terence the Target Setter holds a pragmatic view—'let's perform to what is measured,' whereas Malcolm the Moralist holds a learning paradigmatic view—'keep the results out of the conversation.' I admit that I do lean towards Malcolm the Moralist's views, since beginning this study. This is my bias. Terence the Target Setter's moral imperative comes from a place that would be a minority view with teachers; that is, getting the best results for 'a ticket to the future.' Hence, little influence and his great tiredness: 'I am not sure how long I can do this job ... you know you get tired' ... 'I don't bulldoze ... well I suppose I do sometimes.' Whereas Malcolm the Moralist, while an ECP with energy and vitality, reports a quiet sense of determination and confidence of success in influencing teacher thinking: '... but we will get there eventually.' In my mind, Malcolm the Moralist's learning paradigm would be more consistent with the majority of teacher thinking (than Terence the Target Setter's views) and hence, hold more influence, with less energy required; possibly no bulldozing would be needed.

In this case, Malcolm reveals that his confidence is a result of what the experts say. Malcolm defines the experts as academics and researchers.

While both of the Principals display a sense of confidence in their approaches, their reasons for this confidence are different. Malcolm, an ECP, with a seemingly unproven record indicates high levels of confidence about his influence with teachers and reports no resistance from teachers. Whereas Terence uses language of needing to bulldoze, to sell his ideas, unlike Malcolm we do not know whether Terence's strategies are successful in his persuasion. These two examples evoke the power of influence in two very different ways.

THE LADY OF LIGHT   155

5.4   *Building Aspirational Stories*
Now ... I can hear the cries of people **complaining with teaching to the test.
But 'the reality is, if you don't, the kids perform poorly.'** (Terence the Target
Setter)

6   Anomaly: Aspiring for Grades as Brilliance

One Principal places constraint around the public league tables. Instead, he
works towards building aspirational practices with students. The aspirations
are described in grade targets set by students: where they are asked to set their
targets for the grades, they want to attain for their work each year:

> ... getting to the point about **negotiating that public discourse, about
> league tables,** we say, well **we are not buying** into that ... if we **can be
> really, really clear** about what every [students'] aspirational target is, then
> we don't have to give a toss .... If Joseph gets a B when they set an aspira-
> tional target for a C and they were operating as a D last year, I challenge
> **anybody to tell me that's not** [expletive] **brilliant.** (Barry the Buffer)

At various times Principals disclosed that some of their peer Principals
encourage practices of 'teaching to the test.' 'Wisdom would be **perhaps I
should [teach to the test] and say that's the measure we want. Some [princi-
pals] would do that I suppose'** (Owen). Charmaine reports, '... and I know that
there are some schools **around here that teach to the test in** NAPLAN, **and we
don't.'** One Principal openly acknowledges using this practice of 'teaching to
the test.' The Principal explains that while teaching to the test was unpopular
among educators, they justify this practice as a moral imperative, to improve
students' life outcomes:

> Coming back to when I said **about teaching to the test. If that's your
> measure** ... you are not going to fire a 100-metre sprinter at the Olympics
> doing 800-metre training. They'd be doing 100-metre sprints. The **speci-
> ficity is a key criterion in performance. So, if you are going to perform
> in the** HSC **in this exam and this is what it looks like, then you've got to
> then give everything towards that.** Now ... I can hear the cries of people
> complaining with teaching to the test. But the reality is, if you don't, the
> kids perform poorly. So, I'm sorry. **The moral imperative** is to **provide the
> kid with the best opportunity** and no matter what **your philosophical
> position is, I don't care.**

7   Anomaly: Principals Set Performance Results as Targets

Terence is uncomfortable in being judged on performance results; however, he has a remedy to manage these judgments: 'we are **going to be judged; therefore, we have to perform** ... [in the ways they are judged] .... We need **to set targets.**'

One notable difference in Terence's view compared with the majority view is the way he explains his leadership practices; he is focused on strategies to lift the external results rather than responding through school wide learning programs. His strategies, while an anomaly, are understandable. Terence expresses feelings of resignation and argues that working to performance goals is his only alternative if the number from a performance result is used to judge his competency as a principal and the teachers' competencies.

Likewise, Barry, the Buffer explained the implementation processes of his initiative in setting targets in the form of grades:

> ... we'll have parents in, and we'll explain to them a process of **target setting** for their [students], which will take place on [date] where we bring them in and we'll set a target for every student [Years] seven to 12 for every subject, as A to E **grades.**

These two findings taken together, illustrating Terence's and Barry's pursuit of student performance results, are important. Insights into the reasons for them responding in this way is presented later in this chapter through the case example of Terence.

A consistent anomaly emerges when Principals are trying to create coherence in their communities considering the external demands. Terence and Barry are very prescriptive in the ways they go about building their aspirational and performative cultures. Most of their reports about their work with teachers is to set targets for themselves and their students in the form of grades or bands in performances. This finding, taken together with their other views demonstrate ways of leading learning that are quite different from those of the rest of the Principals. This divergence is a point of interest and prompts a question about what is common to Terence and Barry. There are several common elements.

One is the magnitude and frequency of thoughts and feelings about being judged professionally by their School System from the results that their students achieved. Another is their apparent lack of emphasis on the importance of learning and teaching processes to improve learning. Neither looked to their teachers for improving results through their pedagogical practices.

Figure 16 maps how Principals were giving sense to their communities.

THE LADY OF LIGHT

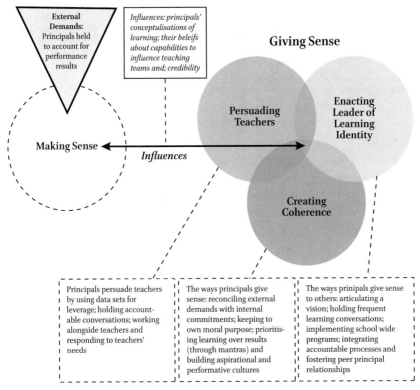

FIGURE 16   Principals giving sense to accountability

The experiences of the Principals so far do not reveal the actual influence of the Principals' sensemaking of their accountability on the way they respond (sensegiving acts) to the performative demands. A comparative analysis of four case examples is used in the next section to tease out this influence.

8   Sense Leaders: Sammy, Charmaine, Barry, and Leonie

It is such a vital question to know the effect of Principals' sensemaking of their performative accountability on their leadership practices. To address this aspect, four case examples are tracked to elicit the relationship. The case examples are Sammy Savvy, Charmaine Cheerleader, Barry Buffer and Leonie Light. These are selected according to a balance of genders, career stages and *pro rata* representation of each School System.

These four case examples, as summarised in Table 11, illustrate the 'effect dimension,' that is, how Principals' sensemaking (of the accountability expectations) *affect* (or not) their sensegiving leadership practices.

TABLE 11 Relationship between principals' understandings of accountability and their practices

Principals	Sensemaking	Sensegiving acts	Devices: Metaphors, narratives, or mantras	Influences
Sammy (ECP-MCP)	HSC results not a priority; prioritised skills that would sustain; accountability a positive part of educational landscape; need it and needed to accept it; results look after themselves if the conditions for learning are in place	Scoped the internal learning landscape on arrival; supported teachers' passions; high use of data to implement plans for professional growth and learning growth and accountability; staff restructures to support learning	Leader learner: 'don't sweat the small stuff'	Confident in using accountability as a leverage aligned with learning; undertook research studies in deep learning; own understandings grew with the school development
Charmaine (MCP)	Not used to the School System accountability expectations; tension with external tests only assessing small section of learning; authentic learning leads to favourable results	Viewed self as being a leader of learning; vision for learning not achieved through performance results; worked with resistance; paced progress with teachers 'Bringing them, walking slowly with them'	Cheerleader/journey: 'Bringing them, walking slowly with them'	Worked alongside teachers in all professional learning matters; deep understandings of curriculum; previous professional experiences—curriculum pathway

(*cont.*)

TABLE 11   Relationship between principals' understandings of accountability and their practices (*cont.*)

Principals	Sensemaking	Sensegiving acts	Devices: Metaphors, narratives, or mantras	Influences
Barry (MCP)	Lack of esteem for the NAPLAN instrument; accountable to the students, not the School System; felt the pressure to achieve high performance results from School System—how many Band 6s	Explained the performance results through story telling in the marketplace; practised for NAPLAN test; introduced school-wide goal-setting program focused on individual student grades	Buffer, shield: protecting	Teaching experiences—delivery model; not clear about own ability to lead teaching and learning; believed the student demographic suffered from residualism; student 'lefts overs'
Leonie (ECP)	Accountable for student happiness, teachers value adding; accountable to self, system, and parents; reliance on the numbers on the performance results limits curriculum development; valuable education is lost	Aimed to find a synergy between internal and external pressures—working harmony; confidence to work as a collective with staff; school will achieve—will turnaround; targeted areas and distributed tasks in the leadership of learning	Lantern: holding up the light to check the progress in the realisation of the vision	Positive beliefs about self in leading learning

8.1   Leader Identities and Levels of Efficacy of Influence

In making sense of their accountability expectations, all four Principals argue that a number is an inadequate representation of their students' learning. Hence, the instruments, the public disclosures (such as the My School website and newspaper rankings) and the consequent judgements from such disclosures influence their sensemaking. While a numerical score is viewed as an inappropriate accountability sole referent, all four Principals show an unfavourable attitude towards the disclosure of NAPLAN results, more so than towards the disclosure of the HSC results. Barry provides some reasons for this, commenting that the students are only in the school a short while before the testing (i.e., Year 7 students). Other possible reasons are detailed in the discussion in the next chapter.

All Principals in the case examples use the sensemaking devices: metaphors, narratives, or mantras. These provide a self-coherence which aligns with their pedagogical leadership practices. Their sensemaking devices suggest effective tools for the leader identity formation. Barry uses the words 'buffer' and 'shield' and one of his behaviours is to protect his teachers from the School System initiatives. Such a metaphor may in turn support Barry's view that his leadership role is one of protection rather than to be influencing teaching practices.

One other common element between the four is that the Principals' thoughts and feelings towards performative accountability appear to be influenced by their previous experiences of and confidence in their ability to facilitate teaching and learning processes in their schools. The Principals who seamlessly integrate the system expectations are more likely to report high levels of confidence in their own leadership practices with teaching and learning than those who pushed back at their systems' expectations. Those Principals who managed the expectations with confidence placed learning in the centre of their core purpose, with detailed ways of doing this, and acknowledged the importance and need of influencing and working with teaching teams.

8.2   The Contrasts between the Case Examples

In trying to make sense of their public accountability, the Principals either integrate or magnify the systems' expectations to a point of rejection. Sammy, Charmaine, and Leonie use their interpretations to arrive at cognitive settlements of a generative integration, whereas Barry's areas of disagreement are enacted with feelings of anger and resignation. Sammy explains that he needs and accepts accountability, and his strategy is manifested in the way he uses accountability as leverage for data use and the professional growth for staff. Charmaine disagrees with the public league tables, and she ignores them: 'I don't care about the *Sydney Morning Herald* [HSC] marks.' She firmly believes that if authentic learning is happening, the results will take care of themselves. This sensemaking strategy is manifested in Charmaine's quiet persistence in pacing her work with her staff, working alongside them, and knowing their needs.

Leonie's sensemaking strategy is to prioritise her responsibility for the students' happiness and the teachers' value adding or pursuit for student performance growth, rather than push for higher performance results. Leonie's strategy is manifested in the way she targets specific areas for growth and works on building staff confidence, through staff restructures and distributing specific leadership tasks to enable improvement. In contrast, Barry's perceptions are reconstituted into anger and injustice at being judged by students' performance results. He appears to be paralysed in his anger, resentment, and resignation about the accountability expectations and how the students' results in his College will not (or could not) meet the expectations. His sensemaking strategy is constraining the School System, keeping them at arm's length, maintaining a sense of autonomy. This sensemaking strategy is manifested by boundaries being placed on teachers and their interactions with the School System and by developing goal-setting programs that target grades rather than the results of external testing. To ease the perceived pressure from the School System, Barry ensures that students practise and drill for the external tests.

The link between the Principals' sensemaking of performative accountability and the influence of these on their leadership practices may seem to be obscure at this point. Yet it affirms previous propositions that: Principals' beliefs in influencing their teaching teams would seem to suggest more effective outcomes for student learning and teaching processes. Their beliefs about the influence are determined by their career trajectories. Comparing Leonie's and Barry's perceptions of their school contexts and the demands the influences become clearer.

8.3 *Sensemaking Influences Leaders' Sensegiving Practices*

Both Barry and Leonie have common school demographics. They reported poor performance results over the last 5 years. These poor performances have affected their school's growth and morale. At the point of the Norris research (2017) their public accountability was high stakes. Understandably Barry's descriptions of his school environment of 'student leftovers' (residuals) fuel his cognitive schemas and emotions. However, Leonie, as an ECP, is facing equal if not greater consequences with loss of enrolments and low staff morale because of staff losses. If the school environment factors are removed from the equation, what is left to be examined are their beliefs about learning and their self-efficacy in their own leadership practices in the face of difficult conditions and pressures, to effect change with teaching teams.

TABLE 12   Summary of findings

Core categories	Processes	Description	Influences
Sense making	Contextualising	Interpretations of expectations considering student demographics, teacher receptivity, parental and School Systems' expectations, enrolments, performance results, competition	Beliefs about learning, previous leadership experiences, peer leaders' views, framing or ability to translate the expectations
	Prioritising	Paying attention to certain expectations or people in the school community over others. Placing boundaries (Weick, 1995) on the translation of the School Systems' policies (external); Boundaries on to whom and how it is expected to be implemented	Beliefs about learning: do they align with external expectations? Interpretations of their school environments: can they manage this? Leaders' relationship with leaders in School Systems; peer leader relationships, self-efficacy in carrying other key functions of their role and their ongoing framing of expectation
	Framing expectations	Expectation frames include acceptance, personalising, responsibility, and agency	Educational leaders' views of their contexts (contextualising), valuing one expectation over another (constraining) and the ways they perceived themselves (identity) a leader of learning, including their creation of metaphors and mantras

(*cont.*)

TABLE 12   Summary of findings (*cont.*)

Core categories	Processes	Description	Influences
Sense giving	Making Meaning: Metaphors, Mantras and Narratives	Positioning learning in the centre: Articulates visions for learning, conversations lead to learning; ignoring, deflecting, diverting opposition; implements learning initiatives that meet external expectations through internal goals and targets; creates integration between external with internal (ranging from seamless to disruptive)	Teacher receptivity, enrolments, result patterns, their identity as a leader of learning, their views, skill, and knowledge about teaching and learning and the ongoing ways they frame their expectations
	Enacting their Leader Learner Identity	Leaders establish self-coherence; Perspective taking; Fostering relationships with peer leaders; Signalling credibility	Teacher resistance; Principals and teachers' expectations of students; leaders' levels of self-efficacy in understanding learning; Principals' self-efficacy in leading learning; Principals' motivation to seek knowledge and skill about learning and teaching
	Creating cultures of coherence	Leaders build community coherence: Working closely alongside teachers Utilising data and embedding school wide programs Employing gambits Building aspirational and performative cultures	Reconciling beliefs about learning and external expectations of learning; self-efficacy in the leader of learning role, views about learning, previous leadership experiences, Capability in enacting metaphors and images, and narratives and mantras ('walking the talk')

164 CHAPTER 7

Clearly, Leonie perceives her previous leadership experiences (pedagogical) have prepared her well for the task in front of her. Barry acknowledges that he cannot identify how to improve the learning and teaching processes in the school and his metaphor when he is 'at his best in leading' does not embed the leader of learning function. Barry also makes no mention of his curriculum leadership experiences or the practices of his teaching teams. In comparing these two case examples it is reasonable to propose that Leonie's previous pedagogical experiences equip her to deal with the high-level consequences brought about by performative accountability, in contrast with Barry's previous experiences and reported low levels of self-efficacy in this area. Barry's sensegiving acts rely on pushing for grades whereas Leonie is clear with a pedagogical plan to integrate the expectations for results and the school's learning agenda. Barry is silent on this detail. Hence the two key influences, which intersect with each other, are the principal's beliefs about learning and expectations of students' learning and their perceived levels of efficacy in influencing the teaching practices to improve results. While this is one case example of two Principals it sheds light on possible influences and differences between Principals.

8.4   *Emerging Proposition*

Principals differ in their foci when it comes to managing their accountability demands for performance results in high stakes environments. Some enact practices which focus on teaching practices others focus on peripheral measures such as grade setting. The moderating factor in these examples is their belief in their capabilities in influencing their teaching teams.

Table 12 is an eagle's view of the key findings in Chapters 6 and 7.

The participating Principals' perceived knowledge and skill about learning are a consistent reference point for many of the Principals. Their perceived capabilities about learning determine the ways they see they can influence teacher practices and their perceived capabilities in building community coherence challenged by perplexing and inflexible external demands.

Overall, the findings indicate that the Principals who are relentless in their pursuit of learning in their role as principal are injected with a sense of confidence, which in turn enhances their influence in the learning and teaching processes with students and teachers. Importantly, the more they identified in themselves as leaders of learning by embedding metaphors aligned with the leader of learning identity the less likely they were to be affected negatively by the external expectations for favourable performance results. Hence their identity formation focussed on leading learning plays a key role in making sense of and giving sense to the external demands, especially when on the surface the demands may be at odds with their beliefs about what is important about learning and young people.

These findings demonstrate that the more these Principals internalise their professional identities in emancipating ways, stemming from a strong moral purpose, the more likely that they will be accomplished in their sensegiving acts to their communities; accepting and personalising their responses to the accountability expectations, using this as a leverage to create coherent cultures that reflect their own conceptualisations of authentic learning and teaching. These Principals arrange their accountability environments as constructions of optimism, keeping the vision clear, 'I am the Lady of the Light' (Leonie) rather than armaments of shields and buffers.

CHAPTER 8

Not How It Is, But How I See It Is

> Situations of ambiguity and uncertainty—as well as change, contrast, surprise, discrepancy and so on—interrupt ongoing flows of experience and automatic processing, thereby prompting people to extract puzzling clues from their environment in an effort to reconstruct their understandings of a situation.
>
> MANDLER (1984, in Spillane & Anderson, 2014, p. 4)

∴

Not only do novice principals engage in deliberate sensemaking, as Spillane and Anderson found, but sensemaking is also a conscious process for school leaders when disruptions occur, when normal approaches no longer work. The disruptions to the continuous flow of experiences for the Principals were their expectations of accountability by their school systems. Like the Principals, school leaders' sensemaking may involve *contextualising*. They can search for tiny indicators in the school to support their hunches (*salient clues*), develop internal strategies to assess support, or predict whether there is a common relevance for staff in their hunches (*social context*). School leaders' sensemaking in such disruptive circumstances may require constraining, that is, placing boundaries over some events or objects (*ongoing projects*), where they engage framing exercises, such as building convincing stories in preparation for the community (*plausibility and enactment*).

Weick's Sensemaking Framework along with other extant literatures on school leadership are presented here in this discussion in exploring school leaders making sense of external demands.

1 Not How It Is, But How I See It Is

> So, having given all that context, we are in a situation now where we want an A-grade school. (Barry, the Buffer)

Context is everything! There is little empirical support for the claim that context is the most influential variable in what leaders decide they will do. Yet the rhetoric about context is often the opposite. Making sense of a school environment *and* within an environment calls on school leaders to do more than just consider their context. School leaders need skills. They need to translate expectations, integrate information simultaneously (Thiel et al., 2012), yet be astute at interpreting the school environmental factors, such as student demographics, enrolments, students' performance results, competition with other schools for enrolments or teacher receptivity. The Principals' explanations, in Chapters 6 and 7, appear consistent with contingency leadership theories (Fiedler, 1964), which privilege leaders' contexts as determinants of their actions (Bush, 2010). However, their interpretations of their contexts were just that; subjective and reflected more about who they were and less about the reality of the contexts.

1.1   *Policy in Situ*

Contextualising is more than a school leader interpreting their school context. Leaders need to firstly reinterpret or translate the policy expectations. For instance, Barry and Terence have very different interpretations of school system expectations about their performance results. Barry interprets that he could buffer the expectations and Terence interprets that that there are few options other than 'driving for results.' This example of re-interpreting and 'translating' policy is supported by several studies: Ball et al. (2011) found that a principal's own 'take' on policy is important; a comparison of England and Scotland policy makers by Ozga (2012) shows that leaders are not limited to the situated necessities of the policy, often not being able to transform data into 'efficient initiatives' (p. 439); Spillane, Diamond, et al.'s (2002) findings indicate that leaders may adopt, adapt or ignore imposed policy, and with 'policy coherence often cited but a seldom achieved education policy goal' (Honig & Hatch, 2004, p. 16).

This policy to practice gap points to what school leaders decide to implement. Certainly, school leaders weigh up the broader contextual organisational factors, yet the weighing up has the leader's filter. Initially implementation 'fidelity' is filtered by the leader's existing knowledge, purposes or visions they have for the school community and their beliefs and values they consider fundamental (professional commitments) (Leithwood, 2018, p. 391). Another filter is the school leader's judgment of the school's capacity:

> ... a school may look like it is straightforwardly adopting a number of policies, [but] schools have different capacities for "coping" with policy and assembling school-based policy responses. (Ball, Maguire, & Braun, 2012, p. 586)

While context may appear 'everything,' there needs to be consideration that school leaders' interpretations of their school environments are influenced, and I argue more so, on their own take on policy.

Perceived difficulties and confidence levels in implementation fidelity are two factors which influence a school leader's sensemaking of external demands. The ways school leaders make sense of their school environment factors in light of policy demands are dependent upon the level of difficulty that they perceive about their school environments (such as teacher resistance) and crucially their self-belief in their capabilities to resolve these challenges (Hallinger, Hosseing-holizadeh, Hashemi, & Kouhsari, 2018). Leonie, in the examples, acknowledges that a priority for her is to prevent staff losses, caused by shrinking enrolments due to the publicly disclosed poor student performance results. While the task of resolving this dilemma is difficult to address quickly, Leonie believes that it is possible for her with the leadership team to manage. This finding is consistent with Fiedler's contingency model (1964), whereby there is a relationship between the individual's leadership style (possibly democratic, 'with the leadership team') and their attitude towards the situation (in Leonie's case the attitude is favourable). Fiedler's dimensions are employed here as they can shed light on school leaders' management of challenging situations.

1.2   Fiedler's Model

The first of Fiedler's dimensions describes the level at which the leader is accepted by their followers. In this case, Leonie perceives her acceptance by the school and community is high; she has built credibility within a short time, which, as an aside, is reported to be important in improving students' performance results. She reasons, 'I think they are happy to work towards [results] it because they know we don't have choice because we are losing staff.' Fiedler's second dimension is the degree of success with the task structure—it is high if the task is well structured. Leonie reveals that the School System employed her at this school because she has pedagogical leadership knowledge and skills; so, she adopts this style of leadership to set up her plan which is focused on a growth plan in literacy and numeracy. This finding is consistent with Fiedler's third dimension of the leader's positional power, when a great deal of authority and power is formally attributed to the leader's position. As all three dimensions are in the high range in Leonie's case, she would be likely to view her context in favourable terms. If Leonie possessed different knowledge and skills, she could have perceived her context in negative or even desperate terms given the poor results, with declining enrolments and staff losses.

Conversely, Barry, the Buffer's ways of contextualising his accountability demands with his school context are low on two of Fiedler's dimensions. He is silent on the second dimension, regarding having a well-structured plan, and the third dimension aligns unfavourably when Barry reports a sense of resignation and despair about his diminished power over declining enrolments. Irrespective of the ways school leaders view their environments, the amount of planning to meet their school's internal needs are considerable and similar to insights by Spillane and Lowenhaupt (2019); school leaders need to have significant management skills to meet the internal needs as well as adapt to the circumstances of demanding external expectations.

1.3 School Leaders Believe, Teachers Achieve

School leaders' expectations of student performances change the outcomes for students' successes. For example, the Principals' beliefs about what their students could and could not achieve appear to have consequential effects for the student results. Owen, the Opportunist's mantra of 'just one more mark' meant he expected students to improve, whereas another participating principal's perception is that their students will do as well as they can, given that they '... will never be anything better than average in terms of the students' capacity overall.' This principal's perception stems from their belief that a low socio-economic status of the student population can only result in poor performance scores. This last finding of 'never being better than average' supports a key finding by Branch, Hanushek and Rivkin (2012), in which principals who are expected to add value to student achievement in schools with low SES, are likely to lower their expectations of their students' performances (Branch, Hanushek, & Rivkin, 2012). Leaders' beliefs here also align with Leithwood's (2018) findings (as outlined above). There are still some school leaders holding low expectations of students in Australian disadvantaged schools in the second decade of the 21st century. Such beliefs are concerning given the potential harm for students and their success in those schools. What is even more concerning is that senior leaders are not aware of the impact that their beliefs and expectations have on students and the possible ramifications for teachers. If my school leader does not believe I can improve the outcomes for my students, what implications would this have on my teaching? Taking insights from Donohoo and Katz (2017) 'When teachers believe, students achieve' could be transformed to 'When school leaders believe, teachers achieve.' There is a call here for those who guide and support school leaders to challenge such assumptions by showing the empirical evidence of the dangers for such views for students and teachers.

1.4 Normalisation Not Acceptance

Testing instruments, such as the HSC, may over a long period of time may become normalised. However, the consequences surrounding such testing regimes still hold challenges for leaders which is far from acceptance. The public disclosure of performance results, for example, is likely to influence the ways school leaders contextualise their accountability expectations. Consistently, the Principals referred to the disclosure of the HSC and the annual public ranking through the *Sydney Morning Herald* newspaper, consistently. One possible reason for the consistent conversation about HSC ranking was that the first round of interviews with the Principals occurred in February, when the HSC rankings were presented in the *Sydney Morning Herald*, a metropolitan newspaper. Several studies were found about the HSC and effective teaching; one study by Manuel, Carter, Locke, and Locke (2015) describes the context as a high-stakes, external and standardised testing regime and they challenge normative definitions of assessment. The second study by Ayres et al. (2004) also references the HSC as a high-stakes examination. The paucity of research on the topic of the impact of the public ranking of HSC results on leaders, and educators in general, is curious. The paucity could suggest the impact of a long serving testing instrument, such as the HSC, has become normalised into the psyche of educators in their jurisdictions.

In contrast, there have been numerous research studies on the impact on educators and principals due to the public disclosure of NAPLAN results through the My School website. MacBeath et al. (2006) found that 'Schools will continue to compete for pupils in order to gain advantage in league table positioning' (p. 27). McGuire (2012) found that 54.2% of principals felt an increased sense of competition with other principals: 'My School has significantly increased negative competition ... why would a "like" school achieving better results than me want to support us?' (p. 46). The difference between the number of research studies on the impact of NAPLAN and HSC results (albeit that the latter is a state-based instrument) is significant. One possible reason is that the 'NAPLAN accountability' instrument was introduced in recent times, and was far more reaching as a national one, along with the public disclosure of results with a comparative tool acting as the pseudo accountability device (My School). Hence unlike the normalised HSC performance disclosures, NAPLAN had not been normalised, at the point in time of interviewing the Principals. Normalisation here does not necessarily mean acceptance or non-consequential. It needs to be remembered that normalised instruments such as the HSC, with a high stakes tag, can result in negative consequences.

Drilling down, the high-stakes consequences for students and educators from HSC results are the students' post-school pathways and the teachers' career pathways (respectively). Students' results determine their choices post school. Teachers will either keep their senior class load and reach the expectations for 'positive' results or relinquish their senior classes under the pressure and teach only in junior classes.

The tools for analyses of HSC results are now more available. School System's expectations are that their prescribed tools are employed and integral to teaching processes and structures within schools. School System expectations now hold principals to account not only for the students' results but also their evidence of their implementation plans and the resulting outcomes. A decade ago, this was not happening: 'It's probably been 10 years now since we were first introduced to DeCourcy—it's just a matter of course now' (Bianca, the Balancer). The effect of this system-wide and state-wide (Catholic) analytical tool (DeCourcy, 2006) is evident, with all of the Principals using the DeCourcy tool as 'a matter of course.' It is not only a common practice but also a common language between principals and their governing school systems. As such, data analyses with implementation plans followed by evaluation are normalised processes for principals in school systems in the NSW state. These normalised processes in NSW raises the question of the extent to which all school systems across Australia place such expectations on school leaders, how the leaders respond to these expectations and how leaders in school systems navigate such responses, especially if implementation plans and executions are not as school systems leaders intend—which is a strong possibility knowing other research nationally (Hogan & Thompson, 2019) and internationally (Long, 2019; Shipps, 2012; Spillane, Reiser, et al., 2002)

1.5 Teacher Receptivity Versus Resistance

The sensemaking act of *contextualising* is influenced by school leaders' beliefs about certain perceived factors in their contexts, such as their teachers' receptivity or being judged professionally on performance results or their career stage. Teacher receptivity here is a teacher's willingness to utilise data, take them seriously and act upon them, specifically the data from external assessments. Some school leaders use system expectations as leverage to hold teachers to account. This finding is consistent with the study by Dulude, Spillane, and Dumay (2015), which found that principals use policy mandates as a tool to make known logical and authoritative expectations and to clarify conflicts between the external expectations and their own internal schemas. Dulude et al.'s (2015) and the Principals align with Weick's (1995) property of social context, whereby the leader seeks sensible meanings through support as well as consensual validation and relevance with their communities.

The more acutely principals think they are being judged publicly by their results, combined with their low levels of self-efficacy to influence, or believe in, their teaching teams, the more likely they are to prioritise performance results as their top referent. Simply put, a school leader's lack of confidence in their capabilities of influencing teaching practices results in them esteeming or driving for student performance results viewing them as the most important aspect involved in the pedagogical processes. Moreover, school leaders lacking confidence to influence teachers are likely to experience negative feelings regarding the external expectations. McGuire (2013a) found that 62% of principals were morally outraged regarding their students' performance data being made public. Their reasoning, like the Principals, is that a single number is merely a snapshot of a student's performance and does not tell the student human story. In some ways being judged on a score is a threat to a school leader's professional identity. That is, the judgment does not match with their own ideas of leadership. The levels of self-efficacy here can be aligned with Weick's sensemaking property of personal identity, with leaders recognising threats or enhancements from their sensemaking of their expectations and in being able to meet these (Weick, 2001).

1.6   *Early Career Leaders and Sensemaking*

In the early stages of school leadership the multi-layered demands can be overwhelming. Oplatka (2012), reports that early career principals' experiences are a 'surprise, reality shock, [with] high levels of stress' (p.129). Early career school leaders need to learn how to diagnose the school culture and the environment quickly, along with working out ways to develop their capabilities to manage the diagnosis. Similarly, Spillane and Lee (2013) found that novice principals experience major reality shocks regarding their ultimate sense of responsibility in their first years. Peer Principals often 'feel' for ECPs, recognising their own challenges in their early careers, and are eager to nurture them through those taxing early years. So too did the example Principals where they held genuine empathy for the challenges facing the ECPs and how they may be managing the pressures of accountability and the impact on enrolments and staff retention.

The influence of school leaders' sensemaking of their school context about their leadership practices is worthy of attention. Some leadership studies highlight the importance of contextual factors as being influential over leaders' behaviours (Hallinger, 2018; Hallinger, Bickman, & Davis, 1996), yet much of the literature over the last 20 years has shown that this influence has less effect on leaders' behaviours than one may expect (Ozga, 2012; Porter & McLaughlin, 2006). In this book, while a school leader's sensemaking of their school environmental factors can be shown to influence their professional practice, what is more pertinent than the 'context influence' are the other influences on leaders' sensemaking. It is of interest because understanding these non-contextual influences, principals' likely practices can be predicted to a certain degree. These influences, as demonstrated by the Principals could be about themselves such as beliefs about the representation of learning or their levels

NOT HOW IT IS, BUT HOW I SEE IT IS

of self-efficacy about influencing their teaching teams. These personal 'effects' then in turn affect the ways a leader makes sense of their school environmental factors.

In a nutshell school context is important to school leaders but what is unique and individualistic is the way leaders make sense of these contexts: my world is determined not how it is but rather how I see it is.

2 Constraining, an Authoring Act

Constraining in the school context describes the ways school leaders attach worth to certain issues over others. They are in fact placing constraints on or boundaries around what they pay heed to or not. As such constraining is an individual act, an authoring act (Weick, 1995), requiring an internalising reconfiguring action, where the author takes control and writes how the story should be told. In the context of leadership and accountability, authoring could be a form of liberation. The sensemaking strategy of *Constraining* by the Principals holds consistencies with the study by Leithwood and Riehl (2005) who found that the way principals responded to accountability expectations was by attending to certain expectations and disregarding others, balancing competing demands and making choices. Yet, not uncommon from other research studies (Berkovich, 2021; Ganon-Shilon & Schechter, 2019a) the Principals, school leaders' and teachers' own sensemaking strategy of constraining can be out of step with school systems' expectations. Misalignment in sensemaking between regulators and implementers have consequences.

2.1 *How Priorities Misalign*
There are variations and inconsistencies about the ways messages of external expectations are received by school leaders. Studies such as Seashore Louis et al. (2012) and Spillane, Reiser, et al. (2002) also found that implementers did not necessarily decode the policy message accurately, that is, the intent of the policy makers. The Principals' beliefs and practices of their expectations, for example, were misaligned with school system expectations. A misaligned priority for the Principals centred on student learning; most Principals encouraged diverse learning experiences for students and discouraged the drive for performance results. Yet School System advisors' expectations considered that performance results indicated the 'health' of the school. Such variations in these school leaders' sensemaking poses an argument that there is no single line of authority or message being conveyed by school systems' authorities, or the message is obscure. Yet this argument is not strong. School System

174   CHAPTER 8

authorities in my study were confident that their accountability expectations were clear to their Principals. These priority misalignments raise the question about school leaders' internal processes in not being able to or not wanting to absorb and integrate demands as intended. For system authorities, the misalignment raises the question about what it takes to make the expectations clearer to leaders.

2.2   *Aligning School Leaders' Priorities with Sensemaking and TPB*

Such priorities established by school leaders align with Weick's sense-making property of *Ongoing projects* and *Social context* (1995) and Ajzen's *Subjective norm* (Ajzen & Madden, 1986). *Ongoing projects,* described as how the individual makes sense of their environment by placing boundaries on external stimuli, the Principals placed boundaries around what they accounted for and to whom they accounted. These processes of *prioritising* and *constraining* expectations align with Ajzen's determinant of the *subjective norm*, in which the individual places value on certain social referents over others (Ajzen & Madden, 1986).

Weick's property of *social context* is defined as sensible meanings, in this instance where school leaders seek support and consensual validation and relevance with their communities. These are the social anchors in making sense of external demands (see Table 13). The social context aligns with Leonie's reports in the early, urgent interventions needed to prevent staff losses and Terence in his appeal to teachers and students to drive for results. A common theme with the Principals' experiences is that they interpreted their School System expectations in different ways, which is consistent with the research studies by Spillane (2009, 2014, 2002) and his colleagues (Firestone & Shipps, 2003; Firestone & Shipps, 2005) and in more recent times the studies by Ganon-Shilon and Schechter (2019a) They found that school leaders not only varied in degrees of aligning between the different levels of accountability but also with regard to what they decided they were accountable for. Spillane, Reiser, and Gomez (2006), in the context of school interpreting and implementing policy, explain:

> What is paramount is not simply that implementing agents choose to respond to policy but also what they understand themselves to be responding to ... individuals must use their prior knowledge and experience to notice, make sense of, interpret, and react to incoming stimuli— all the while constructing meaning from their interactions with the environment which policy is part of. (p. 49)

Note how Spillane et al. (2006) adopt Weick's sensemaking words here: 'prior knowledge and experience' (retrospect) and 'to notice' (salient cues). As they

TABLE 13   Aligning Weick's sensemaking properties with leadership examples

Property	Operational definition	Examples from the discussion
1 Social context	School leaders make sensible meanings of their accountability environments, seeking support, consensual validation, and relevance with their communities. These are the social anchors in making sense of accountability expectations	Leonie in the beginning and urgent phases of change and Barry in his appeal to teachers and students for aspirational grade setting
2 Personal identity	School leaders make sense of who they are in relation to the accountability events, whereby they recognise the threats or enhancements in their school contexts, which may determine their sense of efficacy, with 'judgments of relevance and sense' emerging (Weick, 2001, p. 462)	The Principals representations of learning and levels of self-efficacy in leading learning considering the accountability expectations and their school environment factors
3 Retrospect	School leaders notice elapsed events, going back and remembering what they are doing in making sense of the accountability expectations. For example, leaders draw upon the past year's student performance data to make sense of current experiences	The Principals reported in detail their past performance results and where they would like these results to be in the future
4 Salient cues	School leaders use their resourcefulness to extract salient cues (Shipps, 2012). They shore up stories (Rigby, 2015) about the accountability expectations (Koyama, 2014). When these stories become contradictory (e.g., poor parallels in education systems), the grasp of making sense loosens	The Principals drew upon empirical research about the negative consequences of national testing in other countries
5 Ongoing projects	School leaders make sense of the accountability expectations by placing boundaries on what they account for and how (Spillane, Diamond, et al., 2002) and/or by updating their actions and interpretations of the accountability expectations. They may negotiate and appropriate external accountability in innovative, sometimes savvy, ways (Koyama, 2014)	The Principals varied in what they accounted for and to whom they accounted. These variations indicated the boundaries that they were setting to make sense of their expectations at the same time as constructing ways of implementing these expectations

(cont.)

176　　CHAPTER 8

TABLE 13　Aligning Weick's sensemaking properties with leadership examples (*cont.*)

Property	Operational definition	Examples from the discussion
6 Plausibility	School leaders make sense by developing coherent stories (Elmore et al., 2013) about their expectations. These stories hold certain levels of credibility and reasoning. The principal's level of coherence in the story is constrained by the agreements of their communities, their own stake in the expectations, familiar scenarios, action and credible effects Over time, these developments could become unconscious (Steinbauer et al., 2015)	The Principals developed cognitive schemas or frames about assessment-focused accountability. Their accountabilities for performance results were transformed into plausible frames: personalising, accepting, being responsible and an agent
7 Enactment	School leaders take action to see what they may be up against, try negotiating an idea or makes a declaration (possibly regarding the policy makers expectations)	The Principals provided examples of how they enacted their sensemaking, such as Barry ignoring the Year 7 NAPLAN results and speaking of such to the system advisors

explain, and like the experiences of the Principals, they first need to understand what the expectation is asking for, which is dependent on their knowledge and past experiences of such expectations. At the same time, they are working at ways of 'constructing' their environments and evaluating (Ajzen, 1990) the impact of their implementation processes, their ways of leading them and their self-efficacy in doing so.

2.3　*Rationale for School Leaders' Priorities of Accountability*

An important discussion point here is the reason behind a school leader's priorities. These could be linked to their beliefs about what constitutes learning, their levels of self-efficacy in their capabilities influencing their teaching teams or their social justice commitments. For example, the Principals who placed a high priority on diverse learning experiences for students with less priority on performance results, are well versed in their empirical knowledge about how to influence teachers' practices. For example, Charmaine's influencing practices showed the importance she gave to working with her teachers in their professional learning experiences. This finding aligns with a study by Robinson (2011), which found that effective school leaders need to be closely engaged and working alongside teachers in their professional learning. Moreover, I propose a school leader's knowledge or efficacy in influencing teachers are grounded in their own confidence of their knowledge and skill about teaching and learning. Some studies support the relationship between self-efficacy of leadership capabilities and knowledge and skill in their professional practices (McCollum & Kajs, 2007b).

2.4   Self-Efficacy Influences Priorities

> ... predictors of principals' self-efficacy have shown that principals' preservice studies influence their sense of confidence in carrying out their role. (Fisher, 2014)

When comparing the general leadership literature about self-efficacy with the TPB lens, it is argued that self-efficacy is a self-referent construct (Ajzen, 1991). Self-efficacy is a leader's level of confidence in their knowledge and skills to behave in the way they most desire (Schwarzer, 2014). In terms of the influence of the relationship between school leadership practices and their levels of self-efficacy, the study by Lovell (2009) suggests that further research is needed to examine the relationships between principals' levels of self-efficacy and their capabilities in instructional leadership. However there has been a growing interest. Consistent with Schwarzer's findings here, the research by McCollum and Kajs (2007b) found that self-efficacy was a relevant construct in a broad sense to shed light on principals' abilities to lead schools; their abilities were determined by their knowledge base and skill (McCollum & Kajs, 2007b). A School Leaders' Self-Efficacy scale showcased through conference e-proceedings by McCollum and Kajs (2007a), validated by Petridou, Nicolaidou, and Williams (2014) is a growing research field in broader contexts of school leadership. Findings revealed that "supervising and evaluating instruction and monitoring student progress were significant positive predictors of leadership self-efficacy for the entire sample of respondents whereas coordinating curriculum was only approaching significance" (McBrayer et al., 2018). Studies in predictors of principals' self-efficacy have shown that principals' pre-service studies influenced their sense of confidence in carrying out their role (Fisher, 2014). Yet, the Principals report that their leadership of teaching is influenced, not by their pre-service studies, but by their current and postgraduate tertiary studies and professional reading. Knowing what their School System required of their leadership, the Principals' professional readings and study were building their knowledge and skill base about student learning. This 'base' appeared to create confidence in their own sense of legitimacy. And if they did not have that base? They wanted to know how to build it: '... do you know where I can do a course on learning?' (Larry, the Learner).

2.5 Identity Construction

Part of a school leader making meaning of their role and function is how others see the role. Principals were clear about their School Systems expectations of them to be leaders of learning, even though their interpretations of this function differed. Understandably, these differences are to be expected, given that a principal's role identity is integral to their occupational socialisation (Spillane & Anderson, 2014). Part of making meaning of a role function such as a leading learning identity is how school leaders compare themselves with their peer leaders. Sometimes they will esteem their peer behaviours, at other times identifying behaviours they would not adopt: 'I know some really prepare and drill their students for the exams, we don't do that here' (Charmaine). The theories of teachers' social identity support to a limited degree school leaders comparing themselves to their peers (Danielewicz, 2001). In their normalised hypercompetitive environments this comparing could appear competitive. School leaders are not only constrained by technologies of performativity, they are now linked with their professional identities in their measures of outputs in the student success (Gobby et al., 2018).

Comparing and competing are elements which determine a school leader's identity construction, through talking about their identity, either to themselves (self-talk) or each other in their trusted professional networks (Carroll & Levy, 2010; Crow et al., 2017; Crow & Møller, 2017). These researchers here are developing a research field in the identity construction of educational leaders in accountability environments. This interest suggests that some different formation may occur in highly regulated and competitive environments (Crow et al., 2017).

2.6 Socialising Identities

School leaders, like teachers engage in a socialisation process (Cherubini, 2009), which advances the processes in their leader identity formation (Crow & Møller, 2017). Clearly ECPs are in a process of being socialised. Larry, for instance, asks, 'Can I say that [about the system]?' and Leonie, after being in the system for 18 months, says, '... I have been truly systematised. I am not sure if that's a good thing or bad thing.' The process of leader socialisation is about how leaders in their career make judgements about the norms, values and behaviours of their collective group (Van Maanen, 2010). These findings align with Weick's property of *social context* (Weick, 1995), in which the sensemaking is taking place with multiple actors. Malcolm envisages with excitement that the more the group of Principals in their network work together, the more aligned they would be in their thinking about aspects of school life, such as accountability. Here, Malcom shows excitement in building common thought communities. The influence of school leaders' networks is consistent with Zerubavel's (1997) explanation that there are types of groups that influence individuals' social identities. The point of interest here to school leaders and school system initiatives is that peer-leader relationships influence a leader's sensemaking processes, particularly when faced with complex or contradictory conditions or events. Weick's sensemaking properties of *social context* and *personal identity* fit neatly with this point. There is an intersection of these two properties where the school leader's social context influences their personal identity.

While role functions may seem clearly defined by those who set them, it is no guarantee that school leaders will enact or make sense of their role as their superiors may expect. Put simply, school leaders make sense of their role in their own ways. That said, the descriptions put forward by the Principals about their professional practices mirrored some of the characteristics described by Marsh, Farrell and Bertrand (2016) as well as the revised notion of the 'instructional leader' (Thessin & Louis, 2019).

The role of the principal or senior leaders as the 'instructional' leader was well defined in the early 2000s 'the evaluator and coordinator of curriculum' (Thessin & Louis, 2019, p. 434) witnessed through some observable behaviours, such as instructional walks or the provider of explicit feedback on classroom practice. In 2019 the research study by Thessin and Louis supported the view of the instructional leader being similar to Charmaine's and Leonie's notions of leading teachers, acting as cheerleader, coach, modeller and as a supporter of and facilitator of teacher learning (Thessin & Louis, 2019).

In my study (Norris, 2017) however, the role function of the 'Leader of Learning' (set by both School Systems), along with their accountability expectations, seems to have left some Principals feeling somewhat unsure about fulfilling both functions. School leaders across the globe are learning to meet not just dual but a multiplicity of expectations (Dulude & Milley, 2021; Thessin & Louis, 2019). These multiple expectations create internal tensions. Such tensions continue to plague school leaders, about what they spend time on and what they would like to spend times on (Pollock & Wang, 2021). Never more does a school leader's sensemaking come into play in managing their internal tensions. A leader's sensemaking of their role influences their practices, but so too do their understandings and beliefs about their own abilities of impacting teaching practices or their deep convictions about what represents learning. These are some of the set of complexities for school leaders.

180   CHAPTER 8

2.7   *Constraints about Learning—So What?*

School leaders' perceptions about what is an appropriate measure of learning is intertwined with the ways they conceptualise learning. In turn this meaning making influences the ways school leaders prioritise or placed constraints on their external expectations. For example, a principal who views student performance results as merely one snapshot of the learning process is likely to consider the accountability for students' performance results as a less important referent. Moreover, this meaning making is likely to be influenced by a school leader's beliefs and attitudes rather than logical thinking processes (Rumelhart, 1980a; Zajonc & Markus, 1985). These determinations are important for School System advisors who play an important role when working with school leaders to influence them.

Summing up, school leaders in their processes of prioritising and constraining external expectations, are not simply giving preference to one social referent over another. Their *prioritising* and *constraining* also goes further than interpreting cues. It is consistent with the position of Spillane and Anderson (2014), in which principals notice and bracket cues in their environments. Prioritising and constraining are important sensemaking acts. It is every leader's responsibility when faced with professional disruptions, critical incidents, or high velocity events to employ sensemaking acts such as bracketing their interpretive cues and constraining other influences. Furthermore, as in the experiences of the Principals, sensemaking is made visible in school leaders' spontaneous creations of metaphors, narratives, and mantras. Devices which are a lever for sensegiving. Leaders' attempts to make sense for others (sensegiving), through such devices, are based more likely on beliefs than reasoned cognition. As such school leaders here are 'authoring' as much as 'interpreting' (Weick, 1995, p. 8). While I argue that prioritising and constraining are more likely to be based on beliefs, framing on the other hand as a sensemaking act, is an internal cognitive schema.

3   School Leaders Framing Their External Demands

3.1   *Framing in Context*

Framing in a school leadership context involves the way leaders construct schemas to make sense of an event. In this book the 'event' is external demands. Schemas are integral to school leaders' professional identities. Sensemaking devices through linguistic acts (metaphors, narratives, and mantras) are visible indicators of the cognitive schemas that may be constructed by school leaders. The Principals created stories that framed their understandings of accountability. Principals' own personal beliefs and constructs about learning and schooling, along with their beliefs about the 'leading learning' function, were reflected in these schemas. Deeply held beliefs and knowledge about teaching and learning along with their self in their role function were reflected in their professional identity.

3.2   Frames: The Leader Self

Frames become part of a leader's professional identity. For example, Charmaine framed her accountability as a responsibility: 'I answer to the [School] System for results and other things, but I'm responsible to the students [for their learning].' How Charmaine sees herself as a leader in her accountability environment is not one of 'answering to' rather is 'being responsible for' ensures she has self-autonomy and is not beholden to the external forces (School System's drive for results). In some of her choices when she sees herself as 'responsible for' student learning she is not compromising on her core purpose—student learning. In this way her identity of being a leader of learning is supported cognitively. There is internal congruence.

In a similar way to establish or reaffirm their identities through these expectations, school leaders create metaphors for themselves as leaders, to manage the conflicting demands (Ganon-Shilon & Schechter, 2017). Barry, for example, sees himself as a shield to protect his teachers from the demands of the School System, while Leonie sees herself as the lantern beaming light on the vision, so that teachers can see the path ahead and do not lose their way. 'Becoming' the metaphor (Grove & Panzer, 1989) is a novel and creative way for the principals to make sense of their expectations (Ku, Wang, & Galinsky, 2015). Metaphors have this ability to impress on how a school leader may view themselves and how they may conduct their work. Consequently, the metaphor is a sensemaking device that manoeuvres the property of personal identity (Weick, 2001).

Forming a comfortable identity in a school leader's early career is a key professional task. There is a strong need for the leader to gain self-coherence concerning their identity, before being able to provide coherence for the community. Self-coherence here is described as the individual leader's intrapersonal knowledge and skill, that is, their deep understanding of self and how to come to know the self. Intrapersonal knowledge is self-knowledge, and in the context of leadership, coming to know the self which will inform their leader identity. This domain of leadership is important in a school leader's growth and development and in particular for the community, when complex events or episodes need to be managed. Responsible management and leadership depend upon engaging in regular and consistent reflexive practices (Hibbert & Cunliffe, 2015). The more a leader knows themselves, the more likely they are to demonstrate sense of confidence in building coherence in their communities that can integrate their external expectations with their internal school commitments.

182 CHAPTER 8

The creation of schemas by school leaders about external demands itself is a cognisant act of sensemaking. The schema may have a story backing its logic, and emotions in some instances.

3.3 Building Plausible Stories

Conscious sensemaking leads to cognitive schemas that school leaders over time unconsciously adopt to make sense of their environments. One criterion for a school leader's consideration in building the story is its plausibility. Steinbauer, Rhew, and Chen (2015) advocate that plausible stories are part of this sensemaking. Generally, leaders make sense by developing coherent stories (Elmore, Forman, Stosich, & Bocala, 2013) about their expectations. Weick's sensemaking property of *plausibility* decrees that stories hold certain levels of credibility and reasoning for the individual (see Table 13). School leaders' stories are expressive forms of their cognitive schema. When these stories translate in external communicative forms, they become sensegiving acts.

3.4 School Leaders' Mental Models: Reconceptualising Incongruent Expectations

Schemas represent understandings of complex ideas for everyday objects and events (Rumelhart, 1980). In Spillane et al.'s (2002) investigation of school leaders' views of external policy mandates, found that leaders who employed schema such as establishing specific knowledge structures that link together related concepts, enabled the leaders to make sense of the mandates.

As far back as 1995, MacPherson, in helping educators to come to grips with their demands, called for 'urgent rehabilitation' in the conceptualisation of accountability. The schemas that the Principals constructed—'First you have to accept that accountability is part of life'—supports the research by Cairns-Lee (2015), who found that effective leaders develop their own internal models in their leadership development. Cairns-Lee proposes that models minimise external influences or interpretations, which may disrupt their sensemaking. Extending Cairns-Lee's proposition, Lakoff and Johnson (2008) similarly assert that using models is the difference between leaders being effective or ineffective. This raises the question whether these propositions can be equally applied to accountability demands. Darling-Hammond (2010a) specifically advocates the importance of principals adopting mental models specific to accountability, such as the schema of 'reciprocal, intelligent accountability' (p. 301). Likewise, Kuchapski (2001) urges educators to develop a framework for accountability, mapping the importance of a map. Others argue for a different schema of educational accountability, a *pharmakon* requiring balance;

holding teachers to account yet importantly for teachers to give accounts of their work (Lingard, Sellar, & Lewis, 2017). The experiences of the Principals are supported by these empirical and theoretical studies.

3.5 Specificity: Redeeming Enablers

The Principals who constructed sophisticated schema of accountability, with high levels of specificity, were less likely to experience negative feelings stemming from the effects of the external accountability expectations, than those who showed vague or no schemas about the concept of accountability itself. Those who did not speak about accountability in schematic cognition reported thoughts and feelings such as being grilled, indignation, fear, and anger from being judged by performance results. Extending their schemas of accountability, it raises the question of whether cognitive schemata, such a metaphors, narratives, or mantras, increase a school leader's self-efficacy in being able to be influencing teaching teams in their accountability environments.

3.6 Challenges in Making Workable Schemas

The most consistent influence for Principals when framing their accountability, was their absolute rejection that a number on a single test was an adequate representation of students' learning. When they or their students were judged or marketed by numbers, the Principals viewed this as unfair and for some, immoral. Such views are consistent with studies by Biesta (2004); Siegel (2004) who found that when performance results were the single measure used to rank and compare schools, they were interpreted as morally inadequate educational ideals by teachers (Biesta, 2004; Siegel, 2004). Similarly, McGuire's (2012) study found that 69% of Australian principals question the relationship between NAPLAN results and the school's overall performance; 66% report feeling anger when NAPLAN performance results are the only representation of their schools. NAPLAN, in the minds of our participating Principals, lives up to the predicted consequences as purported by Rowe, who warned test scores with performance indicators tend to be focused on a comparative ranking of schools rather than on identifying factors which explain school differences (Rowe, 2000).

It is likely that NAPLAN accountability for most secondary principals in Australia would need to be part of their consideration, yet not an overwhelming concern. Their main unease or concentration is situated with the elevated importance of the HSC (or the Year 12 equivalent) by their School Systems, the public and the student and parent bodies. The perceptions of the examination by these referents appear to be misaligned with the educational philosophies of Principals and their teaching teams.

3.7 Solid Internal Deflect Strong Externals

School leaders who construct or cultivate solid internal (school) accountable learning processes report fewer feelings and thoughts of anger and despair about external expectations than other leaders. The Principals measure and evaluate their own student performances as part of their routine processes along with being explicit about their learning agenda (e.g., Sammy and Malcom who characterise such routines report less anxiety, frustration, and resentment regarding the external expectations of being held to account than the other Principals who do not have such routines). One study showing the progress of a learning improvement agenda, including the responses to environmental pressures, also demonstrates active engagement with what the environment offers, as distinct from a reactive compliance (Knapp, Feldman, & Ling Yeh, 2013). Similarly, Seashore Louis and Mintrop (2012) found that when schools have their own internal accountability processes in place they can align with external accountability systems easily by reordering their goals. Carnoy et al. (2003) also found that principals with their own internal accountability systems in place report in detail the ways in which they adopt or adapt system programs to 'fit' with their current programs (Carnoy et al., 2003). Carnoy et al.'s research supports later studies by Elmore (2005) and Roche (2004), which demonstrate that the stronger the internal evidence and accountability systems within the schools, the less conflict and clashing of priorities are experienced by leaders and teachers when external expectations need to be met. In other words, school leaders will experience less turbulence, mitigated by external demands, if their internal procedures are purposeful, clear, and embedded. As such, a school leader's adaptability to the external demands is more likely.

3.8 Framing Mechanisms

The methods used by school systems to hold schools school leaders to account are often reported as concerning if not commanding for some. The Principals disclosed that they felt grilled, 'on edge' and 'fearful' and that the accountability is 'onerous and imposing.' This finding is surprising, given that the Principals did not consider the consequences of being held to account as high stakes. Accountability 'on its own is neither good nor bad' but rather one of the judgments is the mechanism and its consequences the regulator may employ (Cochran-Smith, 2021, p. 8). Accountability consequences are interdependent with the stake scale. Some empirical research reveals that the 'stakes level' determines the extent of emotion for educators (Klerks, 2013). However, the reactions by the Principals support the findings of Penninckx, Vanhoof, De Maeyer, and Van Petegem (2015), who examined the 'low-stakes' inspection context of Flemish education. They found that when engaged in strategic activities to produce a better image of the school, the staff members suffered from severe emotional side effects due to the inspectorial methods. These side effects were affected by principals' attitudes towards the inspection, by staff perceptions of inspectors' behaviours and by the inspection results (Penninckx et al., 2015). The mechanisms 'to account' and what regulators are accounting for (such as only performance results) and how the system leaders carry out such accounts (such as feedback process) (Penninckx, 2017) are important influences on the detrimental effects on school leaders and teachers. The implications of these negative consequences are examined further in the final chapter.

In closing, *Framing* is a common strategy used by school leaders, a cognitive schema (Rumelhart, 1980b; Spillane, Reiser, & Gomez, 2006; Weiner & Woulfin, 2017). Schemas are evidenced by plausible stories, aligning with Weick's sense -making property of plausibility (Weick, 1995). Creating models for conceptualising external demands, such as the accountability construct, is an effective leadership strategy (Darling-Hammond, 2010; Kuchapski, 2001).

The discussion to this point has drawn out significant issues related to school leaders' sensemaking of external demands: *contextualising, prioritising/constraining,* and *framing.* The Principals' ways of interpreting their accountability expectations raises the question about which of these sensemaking processes would have the greatest influence on school leaders' practices. Even though it would appear that Principals' interpretations of their school contexts (*contextualising*) hold less influence on their practices than their *prioritising/constraining,* their ways of *framing* accountability are interwoven with their priorities and constraints, making it difficult to ascertain this aspect's level of influence. Context as an influencer on leaders' practices is consistent with the research by Pennings (1975), which examines the interaction between organisational structure, environmental uncertainty and aspects of performance, validating that 'contingency' holds minimal influence.

There are a few points that may be of interest here. One, school leaders do not adopt the external expectations of their school systems in their entirety, and in general do not adopt policy as policy makers intend. Two, school leaders' interpretations of external demands from regulators such as system leaders hold implications for policy to practice. School leaders in various studies, including the Principals' in this book, pay more attention to some factors in their contexts than to others (Obstfeld, Sutcliffe, & Weick, 2005; Spillane & Anderson, 2014). This influence of their 'attention' is more dependent on their values, beliefs, and attitudes (particularly their conceptualisations of learning) and their self-beliefs about their capabilities (such as their beliefs to influence teaching teams) rather than the school context itself. At the beginning of this chapter, Spillane and Anderson citing Mandler where the novice principals, often in the interruptions of the ongoing flow of experience, were in their own way taking control of their environments, not the environment controlling them.

The properties of sensemaking are insightful in describing school leaders' practices of *interpreting* external demands. Table 13 presents a summary of the way Weick's sensemaking properties can be redefined with a school leadership lens (Column 1) and then aligning with the way the Principals interpreted their accountability expectations (Column 2).

CHAPTER 9

Credibility, Persuasion and Coherence

> I asked the School System to give me the data on the other girls'
> schools in other clusters, schools that do very well. I said—now, let's
> have a look at these data ... that's just me challenging staff to say
> well stop being so smug, we always need to do better. We always
> need to say when we are doing well. That's great, let's celebrate that.
> But also, where can we improve?
>
> CHARMAINE (Principal)

∴

Charmaine's intention here could be to offer an alternative understanding or
perhaps disrupt the teaching team's current sensemaking about their results
(see Figure 17).

Charmaine appeals to the team's humility to use the data to improve rather
than be complacent. According to the theoretical premises of sensegiving
(Gioia & Chittipeddi, 1991), Charmaine's act reflects her own sensemaking,
Envisioning, with the articulated intention to influence her team to view the
results from an improvement mindset, *Signalling*. The team would in turn
make sense of Charmaine's sensegiving: 'we always need to do better,' *Envisioning* phase. The teaching team's sensemaking on Charmaine's intentions
here are informing, adjusting, and guiding her next cycle of sensegiving, the
Energising phase. The descriptions by the Principals of being 'at their best'
when faced with external demands were their reported practices. These could
be interpreted as sensegiving practices (Gioia & Chittipeddi, 1991; Kraft et al.,
2018).

Sensegiving acts are intrinsic to a school leader's work, whether deliberate
or not. School leaders are key agents in providing sensegiving to their school
communities. Teachers, like employees, expect their leaders to diminish confusion and create sense or coherence. It is often in these uncertain times
that school leaders will be deliberate, and more conscious, in their sensegiving acts. Intentional sensegiving when employed to help others understand (sensemaking—cognitive act) is a fundamental leadership practice.
If the phases of the theoretical components of sensegiving, as illustrated in

© KONINKLIJKE BRILL NV, LEIDEN, 2022 | DOI:10.1163/9789004517202_009

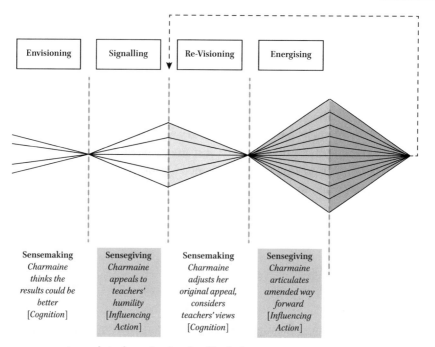

FIGURE 17 A sample in the cycle of a school leader's sensegiving practices

Charmaine's practices (see Figure 17) are enacted by school leaders, then the outcomes are likely to be potent ways of collectively moving forward for school leaders and the community.

In our examples in Chapters 6 and 7 the leadership practices which the Principals perceived were essential to manage their external demands with their school's internal commitments are below. Following the line of thinking that overt leadership practices are potential sensegiving practices these are reasonable examples of sensegiving:

– Exhibiting a moral purpose, through story or mantras
– Articulating a vision for learning
– Demonstrating expertise in data analyses and implementation
– Initiating professional learning conversations
– Implementing shared processes and structures to:
  – create coherence with the community
  – reconcile external demands with internal commitments

Two moderating factors pertinent to these sensegiving practices were the Principals' levels of self-efficacy and their capabilities in cultivating credibility with their teaching teams. These sensegiving practices and moderating factors follow this sequence throughout this chapter. Figure 19 provides a visual summary for this chapter's exploration on educational leaders' sensegiving.

CREDIBILITY, PERSUASION AND COHERENCE 189

The final section of the chapter examines the relationship between a school leader's sensemaking of educational accountability and its influence on their sensegiving acts. To this end, the TPB is employed to validate the theoretical relationship.

1 Persuasive Devices: Narratives, Metaphors and Mantras

Narratives, metaphors, and mantras can develop into full blown stories. The story may come in various forms, a painting, a belief, a vision, or a creative description (Thayer, 1988). However, when articulated to others their intention is making meaning, giving sense to others. Thayer proposes:

> A leader is one who creates human/social alternities by telling a compelling story about what is about will be, about what should be or about what should (or could) be done, about one or the other (p. 259) .... It is the leader's stories that mediate for all those who would follow, an alternative way of being, doing, knowing, having, or saying in the world. (p. 260)

The level of influence a story can have as a sense-giving act depends in part on the leader's ability to communicate. Influential articulation by a school leader depends on two skills. First, is the school leader 'attending' to the listener's context, attuning the leader's 'listening' to the same frequency as the members of their school community. Second, the message itself, which allows the leader to articulate a story in a language that the community can access and understand (Maxwell, 2014).

The use of narratives and mantras were employed regularly by the Principals to influence teachers and students in giving sense to the external demands. Research studies that investigated school leaders' reactions to external expectations, such as Shipps (2012), Shipps and White (2009), Firestone and Shipps (2005) or Spillane, Diamond, et al. (2002) reported on the leaders' management processes. Much of the current literatures have been situated in school leaders' sensemaking, such as Ganon-Shilon and Schechter (2019a) report on metaphorical thought processes, with engaging anecdotes and sensemaking exemplars by Hasinoff and Mandzuk (2018). Expressions of metaphorical thought through oral or text narratives, amongst other overt leadership practices such as initiation of processes or programs, provide windows into how school leaders aim to influence their teachers and students. Sensegiving as presented here is an aspect which may contribute to some other empirical studies (Eren, 2020; Muñiz, 2020; Wong, 2019). The case study (thesis) by Eren (2020) investigates in depth principals' sensemaking, alluding to sensegiving acts. The case study by Muñiz (2020) explores a 'muddy sensemaking' regarding a socio-emotional skills programs resulting from unclear external policies, with a new idea of 'unintentional sensegiving' theorised by Wong (2019).

The way a leader frames or renames (Thayer, 1988) a situation can impact on the way staff members understand an experience and, in the end, how they respond or act upon the event (Fairhurst & Staff, 1996; Neumann, 1995). Public renaming is an overt meaning making act. As such if renaming is overt, with the intention of influencing others, it can be termed as a sensegiving act. Leaders, similar to the Principals, vary in their capabilities of sensegiving. Maitlis and Lawrence (2007) point to three key sensegiving practices that leaders engage in. The first is their discursive abilities. Their skill level in being able to bring an expansive perspective or musings to the experience. The second is their ability to construct and articulate persuasive accounts. Again, the underlying intention is to influence others' thinking (and action). The third of Maitlis' and Lawrence's sensegiving practices is how leaders process the facilitation of routines, practices, and structures in their organisations. These three sensegiving practices align well with the Principal examples and are embedded in the theoretical ELM.

1.1 *Metaphorically Speaking*

Metaphors are powerful conductors for internal change. Even though sense-making is different among the Principals, their 'giving sense' to others is witnessed as though they are 'becoming' their metaphors (Grove & Panzer, 1989). It is argued that if a leader becomes their metaphor their oral and written narratives will reflect that metaphor. In other words, "language itself leads us. Not words as such, but the meaning we have come to attribute to them, the concepts they embody, the mental artifacts they invoke or conjure" (Thayer, 1988, p. 259). Barry embodies his metaphor in the concept of 'buffer.' The mental artifacts aim to appeal to the staff: 'I am the human shield between the [School System and the teachers]—the buffer ... my job is to be the human shield, which protects the teachers from the excesses of [the accountability regime].' Some studies shed light on Australian principals' dilemmas of increasingly being accountable for performance results (Ehrich et al., 2015; McGuire, 2012),yet there are few studies in how educational leaders seek to give sense to their accountability expectations with their teachers and students. The Norris study (2017) does this to a point.

1.2 *Narratives as Windows*

Sensegiving acts articulated through oral and written narratives were aimed at mobilising teacher practices. A plethora of empirical and theoretical studies,

CREDIBILITY, PERSUASION AND COHERENCE

Dinham (2005, 2016); Hattie 2015; Le Fevre and Robinson (2014); Sun and Leithwood (2015) and Dinham et al. (2013) draw indirect parallels regarding school leaders' ways of influencing teaching practices. Direct parallels can be drawn regarding the examples of Principals' styles and expressions of leadership, such as instructional leadership (Bendikson et al., 2012; Brown & Chai, 2012; Thessin & Louis, 2019), accountable leadership (Elmore, 2005), pedagogical leadership (Male & Palaiologou, 2012) and data-informed leadership (Pettit, 2010; Phillips, 2014). Notably, Pettit's Australian research and ongoing work, has opened a research stream on the topic of educational leaders' use of data from external assessment programs. As is known, the expectation by Australian school systems of their principals is that they are 'Leaders of Learning.' Integral to this function is the expectation that principals will be accountable for learning and for utilising data to inform practices. However, an Australian study by Pettit (2010) indicated that principals fall short in meeting these expectations.

A school leader's mantra reverberates in the psyche of a school community. Ask any teacher what messages they hear from their leaders. They will recall these with verbatim, especially those that are in the form of a mantra. If the mantra also has an underling morality it will most likely be recalled more vividly yet judged with greater scrutiny. The judgment is often made according to how well the 'talk' aligns with the 'walk.'

1.3   *Exhibiting a Moral Purpose*

Some mantras by the Principals indicated an underlying moral purpose. The following mantras would offer a secure sense of purpose to the community even when the external demands for high results were pressing: 'It's immoral the way schools use results to market their schools' (Malcolm); 'I don't pay too much attention to the results' (Sammy); 'I don't listen to the naysayers, if it's not about learning' (Malcolm); and 'If authentic learning is happening, results will take care of themselves' (Charmaine). These mantras are a reflexive enactment and require that leaders have already behaved in certain ways and have 'looked back' (*Retrospect*, Weick, 1995). The mantras, when used by these Principals to intentionally influence teachers and students, as a sensegiving act, are an example of the phase of *Signalling*.

2   Sensegiving Act of Articulating a Vision for Learning

The Principals who reveal that they are at their 'best' when they can articulate a vision for learning also emphasise the importance of remaining contemporary in their knowledge of learning and pedagogy. These same Principals also explained how they work closely with teachers on learning projects, professional learning and general teaching and learning processes. Hershey's and Blanchard's (1988) leadership framework of 'selling' is a behavioural task. The Principals were 'selling' a vision for learning and informing people about it are often couched in persuasive terms, such as a 'selling' task. Selling can align the theoretical phases of sensegiving. Notably articulating the 'sale' aligns with three phases of sensegiving: *Envisioning, Signalling* and *Re-Visioning*.

The ability for the Principals to give sense to their communities through forming their vision (*Envisioning*), to articulating the vision (*Signalling*) followed by adjusting the vision if shared (*Re-Visioning*) positioned themselves in a more grounded position in managing their external demands. These Principals reported negative impacts of external expectations less frequently, indicating that being able to articulate a vision of learning is also a progressive step in helping teachers to keep their focus on their purpose, to avoid 'interrupting conditions' blur their purpose (Weick's *Ongoing projects*). The Principals did not emphasise that the vision was shared with teachers and students, other empirical studies demonstrate that a shared vision, reflected through shared language and actions, is likely to hold more impact for influence (Boyatzis, Rochford, & Taylor, 2015; Roueche, Baker III, & Rose, 2014). The fourth sensegiving phase of *Energising* would reflect the enactment of a shared vision.

Yet school leaders need to do more than simply articulate a vision. In response to a Norris blog (Norris, 2018), which pertains to the importance of leaders articulating a vision, a post graduate student and teacher-leader in the field, Kahli Schroder offers her sensemaking:

> It has to be more than articulating a vision for learning. Leaders need to be part of the learning process/journey. Having a clearly articulated vision is not worth the paper it is written on, if it is not enacted. Too often, I have heard leaders give tours to prospective families and talk about the learning process that does not match what is occurring. What I have noted during these times, is what leaders are advocating to families, is what they wish to be happening, which at times is wonderful however, the implementation of creating such a learning environment has fallen through. Time needs to be taken. Leaders need to be in the thick of the learning design and be part of the process with students to really understand what teachers do, how to best support teachers and, to allow leaders to give teachers the feedback they are entitled to. (Norris, 2018)

Kahli clearly is offering her own sensemaking here on the leadership in her school.

CREDIBILITY, PERSUASION AND COHERENCE   193

3   Sensegiving Act of Modelling Expertise

School leaders are often judged not on what they say, but on what they do. Modelling behaviours in leadership with teachers can range from speech giving to pedagogical practices. Specifically, modelling by working with teachers within data-driven cultures is a leadership ability to give meaning to data, especially.

Brian Broadview models the importance in the utility of data:

> We're digging deep to ensure that our students at this school in this context are working towards achieving their potential. It will be reflected on the cross [the DeCourcy cross chart] and we have shifted. We understand where we were and where we're going to ... So, on that yardstick, we're ... which is what [School System] ask us to look at ... we know we've shifted a lot, so at this school, we're always quite high in learning gain between Year 10 and Year 12 .... But now we're actually moving whole cohorts into far higher and greater levels.

The Principals took data and what they could offer seriously. They employ data sets as leverage for persuasion and notably, how data could inform teaching and learning practices. Empirical research was also considered data. Most of the principals described the importance of using and personalising data (Kaufman et al., 2014; Sharratt & Fullan, 2012), acknowledging the influence of educational research in their understandings of learning and the impact of teaching on student learning (Bendikson, Robinson, & Hattie, 2012; Hattie & Timperley, 2007; Richmond, 2007; Timperley, 2007). Yet some Principals only used data to inform performance target setting. Koretz's (2008) study found that in regimes with higher stakes consequences, accountability in driving for performance results gradually superseded the 'diagnosis of the strengths and weaknesses of individual students' learning' (p. 47). The Principals who employed data for the purpose of performance target setting were the same Principals who believed that the external expectations were a tool for judging and being 'sized up' in their competencies as principals. This is an important finding, validated by Koretz's study.

The teacher needs to see a benefit for themselves in changing a teaching practice (Dinham, 2008), in this instance using data from performance results. Teachers are more likely to see a benefit if implementation plans are established collectively and agreed by community members. The Principals who reported their pursuits in solo terms (I and me) were more likely to demonstrate frustration and anger regarding their attempts to either persuade or influence teachers or they shield or buffer system expectations. Such constraints may be self-defeating and self-depleting for leaders. One principal reports their solo pursuit as exhausting: 'I have been going in this job now for [xx] years I don't know how I will continue' (Terence). Finally, and importantly, the students need to know clearly what the expectations are in their school, with a unified approach from all teachers across all their subject areas.

The Principals reported that students' performance results were part of their learning goals, but only a small part. Owen 'tried a whole school approach—it's a great scaffold for writing—so it will help in all subject areas but also should improve our results.' There are many studies about data informing leadership practices to address results, from *No Child Left behind* (Anderson, Leithwood, & Strauss, 2010; Stobart, 2008) and Ofsted (Earl & Fullan, 2003) to NAPLAN (Carter, 2015; Harris et al., 2013; Klenowski & Wyatt-Smith, 2011) and the one study about the HSC (DeCourcy, 2005). While the Principals who were in the funded national partnership school program verbalised the processes that they use to measure their performance growth, they also reported positive esteem for the incidental learning that occurred and the difficulties when students' performances were the only targets. In this instance this indicates that targets other than students' performance results are needed. Other Principals carry out their evaluations according to their own learning goals, rather than basing them on improvements in students' performance results. This represents an increase in data informing practices, with the Principals needing to present evidence of not only their implementation plans but also the evaluations and outcomes of those plans. This magnifies the level and specificity of data and accountability. Being capable and confident in their capability of utilising data to inform their sensegiving practices requires explicit modelling and coaching and skillful facilitation of teacher learning (Thessin & Louis, 2019). Underpinning the practices of modelling, coaching and facilitation is the leader's levels of self-efficacy to embed these into their professional practice.

4 Sensegiving Act of Facilitating Professional Learning Conversations

4.1 *Knowing Teachers' Needs, Motivations*
Knowing teachers' needs and motivations creates opportunities for school leaders to influence teachers and their teaching. Conversations based on inquiry are avenues to help leaders' understandings. However, a study by Le Fevre and Robinson (2014) found that principals demonstrated low to moderate capacity in holding conversations about performance; they are more skilled in advocating their own viewpoints than being able to inquire into and check their understandings of the views of the teachers. This is 'monologing,' where school leaders articulate their viewpoints without seeking out or adjusting to

others' thoughts or feelings. Monologuing by school leaders is antithetical in the cyclic nature of sensegiving, falling short in phases 3, *Re-visioning* and 4, *Energising*. School leaders' actions do impact on teacher motivations. Such impact is evidenced around the reasons that some early career teachers leave the profession altogether (Ford, Olsen, Khojasteh, Ware, & Urick, 2019).

4.2   *Levers for Accountable Conversations*

The DeCourcy data are esteemed by the Principals in the Norris study (2017). The tools associated with the data are accessed easily, are not complicated, and have few items to analyse, yet moreover having a teacher accountability function. The Principals used the DeCourcy data for not only the provision of a different analysis from the HSC results but also as guide for questions to conduct a 'conversation of account' with teachers. While only one Principal reported that they held conversations focused on teacher developmental issues regarding unfavourable performance results, Sammy revealed that making the time and a structure for these conversations, even when they are difficult, resulted in positive outcomes. Le Fevre and Robinson (2014) found that one reason for a school leader's reluctance to address poor performance issues was owing to their tendency to avoid negative emotions. Addressing a leader's fear of negative emotions is important, given the consequences of not addressing poor teacher performance.

4.3   *Perilous: Avoiding the Accountable Conversation*

Addressing issues of performance is important as in not doing so creates negative consequences for leaders. Ignoring it may create more problems than the problem itself. Ignoring may erode other's confidence in the leader. The implications of not addressing concerns about performance are noted in Bryk's and Schneider's study (2002), which found that teachers trust of leaders is diminished when leaders avoid dealing with poor teacher performance or deal with it inadequately (resulting in no change). Hence and possibly ironically, when school leaders avoid holding their teachers to account, there is a decrease of trust, and possibly credibility and legitimacy in their leadership, not only with teachers but parents and students. Legitimacy as proposed by Kraft et al. (2015) is a moderating factor of a leader's sensegiving.

5   Sensegiving Act: Reconciliation

5.1   *Self-Beliefs Influence Leadership Capabilities to Reconcile*

A leader's perception of their legitimacy is important when faced with contradictory conditions such as reconciling external demands with internal commitments. Leaders are more likely to employ clear and autonomous sensegiving practices if they perceive that they have a high level of legitimate power (Kraft et al., 2015). Some Principals seamlessly integrated their external expectations with their internal school learning goals. These Principals noted the importance of gaining collective agreements from teachers and simultaneously being responsive to the current sets of data and their analytical tools, *consensual validation* (Weick, 1995). School leaders at all levels need to have sophisticated integration skills to create schemas between what is being asked of them and meeting their own existing school commitments. Supporting Kraft et al.'s (2015) propositions the Principals were more likely to use direct, unilateral sensegiving strategies if they perceived that they had strong levels of legitimate power. For example, Charmaine perceived she held credibility as a leader of teaching given her predecessor was an acceptable and credible leader of learning. Yet for others they were more likely to use indirect, multilateral sensegiving strategies if they perceived that their level of legitimate power was low (Kraft et al., 2015). Larry perceived his legitimate power as low; he admitted he would ask other senior leaders to manage the leadership involving the performance results, given his perceived limited knowledge about teaching. Larry's legitimate power hindered his influence (sensegiving) with his teachers' learning and work with students.

5.2   *High Legitimate Power Reconciles Seamlessly*

School leaders who are at ease with the demands due to their perceived high levels of legitimate power of influence will likely ignore the pressure to set performance results as their target, substituting it with meeting their own professional commitments. Leithwood and Riehl (2005) found that the way principals manage the external and internal expectations is by attending to some concerns and disregarding others, thus balancing competing demands and making choices. Weick (195) proposes in the property of *Ongoing Projects* to keep the task from loosening it is important to not focus on interrupting conditions. Leaders reorder goals (Seashore Louis et al., 2012), negotiating and appropriating for example, external accountability in innovative and 'clever and savvy' ways to meet multiple demands (Koyama, 2014). Sammy Savvy demonstrates such skills. Being competent in understanding information and being able to integrate this to the current situation is an essential leadership strategy. Thiel et al. (2012) argue that an essential strategy for leaders who are making decisions is their capacity to integrate the plethora of information from their environments. Understanding yet suspending their expectations allows adequate information integration, which enables school leaders to remain considered, yet creative, in their approaches and decision-making.

CREDIBILITY, PERSUASION AND COHERENCE   197

Reconciling by overtly meeting internal commitments with external demands is a critical sensegiving act for school leaders. It demonstrates to teachers and students that they honour their work. Indeed, such an act is a gift that makes sense. Moreover, such acts may bring a sense of coherence to a learning community's directions.

6   Sensegiving Act: Leaders Creating Coherence

6.1   *Atomised States to Coherent States*
Examples of school leaders *Creating coherence* were where the Principals found plausible ways to enact their external demands that aligned with the community's strategic goals. The terms 'plausible' and 'enact' align with two of Weick's seven properties: *plausible* meaning that speech acts are credible and convincing, rather than being accurate; *enactment* meaning that the individual takes action to see what they may be up against, tries a negotiating gambit or makes a declaration (see Table 14) (Weick, 1995). It is here that sensemaking and sensegiving intersect. Plausible meanings, constructed by leaders is sensemaking, a cognitive act. Speech acts demonstrating the leader's plausibility is the sensegiving phase of Signalling, an influencing act. In the context of leaders attempting to align external and internal expectations, Elmore (2005) describes coherence building as 'moving from an atomized state to a more coherent organizational state' (p. 135) and in another study, describes coherence as 'a school's capacity to engage in deliberate improvements in instructional practice and student learning across classrooms over time as evidenced by educator practices and organizational processes that connect and align work across the organization' (Elmore et al., 2013, p. 4). The Principals conjure images to support their self-coherence (sensemaking—*Personal Identity*) and use communicative acts (sensegiving—*Signalling*) such as mantras, and narratives to bring about coherence for their communities.

6.2   *Default Modes as a Sensegiving Encultured Practice*
School leaders, like the Principals, do not necessarily commit to building coherence between school system expectations of their drive for high performance results and their own expectations of their students' performances. The Principals' *Creating coherence* was not necessarily aligned with student achievement in the form of scores, as the School System expected. A study by Carnoy et al. (2003) found that schools facing external accountability demands keep to their internal 'default modes'; the school community may exhibit a huge degree of

alignment around student performance results or may organise itself around behaviour management with little or no coherence with their academic goals (p. 5). 'Default mode' in this sense is a school's encultured practices. Similarly, Duignan (2010) explains the importance of a leader's skill in building coherence, although silent about the effect of this coherency on learning. However, Duignan argues for the importance of creating coherence as leaders establish a sense of order, creating patterns of predictability and ensuring feelings of calm.

Order, patterns of predictability and calmness for school communities have been threatened through the pandemic. In some instances, the school's 'loosening' is reflected across all Weick's properties. School leaders, especially early career leaders, have experienced the anguish, uncertainty, and seemingly unsurmountable challenges (Bagwell, 2020; Chennamsetti, 2020; Harris & Jones, 2020) in trying to make sense and give sense during these times. For school leaders this appeared to be a perfect storm with imperfect responses (Harris & Jones, 2020).

However it is at times of great upheaval do we see authentic and liberating forms of leadership (McLeod & Dulsky, 2021). Exemplary leadership behaviours have been witnessed with leaders who offer feasible plans (*Plausibility*) and shared relevance (*Social Context*), place restrictions 'on some portion of the flow' (Weick, 1995, p. 462) (*Ongoing Projects*) can articulate these plans (*Signalling*), offer hope through adjusting and amending from stimuli in school contexts (*Energising*).

7 School Leaders Give Sense by Articulating Perspective

> The lantern as a metaphor: Novel and creative perspective taking, she **becomes** (Grove & Panzer, 1989) the lantern, shedding light on the direction to take.

Some of the ways the Principals report that they were *Creating coherence* included developing cultures of perspective taking; integrating external expectations with internal processes and goals; embedding a culture of learning; and assembling performance cultures.

The Principals revealed that to 'manage' the external accountability expectations, they created cultures that encourage teachers, parents, and students to keep the students' performance results from external programs in perspective. Perspective taking—seeing the other person's view (Grant & Berry, 2011)

CREDIBILITY, PERSUASION AND COHERENCE

is a potent skill. When employees are 'guided by prosocial motivation (for example being encouraged by leaders), to take others' perspectives, they will channel their intrinsic motivation towards producing ideas that are not only novel, but also useful, thereby achieving higher creativity' (Grant & Berry, 2011, p. 74). Ku, Wang and Galinsky (2015) describe perspective taking in similar creative terms as imagining the world from 'another's vantage point or imagining oneself in another's shoes to understand the visual viewpoint' (p. 79). When school leaders, faced with difficult external expectations, offer perspective taking to their school communities, the community may engage and in turn offer novel and creative solutions in meeting their own needs at the same time as meeting the external expectations. This interchange is where the momentum of a movement happens, between *Energising* and *Re-Visioning*. As such with leadership distributed through the staff group more powerful solutions can emerge in what can be the antithesis to a controlling and regulated environment.

7.1 *Giving Sense by Enacting an Acceptable Schema*

Consistent with the Principals' experiences is the working theory of Carnoy et al. (2003) in the ways that educators conceive accountability. They hold the assumption that schools (educators) embed their internal accountability into the patterns of their day-to-day operations, which significantly influences the way the teachers deliver education. Their assumption is that school leaders and teachers must solve the problem of accountability in some way or another, to carry out their work. Malcolm's narrative solved his problem of accountability through embedding and articulating all works as a learning act; on attending an interview following a student's suspension, 'the parent breathes a sigh of relief when the conversation is about taking up the offer of learning' (Malcolm).

7.2 *Giving Sense by Marketing School Data in a Positive Image*

The Principals revealed that part of their work is to manage judgements made about the school image and their students resulting from the disclosure of their students' performance results. As a sensegiving act the Principals build coherence by ensuring their school looks positive, such as presenting their performance data in their annual report in the best possible light: '... well, I present the data to represent the school as best I can' (Brian Broadview). This finding, consistent with the study by Teddlie and Reynolds (2000), found that principals always present the best data available, even at times with 'deception or manipulation of data [in order] for a school to look good' (p. 276).

7.3 *Giving Sense by Resolving Clashes: School Versus School System*

The various influences that affected the ways the Principals built their cultures of coherence were seeking clarity and specificity about school system expectations, finding some sense of self-coherence and decisions regarding their styles of leading.

The Principals reported that in meeting the system accountability expectations, their school priorities clashed with the system priorities. These clashes created anxiety and frustrations, accentuated due to the accountability system also being their employer. Marks and Nance (2007) found that principals were likely to perceive the influence of the state negatively when states used mandates, regulations, and sanctions as policy levers. However, Carnoy et al. (2003) found that educators perceived educational accountability negatively where there appeared to be an absence of their own internal accountability school processes. The Principals who reported a greater negative effect of system accountability expectations than others were the same Principals who spoke the least about their responses to accountability from a learning perspective, such as the utility of data and influencing teaching. The moderating factor for sensegiving here in this instance could be a school leader's knowledge and skill in pedagogical processes of their levels of efficacy in pedagogical processes.

7.4 *Giving Sense by Co-Designing Internal Accountable Processes*

One aim of external accountability systems in Australia has been to push low-performing schools to do better (Ministerial Council for Federal Financial Relations, 2009). One may predict that schools that are least aligned internally would obtain the greatest benefit from the imposition of external accountability. However, Carnoy et al. (2003) found that it was precisely these schools 'with non-aligned internal accountability systems that were least likely to be able to respond coherently to the external accountability demands' (p. 8). Their research supports previous studies by Elmore (2005b) and Roche (2004), which found that the stronger the internal evidence and accountability systems within the schools, the less conflict and clashing of priorities are experienced. The moderator here from a sensegiving perspective is the strength and consensual validation with teachers about their internal processes.

Additionally, and like this investigation, Carnoy et al. (2003) found that poor integration between external expectations and internal processes and goals was exacerbated when the external system expectations were not consistently strong. Likewise, Pettit (2010) found that clear and well-articulated school system expectations are essential for school leaders to meet their regulated accountabilities, to take data seriously and to use data for implementation for

CREDIBILITY, PERSUASION AND COHERENCE

change in student learning. A possible moderator for sensegiving here could be clarity by the school leaders. While Kraft et al. (2015) do not comment on clarity as a moderator it is understandable that school community members seek out or expect their school leaders to be clear about intentions or their own sensemaking of events, particularly if it is a critical event.

7.5 *Clarity as a Sensegiving Expectation*

Leaders are often confused about what is expected of them by their regulators such as school system leaders. Studies along with the Norris study (2017) indicate that school systems need to be clear about their expectations to help schools. In fact, not being transparent about expectations creates further problems for educational leaders. Sensemaking such as boundary setting can follow when the expectations are clearly articulated to leaders. This seemingly lack of clarity of system expectations may be surprising, given the empirical research (Comber, 2012; Comber & Cormack, 2011; Smeed, Bourke, Nickerson, & Corsbie, 2015) and discourse (Lingard et al., 2013) about the negative effects of NAPLAN and PISA testing on the work of teachers and educational leaders. Perhaps their messages indicated unintentional sensegiving. Ambiguous messages, disparate verbal and written expectations (public versus private) and silence are characteristic of unintentional sensegiving stifling system reform (Wong, 2019).

The school system advisor-principal relationship by its nature involves all the elements in an accountability cycle: disclosing, explaining, and justifying and redress. If left there however many opportunities for a productive relationship is missed, for both. The relationship at its most effective is a relational partnership, with school leaders working to the same end (Gurr & Drysdale, 2015). Working on the same goals, as opposed to buffering or blocking the relationship, is a vast source of energy, and ultimately outcomes for teachers and students. Some Catholic school systems envisage the partnership as a covenant (Whelan, 2000)—with the accompanying mantra: 'I will be good for and you will be good for me'

The need for clarity for leaders by school system advisors is explored further in the final chapter.

8 Two Moderating Factors of School Leaders' Sensegiving

Two moderating factors of Principals' sensegiving identified were Principals' levels of self-efficacy about teaching and learning and the second, was their perceived capability in cultivating credibility with their teaching teams.

8.1 Self-Efficacy: A Sensegiving Moderator

Investigating the Principals' levels of self-efficacy was not an immediate goal in my study. However, this factor appeared to impact on their leadership practices. Principals' levels of self-efficacy about their practices in achieving student performance results are influenced by their confidence levels regarding their understanding the teaching and learning processes. Self-efficacy is an important determinant for behaviour in school leadership. The study by Tschannen-Moran and Gareis (2004) found that self-efficacy influences principals' efforts, persistence and resilience in managing demands and expectations. The self-efficacy construct is relevant in a broad sense of a school leader's ability to guide and support teachers and students (McCollum & Kajs, 2007b). In comparing the general literatures on self-efficacy, the position taken here is that a leader's *level* of self-efficacy is a self-referent construct (Ajzen, 1991) and self-efficacy taken as a leader's confidence in their knowledge and skills (Bandura, 2014). There is some relationship between a leader's practices and their levels of self-efficacy (Lovell, 2009), and further research is recommended to examine the relationship between a school leader's sense of self-efficacy for enacting the instructional leadership style and their sense of self-efficacy in their general leadership practices, particularly in secondary schools.

When tasked with leading teachers and meeting accountability expectations, school leaders need to balance competing priorities (Leithwood, 2005), reorder goals (Seashore Louis & Mintrop, 2012) and be creative in integrating information (Thiel et al., 2012). Many studies on the topic of leader effectiveness in creating growth trajectories in student achievement offer insights here (Hattie, Masters, & Birch, 2015; Le Fevre & Robinson, 2014; Robinson, Lloyd, & Rowe, 2008). However, not much of the literature explores the influences on a school leaders' agency on teaching and learning while at the same time being accountable for results. Yet, it may simply be an assumption (and a fair one) that building credibility with teaching teams, is an essential task for school leaders in any contextual environment.

Instead of the term 'building' credibility, the term 'cultivating' is adopted because of its organic imagery, avoiding the industrial and construction imagery.

8.2 Cultivating Credibility: A Sensegiving Moderator

8.2.1 School Leaders' Credibility Is in the Eye of the 'Sensereceiver'

Another assumption is that credibility practices as sensegiving leadership acts are determined by what the leader says or does. To a degree this is a reasonable assumption. However, the determinations of credibility as a sensegiving act it is argued, is determined by the sensereceiver. This argument, validated by Kraft et al.'s (2015) notion of legitimate power is given by the sensereceivers. Hence to

CREDIBILITY, PERSUASION AND COHERENCE

develop their credibility in their leadership practices, school leaders' sensegiving practices need to be explicitly attentive to the sensereceiver, knowing their needs and motivations. Credibility practices that a formal leader engages in is a moderating factor in the momentum or energy (Gioia & Chittipeddi, 1991) that can be gained in their sensegiving acts. It is recommended that first and foremost the school leader shores up their own sensemaking, followed closely behind is understanding the needs and motivations of their sensereceivers and finally the leader wraps and presents their sensegiving as a reflection of the sensereceivers own sensemaking.

High levels of legitimate power are needed to impact on employees' work (Kraft et al., 2015). In schools the impact is focussed on teachers' work, and to a lesser degree students' work. Essential to this legitimate power is cultivating credibility with teaching teams. Cultivating credibility, as a sensegiving act, refers to the degree to which school leaders themselves can make meaning of events to sufficiently give sense, and be received by teachers' sensemaking to the point of influencing and helping teacher learning and teacher enactment. For example, the Principals perceived that being credible with teachers was essential in influencing and persuading teachers in their thinking and acting to meet the external accountability expectations, and yet remain faithful to the schools' learning goals.

The impact of a school leaders' credibility also depends on the benefit teachers perceive in the leader's messaging (Dinham, 2008). As such, the degree of credibility could be said to be determined by the teacher's perception of the leader's sensegiving practices. The importance of cultivating credibility with teachers was often reported by the ECPs and those new to their school communities: 'They don't know me, so I am not sure of my creds [credibility] yet.' Clearly school leaders know about the need for credibility. In the early stages of their formal leadership appointments, this need could be all consuming. Sensegiving and the cycle of sensemaking to sensegiving offers a framework for early career and aspirant leaders, especially in times where external demands or critical events may seem overwhelming.

8.2.2 School Leaders Cultivate Credibility by Working with and Alongside Teachers

Working beside teachers, such as engaging in professional learning with them, provides opportunities to not only be in close working relationships but also to know and remain current about the nature of teachers' work. Charmaine describes herself as 'a hands-on leader,' attending staff professional studies days, along with the teachers, as a part of the team on these days. In this way, Charmaine is building and maintaining relationships through common tasks with equal power relationships. School leaders working beside teachers aligns with Hersey's and Blanchard's (1988) behavioural task of *participating*, which is described as shared decision making to task accomplishment, fewer requests for a task to be completed, while maintaining high relationship behaviour. Similarly, Hargreaves and Fullan (2015) assert the importance of working together to remain strong for a common purpose. Influential research, impacting on leader practitioners' practices, by Robinson (2011) found that the characteristic of 'being close' to teachers and their professional learning and work results in improved student achievement.

However, the professional learning should not be a stand-alone experience. The research by Thessin and Louis (2019) found that professional learning is most effective when leaders engage with teachers in a series of connected professional learning not just 'one-shot-single' experiences. This research of knowing teachers' needs and aspirations, working besides and being close to teachers' work, participating in the team, leaders and teachers co-constructing connected professional learning would indicate effective sensegiving practices for school leaders when tasked with being accountable for performance results.

8.2.3 School Leaders Cultivate Credibility through Their Knowledge and Skill Base

School leaders who have a sound knowledge base and skills set in pedagogy are likely to not only manage their performative demands but are likely to be credible in the perceptions of their teaching teams. For example, the greatest influence in the Principal's agency in managing their accountability expectations is found to be the Principals' perceived knowledge and skill about the teaching and learning processes. Larry the Learner, for example, discloses, 'I don't know much about that [learning and teaching].' Sammy reflects on his past: 'Look, when I first came into the job, I was told that [learning and teaching] was an area I needed to develop—and I did.' There appears to be a dependent relationship between the comfort or confidence in being accountable for results and their leadership agency with the Principals' knowledge regarding learning and teaching. Several studies point to similar dependent relationships in school leadership. The study by McCollum and Kajs (2007b) found that the self-efficacy of principals was related to their confidence in their knowledge base and skill. Likewise, Nelson and Sassi (2005) and Stein and Nelson (2003) found that a barrier to more effective instructional leadership is the adequacy of leaders' knowledge of teaching and learning processes. They found that school leaders who demonstrate lack of confidence are likely to be reluctant to observe teachers and give them feedback. Spillane and Seashore-Lois (2002) found that if leaders do not demonstrate knowledge and confidence, their

CREDIBILITY, PERSUASION AND COHERENCE

probabilities of being influential with teachers are not high. If school leaders are to be influential agents in leading in increasingly complex and contradictory conditions, then they need to be confident and convinced in enacting their own knowledge and skills regarding teaching and learning.

This raises the question about whether the school leader is self-aware of their strengths and challenges. And if they are aware that they do not have the knowledge base or skill set to manage events.

School leaders may manage this deficit either directly or indirectly. Ralph, for example, delegated this function to others. This delegation is not unusual, as secondary school principals regularly devolve or distribute the tasks before them (Jäppinen & Maunonen-Eskelinen, 2011). A plethora of literature describes how school leaders influence (or do not influence) teachers and teaching (Le Fevre & Robinson, 2014; Robinson, Lloyd, & Rowe, 2008). How well school leaders influence and mobilise their teaching teams can be evaluated through their effectiveness of their sensegiving practices. One of the purposes of sensegiving for school leaders is to help teachers understand the events around them, in doing so, leaders need first to know and understand teachers' work.

8.2.4 School Leaders Cultivate Credibility by Knowing and Understanding Teachers' Work

Understanding teachers' work, what they know and how they do it, is a basic need for teachers in their relationships with the school leader. Leaders cultivate credibility through indirect and multilateral sensegiving practices (Drori & Ellis, 2011). An effective sensegiving practice for a school leader is first to seek to understand teachers' work, and then for to provide an eagle's view (discursive skills), above the minutiae to engage in communicative acts which show they understand the teaching processes and in this understanding be able to offer insights, such as renaming a problem or providing liberating views (Thayer, 1988). However more important than a leader's discursive ability is their ability and desire to meet teachers' needs by understanding their work and esteeming such work with their students. Aligned with this need is a potent empirical message by Franken, Penney and Branson (2015) who found that teachers are more likely to be influenced by their leaders when they perceive that they understood their aspirations and needs.

8.2.5 School Leaders Cultivate Credibility with Teachers—The Moderator of Teacher Benefit

Related to teacher aspirations and needs, for leaders to cultivate credibility with teachers they need to tap into 'teacher benefit.' The benefit is not necessarily non-altruistic. The perceived benefit for teachers is not just for themselves.

It may be seen by teachers to be a benefit to students, parents, the overall teaching team or to the health of the school. So, for school leaders to engage a sensegiving act they need to understand teacher benefit. When leaders are, for example, encouraging teachers to use data to inform their practice, the teacher needs to see a benefit for their students (Dinham, 2008). A collective enterprise also is attractive to teachers. For example, in rigid performative environments teachers are more likely to see a benefit if implementation plans pertaining to accountability for learning have been established collectively and agreed by community members, than if imposed by the solo leader. The Principals who described their pursuits in solo terms (such as 'I' and 'me') spoke of frustration and anger regarding their attempts to either persuade or influence teachers or conversely, they shielded, buffered, or ignored system expectations. Imposing demands as the solo leader is fraught and energy draining. One Principal reports their solo pursuit as exhausting: 'I have been going in this job now for [many] years I don't know how I can continue' (Terence).

So, where do students fit in here? Students need to know clearly where the expectations for performance results reside in their learning cycle. This clarity can be achieved when teachers agree on the expectations and there is a unified approach from all teachers across all their subject areas. Such collective agreements with a teaching team require effective leader discursive skills with persuasive accounts, fuelled by a well-articulated shared vision and knowledge of learning and teaching.

Figure 18 tracks the previous discussion adapting Kraft et al.'s (2015) moderating model of sensegiving to the points raised above.

9 Theoretical Relationship between Leaders' Sensemaking and Sensegiving

The discussion here explores the relationship between a school leader's sensemaking of educational accountability and its influence on their sensegiving acts. This exploration employs the TPB to validate the theoretical relationships between sensemaking and sensegiving (Ajzen, 1991, 2012; Ajzen & Fishbein, 1980). The TPB's capacity, to validate as such, is premised on the notion that this well-tested theory provides explanations for and predictions of behaviours (Ajzen, 2012).

Ajzen's three determinants, which are the predominant influences on intention, are *attitude, subjective norm* and *perceived behavioural control* (Ajzen & Madden, 1986). These three determinants are employed to 'tease out' the relationships between the Principals' sensemaking of the expectations and

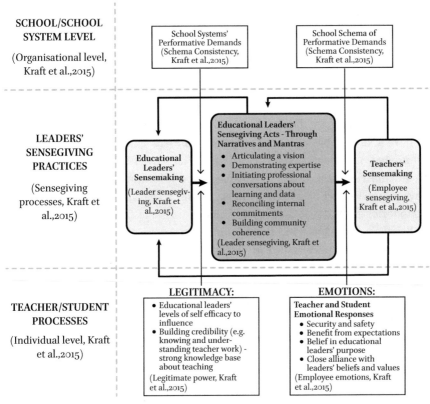

FIGURE 18   School leaders' sensegiving acts and moderators (adapted from Kraft et al., 2015)

their leadership sensegiving practices in their accountability environments. The explanation utilises the sample data predominantly from five Principals: Leonie, Barry, Charmaine, Terence, and Larry.

The first of Ajzen's determinant to align is *attitude*. The Principals' sensemaking of their school environments and expectations are being evaluated in 'favourable' or 'unfavourable' terms. These evaluations, following Ajzen's proposition, determine their intentions in the ways they would lead learning. Leonie and Barry are employed as two case examples to demonstrate how identifying the attitude to the outcome makes it reasonable to predict a principal's intention to act.

Leonie reports that if she ignores the performance results on NAPLAN, their results will remain the same or become lower. Leonie also reveals that school enrolments are dependent upon performance results: 'Parents will choose. They will look at our results. They will look for the pink on that map or the green ....' Staff members are being deployed elsewhere due to the loss of enrolments through poor student performance results; therefore, Leonie views these performance results as unfavourable, and her intention is to improve them. However, she regards teaching to the test and working only towards performance results as limiting the curriculum for students: 'NAPLAN can narrow curriculum and diminish all the interesting aspects of kids' learning.' To avoid staff losses (favourable outcome), Leonie reports that she will implement short-term intervention strategies (intention) to improve the performance results (favourable outcome). Leonie summarises her intention: 'So I said we're going to have a year of basics ... we're going to go focus on improving literacy and improving numeracy in the areas that our kids need ... I've got to get those results up.' Her attitude to the behaviours, both favourable and unfavourable, have a direct effect on her intentions. Having 'a year of basics' is also placing boundaries around teacher action (a characteristic of *Ongoing Projects*).

Barry on the other hand has his focus elsewhere. His sensemaking is that he perceives that poor results in students' performance in external testing led to unfair comparisons of schools by the community and school system advisors, which are harmful for prospective enrolments (unfavourable outcome evaluation): 'It does get up my nose a lot when, as often happens in schools— that always happens, in fact—the job of comparing apples with oranges happens.' Here, being compared is also an unfavourable outcome evaluation. Even though it may be difficult to predict Barry's actions exactly, it could be predicted that Barry's intention would be to find ways of reducing these comparisons. Barry's metaphor of 'buffer' and 'shield' is a window into the ways he acts to diminish the impact of the School System comparing. The public narrative is a mantra that these students achieve above what would be expected (*Signalling*). Barry initiates a school-wide change, persuading the students and teachers to focus on internal school grade growth rather than public performative measures: 'So you could go in as I've done today with the regional director, wander through classrooms and say, "Cooper, what's your target for science?" "It's a C, sir." Says the regional director, "How did you arrive at a C?" [Cooper] said, "Well, last year I was a D." So, it was the aspirational and achievable target for that child.' Clearly, Barry's attitude to the behaviours of being compared, is an unfavourable outcome for him and instead creates an internal accountability of grade setting, which is a favourable outcome in his making sense of high expectations for results. Hence, Barry's outcome evaluation establishes his intention of internal grade setting, which in turn influences his ways of leading learning (behaviour).

Ajzen's second determinant of intention, the *subjective norm,* is applied to the case examples of Charmaine and Terence. Subjective norm refers to an individual's 'perceived social pressure to perform or not to perform the behavior' (Ajzen, 1991, p. 189). Ajzen suggests that the social pressure is more often

CREDIBILITY, PERSUASION AND COHERENCE

individuals and refers to them as social referents (Ajzen, 2012).The *social referents* (i.e., to whom the Principals were motivated to prioritise their accountabilities), are identified as parents, students, School System personnel or themselves. The *object referents* (i.e., what Principals are motivated to account for) range from the students' happiness in learning or the students' results in external tests.

Charmaine's social referents are the students, the parents and herself, followed by the School System. She explains, 'I care about our kids. I care about their parents. Obviously, I am accountable also to [the School System] for the performances of the school but ... I think we're accountable to the students.' Her object referent is the type of learning she considers she accounts for. She explains:

> Yeah, okay, Band 6s are important but it's more important that they're all getting the best that they can get ... That's not just about results, is it? I mean, learning is about everything else that's happening in the school as well, all the other opportunities that the girls get to learn and to grow and get experience in a variety of things.

The referents that Charmaine reveal influences her intentions directly. She reports that as a leader of learning, it is important to articulate a vision for learning, to work closely with teachers in their professional learning and to maintain broad pedagogical learning programs that continue to engage the students. As such, Charmaine's intention is demonstrated through a longitudinal school-wide pedagogical program.

Terence's object referents are high performances in the HSC exam, whereby he explains that the results from the NAPLAN, HSC and Religion Test are the measure and 'that's the measure and we need to perform in that regard.' At the same time, his social referents are his teaching staff, whereby he needs to persuade them to aim for high percentages for student results and the students are, in one sense, another social referent group: 'I never bulldozed. Or maybe I do sometimes. But the times are tough when you have to ... I said to them I want to know what the targets are we are aiming for, and this was the whole diatribe that came back ....' Terence's two referent groups determine his intentions.

Ajzen's well-tested theory recognises that intention precedes behaviours (Ajzen & Fishbein, 1980). The perceptions of Charmaine and Terence, regarding their referents, influence their intentions. As with Ajzen's factor, *attitude*, the more favourable the referent, the stronger is the principal's intention to enact this in their ways of leading.

Ajzen's third determinant of intention is *perceived behavioural control*. Perceived behavioural control refers to the individual's perceived ease or difficulty of performing the behaviour and is assumed to reflect past experiences as well as anticipated challenges (Ajzen, 2012). As influencing behaviour indirectly, through intention, perceived behavioural control has been shown to have a direct effect on behaviour (Ajzen & Madden, 1986). Larry is employed as the case example because of his explicit explanations of his intentions and reasons for his ways of leading learning through his educational accountability. Larry reveals that his past career trajectory was formed through pastoral and well-being pathways in middle and senior leadership experiences. In his mind these experiences have not prepared him adequately for the principal's role, which hold expectations of being a leader of teaching and learning. Perceived behavioural control is most compatible with Bandura's (1977) concept of perceived self-efficacy, which concerns judgements of how well an individual can execute courses of action required to deal with future situations (Bandura, 2006). In Larry's case, his interpretations of the accountability expectations appear to lack clarity. He seems unsure of his object referent: 'I mean I think growth, yeah, look, to me it's more—yeah, learning growth is probably the most important—is the most important thing ... but I suppose to me, that should include being above the state average. Can I say that?' Lacking clarity in his own mind influences the ways he believes he could lead learning. He reports that he does not know the ways to influence teaching and learning processes because he explains that it was not a strength area in his formation:

> Primarily my role is to work with the staff to lift their learning and teaching practices to help facilitate the students on learning ... my focus is around leading that learning and that requires of me to be competent enough to be able to help facilitate that ... a lot of my formation in terms of leadership was around change and not so much about learning and teaching ... I'm not the expert in learning and teaching and probably never will be.

At this point, it is reasonable to predict, to a degree, some possibilities in Larry's direct course of action. First, it is *unlikely* that Larry would make claims of his knowledge and skill in learning and teaching with his staff and it is *likely* that he would engage others' help or not act at all.

Larry's leadership practices are to devolve the tasks to others: 'to me it's about facilitating that discussion and trying to make sure that the learning and teaching coordinator or where we're going in the learning and teaching team or as a leadership executive—that it's facilitated through the staff and led through the staff ... we have a really good teaching and learning director here.'

CREDIBILITY, PERSUASION AND COHERENCE

Following this, Larry introduces a qualifier: 'one day I would like to see myself as a facilitator of learning.' Larry's case example demonstrates how his lowered levels of self-efficacy about his knowledge of teaching and learning formed his intention of allowing others to lead learning and this intention is realised when others engage in a lead role in the leadership of teaching and learning.

As with the determinants of *attitude* and the *subjective norm*, the determinant of *perceived behavioural control* exposes the relationship between Principals' understandings of accountability (favourable outcome evaluations and social referents and self-efficacy), with this determining their intentions. As with Ajzen's hypothesis, these intentions influence their leadership practices. The "more favourable the attitude and the subjective norm with regard to a behavior and the greater the perceived behavioural control, the stronger should be an individual's intention to perform the behavior under consideration" (Ajzen, 1991, p. 189). Through the demonstrations of these Principals, all three predictors make independent contributions to understanding the Principals' leadership practices in an educational accountability context (Ajzen, 1991; Ajzen & Madden, 1986).

The application of the TPB, using the five case examples, demonstrates that when being held to account for students' performances through external testing, school leaders prioritise their referents, evaluate the outcome of certain behaviours and make judgements about their self-efficacy in being able to lead learning. These priorities determined their intentions and behaviours, as shown in the summary in Table 14.

A key finding in my study (Norris, 2017) is that the Principals reject that a single number could be an adequate measure of learning. Their rejection originates from their beliefs about learning, student expectations and the way the measures are employed to rank schools and judge their competency as a principal. Other studies have also found that school leaders object to performance results being used for ranking, competition and marketing (McGuire, 2012; Stobart, 2008), for judging their professional competency (Perryman, 2009) and the types of instruments used for assessment (often termed blunt) (Goldschmidt et al., 2005; Perryman, 2007). The Principals make sense through framing their accountability expectations in ways that align with these beliefs, reporting the importance of responsibility, personalising and acceptance. They desire a more meaningful relationship to the accountability expectations. Similar to Darling-Hammond's (2010a) and Koyama's (2014) conceptualisation of accountability, they imagine a reciprocity and a creative integration of external and internal relationships. Arriving at this internal agreement is clearly a complex sensemaking event for these Principals and under similar conditions could be likely for other school leaders.

TABLE 14   Application of the TPB to case examples

Determinant	Description	Example findings
Attitude	The degree to which the Principal has a favourable or unfavourable evaluation or appraisal of the behaviour in question	Leonie unfavourably evaluated the loss of staff as being due to loss of enrolments, which resulted from poor student results in external testing. Her evaluation of outcomes formed her intention to improve the students' results
Subjective norm	Ajzen (2012) suggests that often, the social pressure is individuals or social referents. In this study an internal pressure by Principals to perform or not perform a behaviour was the priority that the Principals gave to the object referents	Charmaine's social referents were identified as the parents and students, with her object referents identified as authentic learning. These referents determined her intentions of ensuring that students' results in external testing was low priority
Perceived behavioural control	Principals perceived ease or difficulty of performing a behaviour, assumed to reflect past experiences as well as anticipated challenges (Ajzen, 2012)	Larry predicted it would be difficult to lead learning and account for this, given his previous leadership experiences

Consistent with the empirical findings that school leaders do not adopt policy as policy makers would intend (Spillane, Reiser, et al., 2002), the Principals do not adopt the expectations of their school systems. They prioritise the focus of their accountability environments (Obstfeld et al., 2005; Spillane & Anderson, 2014), constraining certain stimuli which is explained as a sensemaking process. In this discussion, the application of Weick's sense-making properties illuminates reasons for Principals' choices in what they adopt and do not adopt regarding accountability expectations.

Orating their mantras provides sensegiving to their communities (Gioia & Chittipeddi, 1991; Weick, 1995). This exploration offers a different perspective

CREDIBILITY, PERSUASION AND COHERENCE

in Australian school leadership, with the examples from the Principals' use of metaphors and mantras employed as a coherence device for themselves and for their communities when faced with the need to implement external expectations. Similar to the findings of Carnoy et al. (2004), Elmore (2005) and Roche (2004), *building coherence* is less complicated when there are existing internal evidence systems informing the learning processes.

If school leaders are to be influential in leading through accountability demands in their teaching and learning processes, they need to be convinced about their own beliefs and knowledge and confident to enact these in their leadership. Expressions of these enactments are described through *cultivating credibility* with their communities. In the examples this includes articulating a vision (Venus, Stam, & van Knippenberg, 2013), being close and working beside teachers (Robinson, 2011); participating in the team (Hersey & Blanchard, 1988); being the cheerleader (Charmaine); and understanding their teachers' aspirations and needs (Branson, Franken, & Penney, 2015).

In complex and contradictory environments, school leaders are balancing competing priorities (Leithwood, 2005), constraining certain elements, reordering goals (Seashore Louis & Mintrop, 2012) and creatively integrating information (Thiel et al., 2012). There is a plethora of studies point to leader effectiveness in delivering student outcomes (Hattie, Masters, & Birch, 2015; Le Fevre & Robinson, 2014; Robinson et al., 2008), less so on theoretical models or frameworks demonstrating the way school leaders' sensemaking of external demands are likely to affect their agency in their sensegiving practices, such as facilitating teaching and learning processes.

In this discussion, Ajzen's TPB is applied to five case examples. The application of the examples is premised on Ajzen's assertion that an individual's intentions determine their behaviours (Ajzen, 2012). In these examples, the way school leaders make sense of their external demands considering their internal commitments determines their intentions. Ajzen's *attitude, subjective norms* and *perceived behavioural control* are analysed in how the Principals evaluate the possible outcomes of their intended actions (e.g., making decisions whether to target for results), prioritising their referents (e.g., placing a higher priority on teachers than on the school system) and making judgements about their self-efficacy (e.g., being able to lead learning considering their expectations). This analysis demonstrates the Principals' intentions, which in turn are shown in their enactments. This application of the well-respected theory has been a worthwhile exercise.

This discussion through the examples drawn from the Principals' experiences, notably the application of the TPB, highlights the importance of how school leaders' interpretations of accountability expectations, under certain conditions, can determine their intentions. Understanding a school leader's sensemaking is key to determining their intentions and their likely behaviours. My study and others (Eacott & Norris, 2014; Spillane & Lee, 2013; White, 2006) suggest that educational leaders' sensemaking of their external demands are dynamic, organic and unique to what they themselves bring to the demands, such as their professional experiences; knowledge and skill regarding learning and teaching; contextualising within their school environments; and peer and school system relationships. 'We are led not by what is but by who we are ... who we *are,* and the world as we *know* it are two aspects of the same thing' (Thayer, 1988 p. 259).

What is striking are the novel and sophisticated ways that school leaders are likely to adapt and evolve in actively making sense of external demands, and then giving sense to their school communities. These Australian Principals, in response to their accountability expectations, have much in common with the mature Australian Eucalypt, uniquely adapting and evolving their structures, as if integrating the 'weather' to become part of them.

CHAPTER 10

Sense Leaders: Ready for Any Catastrophe

The purpose of this book was to offer a theoretical model in understanding the ways school leaders may react to conflicting expectations and demands. It is a new approach and hopefully contributes to the field of school leadership by watering some of the existing plants of sensemaking (Spillane, 2014; Hasinoff & Manduzuk, 2018; Ganon-Shilon & Chen, 2019; Rom & Eyal 2019) and of sensegiving (Wong, 2019; Anderson, 2020; Eren,2020) with the TPB (Ajzen, 1991; Leavell, 2015). These 'senses' and TPB are all in relation to school leaders' complex work. The Eucalypt Leadership Model (ELM) brings together these three important theoretical premises to authenticate a way school leaders and aspirants may navigate complexities in their schools, and notably through critical events. The abilities of school leaders in their 'sense leadership' affect students, teachers, and parents. Teachers with school leaders cultivate their school communities with the fundamental purpose of student learning. All of those in the field have a role to understand and support their essential work.

This closing chapter has several aims. It extends the relationships of sensemaking, sensegiving and TPB through a hypothetical scenario, with the aim of informing future research. Table 1 from Chapter 2 is drawn upon to demonstrate this extension illustrated in Table 15. From that point the implications and recommendations for school leaders, those who guide and teach them, are presented, followed by suggestions for future research. Following these sections, the metaphor for school leaders in the Eucalyptus tree, inspired by Judith Wright's poem, closes the book.

1 Eucaus Announces Nation-Wide Testing

A national policy (fictitious) *Every Child Deserves a Future* (ECDF) in the country of Eucaus has announced a development of their nation-wide testing regime. The external performance results from the national test will align with the competencies in the Eucausian Teacher Standards. In Eucaus, the Teacher Standards are aligned with teachers' incremental pay scales. The Eucausian public narrative that follows this announcement is that teachers will now be subject to performance pay scales; these performances will now be based on students' test results, as in a numerical score. Eucaus's aim is that this initiative will encourage teachers to improve their students' test results.

© KONINKLIJKE BRILL NV, LEIDEN, 2022 | DOI:10.1163/9789004517202_010

TABLE 15   Examples of the impact of leaders' sensemaking on sensegiving practices

Sensemaking (Weick)	Element 1: Making sense		Theory planned behaviour	Element 2: (Maitlis & Lawrence, 2007)	Giving sense
Properties	*Sub-processes*	*Hypothetical example: Eucaus*	*Attitude, norms, and control*	*Sub-processes*	*Hypothetical example: Eucaus*
Social context—' social anchors'; Plausibility Retrospect Enactment	Contextualising expectations	High parental expectations for high performance results Effects on enrolments Effects on teacher pay scales Teacher receptivity	Subjective norms	Composing persuasive accounts	Capacity to influence teachers through perspective taking, educates and tells good news to parents; possibly through declarations and at time testing the waters
Ongoing projects	Constraining expectations	Higher priority given to parental expectations over policy expectations	Attitude	Facilitating teaching and learning systems	Capacity to set clear and collective internal learning goals; to articulate a vision and implement a school-wide pedagogy
Salient cues Personal identity	Framing expectations	Capacity to evaluate policy expectations and options, considering parental constraints and enrolments; evaluates their own capacity to act	Attitude Perceived behavioural control	Creating coherence	May employ selected parts of the expectations, as an agency for change These actions are dependent on educational leaders' self-efficacy judgements

We follow how two educational leaders (*Leader 1* and *Leader 2*) enact these expectations in quite different ways, even though they perceive their school environmental factors in similar ways. *Leader 1* and *Leader 2* each place constraints and frames around the ECDF initiative in different ways, which leads the reader to predict their likely sensegiving acts (see Table 15).

Leader 1 has tight constraints about the way the policy can influence their current teaching teams and frames the ECDF as an imposition, an unwelcome nuisance lacking transparency, used to close underperforming schools. *Leader 1* has feelings of anger and bitterness that education has been reduced to these measures of learning. *Leader 1* uses the metaphor of the tightrope walker trying to cross between one building (ECDF) and another (their school goals). 'Walking this tightrope' is a fearful experience for *Leader 1* because their employment is at stake, creating insecurity and fear. Knowing these emotions will be difficult to manage for themselves, *Leader 1* recognises that they will need to persuade and mobilise teachers to implement a learning design that will ensure acceptable performance results. Many educators, like *Leader 1*, in rural regions of Eucaus are promoted to leadership positions in their beginning years as a teacher. *Leader 1* has an enormous amount of leadership experience but only two years as a classroom teacher. Although *Leader 1* believes that schooling is the pathway for a student's future, they do not agree that all learning should be focused on the numerical score from external tests.

It is reasonable to predict that *Leader 1* will find designing and implementing learning and teaching structures and processes to accommodate the ECDF a challenge. One challenge that *Leader 1* needs to overcome is their level of self-efficacy, which is likely to be low to middling, during the design and implementation phases. *Leader 1* may delegate the task to others for implementation, thereby risking its success, given that *Leader 1* is not involved or close to the learning and teaching processes (Linda Bendikson et al., 2012). Or on the other hand *Leader 1* may situate the design of learning and teaching processes squarely with the ECDF expectations in targeted performance score goal setting. Hence trying to create coherent performative cultures, at the same time easing the tensions for teachers because performances are what they will be judged upon, may be a sound sensegiving pathway. However, it is unlikely that *Leader 1* can integrate, with ease, the ECDF expectations into the existing arrangements.

Leader 2 seeks to understand the ECDF initiative and what it can offer their school. *Leader 2* frames the new Eucaus ECDF as an opportunity to enable teachers to work towards the standards. *Leader 2* situates their leadership in the centre of the learning and teaching processes. Unlike *Leader 1*, there is no sense of fear regarding the new ECDF policy. They explain their leadership as a bricoleur (Koyama, 2013), whereby they make sense by pulling threads from the ECDF, their school environment, the shared language of learning and the needs of teachers who want to succeed. *Leader 2*'s previous leadership experiences prepared them for this well and they feel a high level of self-efficacy in mobilising their teaching teams. They believe that while data have their place in the learning processes, they should not drive the process; effective learning is related to effective teaching, and influencing teaching is *Leader 2*'s essential purpose. *Leader 2* believes that learning is not an end point but one that should be enjoyed in the present as diverse offerings to students. *Leader 2* perceives and supports that the teachers reject the idea that learning can be measured by a single number and are disappointed that results will be tied to pay scales. However, this is accepted for what it is, and their collective common purpose is not swayed; simply a mild disappointment, yet not influencing their current ways of working.

Given Leader 2's high levels of self-efficacy in influencing their teaching teams and their views about the possibilities that the ECDF policy offers teachers, it is likely that Leader 2's sensemaking will provide a strong and positive base for their sensegiving acts with adapting the ECDF expectations smoothly into the school and add value to their current processes. One reasonable prediction is that *Leader 2* will work with the Eucausian Teacher Standards with a formative rather than a summative focus. *Leader 2* is likely to be clear about their expectations with teachers about how they are positioning the ECDF expectations. Performance results will continue to be used as one form of data to inform the teaching and learning processes. Teachers will have begun to identify ways to hold themselves accountable for their learning goals and at the same time, ensure that performance results reflect these learning goals.

The two leaders' sensemaking and sensegiving showed similar contextual conditions (same policy and similar school environmental factors). Knowing these school leaders' experiences and views about learning and their likely levels of self-efficacy in their sensegiving leadership practices, demonstrate that we can explain leaders' interpretations and reasonably predict the ways they may enact these interpretations.

2 The Theoretical ELM in Situ

In Australia, the principal, or their delegate, is the key agent for external policy implementation in schools. This next section explains how the theoretical ELM clarifies in general school leaders' ways of managing and leading with demands set by external bodies. The theoretical ELM comprises six sub-processes:

(a) Contextualising Expectations; (b) Constraining Expectations; (c) Framing Expectations; (d) Composing Persuasive Accounts; (e) Facilitating Teaching and Learning Systems; and (f) Creating Cultures of Coherence. The theoretical ELM illustrates the relationship between Making Sense and Giving Sense. This relationship contributes to the core of this book in an important way. School leaders' conceptualisations of learning influence the ways they make sense of their educational accountability. These beliefs are mirrored in the Principals experiences where they reject the idea that learning can be adequately measured by a single number. According to these Principals, learning is more than a student's result in a test. It was a belief that learning should be measured and accounted for with a more effective mechanism than their current external testing mechanism. Part of these beliefs about learning and measurement appear to be influenced by a resistance to an economic rationalist perspective that learning is assessed only through a quantitative measure. In turn, this belief is often reinforced by peer principal relationships and their school leader networks. Possibly to a lesser extent, yet notably influential in a school leader's sensemaking, is their self-belief in their agency of mobilising their teaching teams. This confidence is dependent upon being able to integrate the external expectations within their own internal learning processes in their schools. Yet to complete the integration the school leader is dependent their capabilities to persuade and gain credibility with their teachers. School leaders gaining credibility with teachers while multi-faceted, is not surprising. 'Creds' (Leonie) come with effective pedagogical practices as a baseline. The more the Principals articulated the importance of their knowledge base and skill about teaching and learning processes in the context of accountability, the less they reported their external expectations negatively. Indicators of their sensemaking and sensegiving and their levels of ease or dis-ease with their expectations were found to be manifested in their metaphors, narratives, and mantras.

When external demands place school leaders in turmoil they are likely to engage in sensemaking. Understandably their sensemaking would involve *Contextualising*, *Constraining* and *Framing* the demands. For example in accountability environments school leaders would contextualise their expectations by 'taking notice of' (Weick, 1995) particular factors in their school environments, such as student demographics; competition for enrolments; teachers' receptivity; and parental expectations. The way a school leader contextualises their environment has some influence on their professional practices; however, their beliefs about learning and their self-beliefs in their capability to enact some level of persuasion with teaching teams is likely to have a greater influence. School leaders' priorities, which they may attribute to their object and social referents in an accountability example, align with Ajzen's (Ajzen, 2012) determinant of attitude. Congruent with several of Weick's sensemaking properties school leaders in their prioritising, would likely place constraints on for what and to whom they account regarding their expectations. Hence, school leaders' intentions would materialise because of their accountability constraints. They are likely to constrain school system expectations and privilege their accountability to parents, students, and themselves. These intentions (from their contextualising and constraining) are likely influenced by their beliefs about the representations of learning, such as students' enjoyment of learning in the present moment, the importance of diverse learning experiences and the skills and knowledge directed at post-school pathways.

School leaders when faced with complex demands are likely to make sense of their expectations through framing these into schemas. In the case of accountability as defined in this book the frames may include accepting, personalising, and conceptualising accountability for accountability as a responsibility and as an agency for action. I reason, like the Principals, that school leaders' frames could be influenced by their previous professional experiences, career trajectory, professional learning, and ways they understand the nature and meaning of teaching and learning.

When external demands impact on school communities, school leaders need to help their community understand and support them about what may be happening. Helping the community understand by school leaders is theorised as a sensegiving process. Some examples of sensegiving processes could be Composing persuasive accounts, Facilitating teaching, and learning systems and Creating coherence. School leaders are likely to describe their professional practices regarding meeting their external demands through the designs of their teaching and learning structures and processes. School leaders, like the Principals, who report a sense of confidence in being able to meet the accountability expectations (in whatever form) would be likely to report that they integrate their expectations into existing internal processes seamlessly and effortlessly. In turn, these school leaders may also report the importance of remaining up to date with contemporary teaching processes and hold close working relationships with their teachers, focused on learning. In contrast, school leaders, like the Principals who report negative implications from their accountability expectations may be silent about their teaching and learning processes in the school. Instead, these leaders may pursue improvement in student performance through target setting for grades or performances in the external tests.

School leaders' metaphors, narratives and mantras reveal some of the ways they may communicate to Create coherence. Metaphors in accountability environments, as expressed by the Principals could include 'buffer,' 'shield,' 'lantern,' 'cheerleader,' 'salesman,' and narratives and mantras composing plausible accounts such as perspective taking and balancing, and mantras such as 'we can all be aspirational,' 'just one more mark' and 'we need to tell the good news story.' Metaphors appear to be powerful platforms for sensemaking.

The ELM addresses an important purpose in how school leaders' sensemaking affects their sensegiving leadership practices. For example, the Principals' beliefs about learning influenced the ways they interpreted (making sense of) their expectations and their capability and confidence of integrating these expectations in their practices (giving sense to), in their existing teaching and learning structures and processes in their schools.

3   Contributing to Further Research

This book proposes the theoretical ELM, which explains the interpretive, adaptive, and enactive processes of school leaders' interpretations and enactments of external demands, accountability. The ELM demonstrates a particular lens to explain how and why school leaders may make sense of external demands in the way that they do.

This ELM proposes some reasons in how and why school leaders may make sense of external demands the way they do and notably, their likely intentions and sensegiving practices. In Australia, some theoretical models and frameworks offer explanations of how the individual educator may negotiate moral dilemmas in their leadership (Bezzina & Tuana, 2014) or map the various domains that face leaders (Burford, 2015). Using such a model in this way has the potential to make a fresh contribution. A few educational leadership studies have employed other theories to guide their investigations. In this study, Weick's (1995) sensemaking properties and associated frameworks (Thiel et al., 2012), Maitlis's and Lawrence's (2007) guidance in developing sensegiving constructs and Ajzen's (2012) Theory of Planned Behaviour support the theoretical components of the ELM. Applying these well-recognised and applied frameworks, theoretical and some empirical underpinnings (Maitlis & Lawrence, 2007) also offers other ways of contributing to school leadership research in Australia.

Internationally, the ELM makes a theoretical contribution to school leadership research. Situating the theoretical categories within the extant literature demonstrates that school leaders' sensemaking of their expectations with their sensegiving practices mirror many of the findings from studies in other international educational jurisdictions (Firestone & Shipps, 2005; Shipps, 2012; Spillane, Diamond, et al., 2002). This ELM extends these studies with elements of school leaders' interpretations and how these may influence their professional practices. The way each Principal conceptualised learning and their levels of self-efficacy in their knowledge base of learning and teaching processes are the key influences on being 'their best at leading' while meeting their external demands. Therefore, a contribution of the study is the acknowledgment of the likely influence of school leaders' knowledge base and skill of the nature and meaning of teaching and learning on their sensemaking and sensegiving.

Examples from the Principals indicate that beliefs about teaching and learning are also linked with their self-beliefs in being able to mobilise teaching teams. A school leader's level of self-efficacy in mobilising is likely to be influenced by their self-beliefs in their knowledge base and skill in the teaching and learning processes. The focus on school leaders' levels of self-efficacy in their agency in mobilising teachers' practices is worthy of further research. Cultivating credibility with teaching teams is a key leadership task and also worthy of research pursuits.

However, I contend that theoretically, the sensegiving processes for school leaders' offer the most important and rich area of research. The application of a school leaders' sensemaking through their sensegiving phases offers an authentic approach for school leaders in relationship with their teaching teams, students, and parents. If a school leader engaged in the four phases of sensegiving, real collaboration would occur with the power of genuine and co-created outcomes. The phases are a blueprint for successful school leadership if the leader would dare.

Overall, here is a well-supported theoretical model to explain school leaders' sensemaking processes, their likely intentions from this sensemaking (given certain conditions) and knowing these intentions their likely sensegiving practices in response to external demands, or any complex critical event.

4   Implications and Recommendations

The theoretical ELM has potential implications for school leaders and aspirants, policy makers, system leaders and tertiary educators. These referents form the structure below, in which the implications are raised along with recommendations for future research.

4.1   *For Principals*
With school systems increasingly expecting principals to be 'leaders of learning' within the context of a broader performative culture, it is important to know more about how principals' levels of self-efficacy regarding their knowledge

base and skill of teaching processes influences their capabilities in their professional practices. Given the benefits of examples of successful sensegiving practices of the external expectations with a school's processes, it is important to understand what conditions make in-school learning systems agile, yet stable in meeting diverse external expectations. Narratives, metaphors, and mantras are powerful sensemaking and sensegiving devices, respectively, for principals. Metaphors appear to provide some sense of professional identity for the principals themselves, as well as acting as leverage for influence and persuasion regarding internal and external expectations. Future research could investigate the influence and agency of sensemaking and sensegiving devices, such as metaphors, narratives, and mantras on principals' work. The impact of peer principal relationships of comparison and competition is another research area that could lead to understandings, in relation to the level of effect these relationships have in helping principals develop their professional identities.

4.2   *For School Leaders and Aspirant Leaders*

Regarding school leaders and aspirant leaders, the ELM, provides some sway about which career pathways in the secondary school sector could either support or hinder their leadership trajectory. It is important for those in middle-level leadership positions having opportunities in their leadership practices to focus on teaching and learning processes and remaining contemporary in their knowledge base and skill of contemporary teaching and learning processes. Building knowledge in this area cultivates a leaders' credibility with teachers and thus an increased capability in their leaderships skills to work in an 'influence relationship' with teaching teams. Knowing the characteristics of 'leading learning' or being a 'leader of learning' is an important continued area of research. For example, the Principals and other studies reveal some important factors in 'leading learning': being able to articulate a vision for learning and knowing that a shared vision improves collective work (Howard, O'Brien, Kay, & O'Rourke, 2019); being closely engaged in the teaching and learning processes (Robinson et al., 2008), such as being involved in professional learning and identifying with teachers' needs and aspirations needs and the teaching profession. The latest work of Thessin (2020) has extended Robinson's (2011, 2012) previous works, redefining the notion of instructional leadership in performative cultures; privileging coaching, modelling and facilitating teaching processes. These studies point to the research potential in understanding explicitly what is purposeful for school leaders in their formation, notably around leading learning, and becoming 'principal-ready,' equipped to deal contradictory and high velocity events.

4.3 *For Policy Makers and School System Leaders*

In terms of policy makers, this ELM has implications for school system leaders and those delegated to govern and employ. The first implication, confirming other international studies (Shipps, 2012; Spillane, Diamond, et al., 2002), is that principals do not enact policies as the makers of those policies expect. This ELM provides some understandings as to why educational leaders may not enact policy, which ultimately is problematic for system leaders. The Principals and elsewhere (Knapp & Feldman, 2012) are likely to enact policy expectations as makers intend if they understand them, if the policies align with their professional beliefs (Shipps & White, 2009), and if the educational leader has confidence in their abilities to enact it. For example, this involved the Principals' agreements around their conceptualisations of learning and their own capabilities in the teaching and learning processes.

The implication is that a school leader's integration of policy is not only dependent on beliefs but on their confidence in knowing how to integrate policy expectations into their existing school structures and processes. While this confidence is likely to be influenced by their levels of understanding of policy it is more by their perceived capacity to integrate expectations with their internal processes. This integration requires school leaders to have established credibility with their teaching teams, for any likelihood of mobilising. The implication for system leaders is that some school leaders may not be able to integrate the expectations and/or not perceive they can mobilise the teaching teams. Professional learning and attention to recruitment processes would need to be a consideration if these deficits were apparent.

School leaders not enacting policies as intended points to the importance of understanding the reasons for the disparity. It is likely that school leaders' conceptualisations of learning are central to their sensemaking along with whom they think they are accountable to (referents). It may be productive for school system leaders, peer leader networks and associations if they engage in reflective and reflexive processes to understand their reasons. Knowing more fully school leaders' conceptualisations about learning and the priorities they give, for example, to certain accountability relationships over others are avenues to enable such understandings. The Principals' conceptualisation of learning was more than a numerical score. This conceptualisation was misaligned with their public and market accountability where learning was quantified and reduced to a number form.

The relationships of accountability for principals are diverse, including the school system's consultant, the market, the parents and students and teachers and with other principals. It may be helpful for school system leaders and indeed principals' themselves to understand that their conceptualisations of learnings and the priorities they give to certain referents can be a sound platform to inform their professional learning experiences and programs.

4.4 *School Leaders' Professional Learning Programs*

The preparation of professional learning programs is an essential consideration in tailoring to increasing demands and external pressures for school leaders. Demands and pressures will not go away albeit disguised in other masquerades. The following section examines the preparation of professional learning programs. The examination of such preparations is not limited to policy makers and school system leaders but also for those who design leadership programs in tertiary institutions and professional learning associations.

Performative cultures along with volatile conditions are becoming common characteristics in schools and school systems. As such professional learning programs need to be designed in such a way to support school leaders and aspirant leaders in such cultures (Edwards-Groves & Kemmis, 2016; Lambert, Wright, Currie, & Pascoe, 2016). Current professional learning experiences for schools utilising data to inform practice are diverse and substantial, notably the analysis and the approaches with teachers in such implementation. Guides and support in professional practices for principals are helpful for managing accountability expectations including the AITSL Principal Standard for 'Manages High Standards and Accountability' and the leading learning streams in post graduate tertiary programs. Existing programs in Australia such as the DeCourcy modules, RAP analysis and the utilisations of the Principals' Profiles are some of the ways school leaders may learn to make sense of and give sense to their challenges. The Principals reported they engaged in such programs however they also indicated that more specificity was required to enable them to develop a greater internal locus of control through their narrated sensemaking and sensegiving processes to manage their external demands.

The growing empirical evidence (Brookhart & Moss, 2013) suggests that the more school leaders involve themselves in the teaching processes the better they can fulfil their role function of 'leading learning.' This involvement is likely to increase their confidence in their influence with their teaching teams. Hence preparation programs need to find designs or even reasons which enable school leaders to be involved in learning and teaching processes in schools, especially larger schools with complex organisational structures. Action research projects focussed on learning, leader observations with reflection and structured professional learning where senior school leaders engage with teachers and students in their teaching, enacting contemporary characteristics of the instructional leader, are recommended (Instructional Leader: Coaching and Modelling, Thessin & Louis, 2019). These experiences however are not enough.

School leaders need reflective and reflexive strategies to continually make sense of such experiences so that their sensemaking becomes internal and personalised. Engaging in such strategies takes time and sensemaking of not focussing on interrupting conditions (Weick, 1995). Those Principals who demonstrated sophisticated and adaptable ways to manage and lead through their accountabilities also engaged in deeper reflection techniques. The metaphors are demonstrable signs of such techniques.

School leaders' schemas which frame external demands in a way that acts as a generative force are likely to hold liberating conceptualisations of the demand. For example, conceptualising accountability by personalising and accepting it, viewing accountability as a responsibility and accountability as an agency. Such frames strengthen a school leader's internal loci of control which potentially minimises the destabilising agent resulting from external demands. To enable a demanding challenge to be a generative force then it makes sense if school leaders' have time and cognitive space to frame it, such as internalising and personalising it. Professional standards serve a purpose but could be expanded to include other explicit areas. For example, the Australian Principal Standard of Professional Practices—'Manages High Standards and Accountability' identifies what needs to be accountable, however the practice could describe how such management may occur and importantly what kind of capabilities is required of school leaders. It is essential for school leaders to develop capabilities to engage and nurture their internal loci of control, in the face of increasing demands along with the event of high velocity episodes.

To develop such capabilities school leaders could explore their own frames of accountability, or in broader terms their schemata for external demands. One reflective and possibly reflexive strategy to trigger such framing is the utility of metaphors, narratives, or mantras. Given metaphors and symbols are used in psychotherapy (Grove & Panzer, 1989), a similar process could be employed for school leaders' professional learning programs which provide structure and creative guidance, time, and safety for school leaders to explore their metaphors and their narratives that hold meaning in managing challenging conditions.

Looking forward, the sophisticated sensemaking strategies that the Principals employed signal the need for particular preparation in professional learning program offerings for principals, school leaders and aspirant school leaders. Programs need to provide space, time, and simulations for reflection. There is opportunity for professional learning to help school leaders understand how they make sense of any external demands and how this sensemaking impacts on their sensegiving practices. The sensemaking strategies reflect psycho-social processes; individual and internal constructs and social constructs which are likely developed with other peer leaders and social referents in their communities. As such the nature of professional learning programs could offer reflexive strategies to guide leaders to understand how the self makes sense of external demands and to ensure that they do this within a context of a com-munity of learners, their peers or with their school communities.

5   Researching into the Future

The ELM provides a lens for school leaders to evaluate their levels of self-efficacy about their knowledge base and skill in teaching and their commitment to remain up to date in understanding teaching and learning processes. Continued research about what is purposeful for school leaders in their formation particu-larly how their knowledge of teaching and learning needs to be embedded in their sensegiving practices will be important in a world that now is even more unpredictable post COVID-19. Aspirant leaders need nuanced preparation, so they are 'leader-ready' for meeting the demands of external policy expectations or unexpected events. Judith Wright's imagery of the Eucalypt provides a seed for preparing a leader's way of being: 'pivoting,' being 'whip-supple' with 'flesh close to the bone,' so 'she follows a delicate bent of her own' (p. 335).

This ELM proposes that when strong internal evidence systems are effec-tive, school leaders are also likely to be effective in integrating external expec-tations within their current school learning routines, structures, and processes. Further to this proposition, what these strong evidence systems look like and how they are constructed in current educational jurisdictions in Australia are also worthy of further investigation.

Understanding how principals form their professional identities in their environments will assist school leaders, especially early career leaders. Further research about metaphors and the influences of peer leader relationships on leaders' identities will assist richer understandings about leaders' emerging professional identities and those who support them. Fourth, there is no guaran-tee for policy makers that school leaders will implement policies as intended, which suggests that an extension of this research in Australia would be helpful. Australia often follows global trends. Hence national external policy expecta-tions are likely to increase. Investigating further school leaders' needs, motiva-tions and attitudes has merit.

6   A Metaphor for School Leaders' Sensemaking and Sensegiving

The Principals demonstrated a sense of being grounded, resilient and most of all adapting and evolving in themselves as leaders. Seeking an overall metaphor to describe such adaptations by school leaders I have drawn on the wondrous nature of the Australian Eucalypt, the pauciflora. Eucalyptus pauciflora, "*pauci*," meaning 'few' and "*florus*" meaning 'flowered,' commonly known as the snow gum, cabbage gum or white sally, is a species of tree or mallee. It has smooth bark, lance-shaped to elliptical leaves, flower buds in clusters of between seven and fifteen, white flowers and cup-shaped, conical, or hemispherical fruits found primarily in the Snowy Mountains, right along the tablelands in southern New South Wales through Victoria to Tasmania. It can be found in Canberra along the original grassy plains. The pauciflora is chosen as it is symbiotic of the Australian school leader: long-lived with gradual growth; taking a while to establish but begins to grow quicker after the first few years; has a fibrous root system connecting with other species; transplants easily; can withstand snow and ice; prospers in well-drained soil and; able to grow in diverse areas from shallow rocky soils in very exposed dry areas to wet snowy areas on high ridge tops (Maurice, 2003).

The Eucalyptus is eloquently described by our Australian poet Judith Wright:

> She, on the other hand follows a delicate bent of her own. Worn by such aeons, dried by such winds, she has learned to be flexible, spare, flesh close to the bone ... (Excerpt from *The Eucalypt and the National Character*, Wright, 2016, p. 362)

The Eucalyptus learns. Learns to follow 'a delicate bent of her own'; learns to be 'flexible' and 'spare' with her 'flesh close to the bone.' The imagery in this poem 'delicate bent of their own' is captured in the individualistic photographic image in Figure 19. The imagery and photo aim to draw parallels with the Principals unique actions and the nuances of their individual ways of being which are affected by external policy expectations. At times, the Principals' experiences imply they are like 'flesh to the bone': 'How fair is that when you are compared with schools who cherry-pick their students ...?' (Barry) and other times the experiences suggest they are 'flexible' and demonstrated a 'delicate bent' of their own: 'You just have to accept it I guess, it's just part of the landscape now ... and always will be ... but you need to use it ... actually I welcome accountability really ...' (Sammy Savvy). Sammy's excerpt demonstrates his learning of 'bending' by accepting the performative landscape and declaring his interacting position with the environmental conditions of that landscape ('I welcome accountability really'). Given the opportunity to explain their perspectives, the

FIGURE 19   Snow gums, snowy mountains, Australia (contributor David Bigwood, Alamy, https://www.alamy.com/search/imageresults.aspx?imgt=0&qt=Snow+gums+david, used with permission)

Principals make insightful contributions about their experiences of accountability. Their insights are the underlying suppositions guiding this book.

7   Closing Remarks

The theoretical ELM is limited in the contexts in which it can explain and offer the likely understandings and behaviours about school leaders' views and enactments of external demands. Hence, when interpreting the theoretical components, readers may wish to consider their own contexts and ask what aligns. There is no assumption that this ELM is reflective of school leaders' experiences in other cultures, school systems or school sectors. However, the ELM has the useful capacity to focus attention on school leaders' possible sensemaking of any external demand, turbulence, uncertainty, and the importance of then engaging in the phases of sensegiving.

In terms of educational accountability, given Principals' beliefs about learning, it is important to identify the importance of being grounded collectively as a school staff. To weather the storms and give sense to the school community school leaders would be best to invest in establishing and embedding internal learning goals, including their own accountable learning processes. The ELM may offer guidance to aspirant leaders in their professional career pathways; that is, remaining 'fresh' in the core work of schools—learning and teaching. In terms of developing the 'self' as a leader, aspirant leaders may realise the opportunities that metaphors, narratives, and mantras may offer in creating coherence into their sensegiving leadership practices, for themselves and for their communities.

Elmore's comments in 2005 still provide insight to the phenomenon experienced by school leaders today:

> ... schools [school leaders] are always accountable, regardless of the policies under which they operate ... Policies, however, do not determine whether schools [school leaders] are accountable ... all schools [school leaders with teachers] operate with implicit or explicit action theories that determine to *whom*, *for what*, and *how* they are accountable .... (Elmore, 2005, p. 135; emphasis added)

Elmore's point about action theories aligns with the Principals' use of metaphors. The use of the metaphor has been a consistent theme in my study with Principals using the metaphor as an effective sensemaking device and the mantras and narratives as sensegiving acts. As a co-collaborator with these Principals (Corbin & Strauss, 2008), I adopted a metaphor, the Eucalyptus. Like the thriving Eucalyptus, ideally the school leader will be 'ready' and seize those elements in their external environments which not only can be readily adapted but can enhance their own ecological school system (Branson & Marra, 2020). The poem by Judith Wright metaphorically aligns our Australian character with the Eucalyptus:

> Ready for any catastrophe, every extreme, she leaves herself plenty of margin. Nothing is stiff, symmetrical, indispensable. Everything bends, whip-supple, pivoting, loose with a minimal mass ... (Excerpt from *The Eucalypt and the National Character*, Wright, 2016, p. 335)

Wright's metaphor aptly captures the diverse ways that adept school leaders are 'ready for any catastrophe,' 'whip-supple' and 'pivoting' and pliable as a way of being responsive to their environments. The school leader does this to accommodate the expectations of their role within an environment of rapid, constant change, 'leaving themselves plenty of margin' where 'nothing is stiff.' The experiences of the Principals in my study reveal that their unique adaptations could be adequately described and explained as processes of Making sense and Giving sense. Specific conditions influenced their Making sense and Giving sense, such as the profile of the Principal—their experience, capabilities, world views and beliefs, the internal school commitments and to a lesser degree, the school's demographic.

The Australian school leaders' experiences presented in Chapters 6 and 7 could be school leaders anywhere. Naturally, school leaders are likely to establish rich, living dialogues with their communities, through sensemaking/giving devices such as metaphors, mantras, and narratives (Weick, 1989). These mantras can be organic, diverse, and unique, from working closely ('walk with them') to selling ('every child can get an A for effort'). Wright's poem extends the imagery and draws parallels between the Eucalyptus and the original Australians and their rich, living dialogue with this land (Gifford, 2010).

School leaders as sense leaders are 'ready for any catastrophe' (p. 335) bending, pivoting and whip supple (Wright). Like the qualities of the First Nation peoples, through their sensemaking school leaders could 'listen to the land' and what it asks of them, and in their unique ways, speak back, and in doing so, give sense to their complex and contradictory environments.

References

Aas, M., & Paulsen, J. M. (2019). National strategy for supporting school principal's instructional leadership: A Scandinavian approach. *Journal of Educational Administration, 57*(5), 540–553.

ABC News (Producer). (2020, August 24). *Independent schools told to reopen or lose funding as National Cabinet discusses coronavirus impacts on education.* https://www.abc.net.au/news/2020-04-09/independent-schools-told-to-reopen-coronavirus-funding/12138092

ACT Parliamentary Counsel. (2015). *Republication No. 12.* http://www.legislation.act.gov.au/a/2010-55/current/pdf/2010-55.pdf

Adams, J. E., & Kirst, M. W. (1999). New demands and concepts for educational accountability: Striving for results in an era of excellence. In J. Murphy & K. S. Louis (Eds.), *Handbook of research on educational administration* (2nd ed.). Jossey-Bass.

Advertiser, T. (2020). *Vic Premier grilled at hotel inquiry.* https://www.adelaidenow.com.au/news/national/daniel-andrews-doesnt-know-who-decided-on-private-security-guards/video/1c25bf26a0335848f7d918e5b00b1ca1

AIS NSW. (2020). *Empowering independent education.* https://www.aisnsw.edu.au/

AITSL Australian Institute for Teaching and School Leadership. (2016). *National professional standards for teachers.* http://www.aitsl.edu.au/

Ajzen, I. (1991). The theory of planned behavior. *Organizational Behaviour and Human Decision Processes, 50,* 179–211.

Ajzen, I. (Ed.). (2012). *The theory of planned behavior* (Vol. 1). Sage.

Ajzen, I., & Fishbein, M. (1980). *Prediction of goal-directed behavior: Attitudes, intentions, and perceived behavioral control.* Prentice-Hall.

Ajzen, I., & Madden, T. (1986). Prediction of goal-directed behavior: Attitudes, intentions, and perceived behavioral control. *Journal of Experimental Social Psychology, 22*(5), 453–474. doi:10.1016/0022-1031(86)90045-4

Allen, C. D., & Penuel, W. R. (2015). Studying teachers' sensemaking to investigate teachers' responses to professional development focused on new standards. *Journal of Teacher Education, 66*(2), 136–149.

Alvesson, M. (1996). Leadership studies: From procedure and abstraction to reflexivity and situation. *The Leadership Quarterly, 7*(4), 455–485.

Anderson, S. E., & Macri, J. R. (2009). District administrator perspectives on student learning in an era of standards and accountability: A collective frame analysis. *Canadian Journal of Education, 32*(2), 192–221.

Angus, L. (2015). School choice: Neoliberal education policy and imagined futures. *British Journal of Sociology of Education, 36*(3), 395–413.

Appel, M. (2020). Performativity and the demise of the teaching profession: The need for rebalancing in Australia. *Asia-Pacific Journal of Teacher Education, 48*(3), 301–315.

Arnold, C., Atchison, J., & McKnight, A. (2021). Reciprocal relationships with trees: Rekindling Indigenous wellbeing and identity through the Yuin ontology of one-ness. *Australian Geographer, 52*(2), 131–147. doi:10.1080/00049182.2021.1910111

Au, W. (2009). *Unequal by design: High-stakes testing and the standardization if Inequality.* Routledge.

Australian Catholic University. (2017). *Masters of educational leadership.* http://handbook.acu.edu.au/handbooks/handbook_2017/faculty_of_education_and_arts/approved_course_campus_offerings/national_school_of_education/postgraduate_courses/master_of_educational_leadership

Australian Curriculum Assessment and Reporting Authority. (2009). *My school and beyond.* http://www.acara.edu.au/acara_update_14122009.html

Australian Curriculum Assessment and Reporting Authority. (2013). *My school.* http://www.myschool.edu.au/

Australian Curriculum Assessment and Reporting Authority. (2016). *My school.* http://www.myschool.edu.au/

Australian Curriculum Assessment and Reporting Authority. (2020). *My school.* https://www.myschool.edu.au/

Australian Government. (2018a). *The Australian student wellbeing framework.* https://www.education.gov.au/national-safe-schools-framework-0

Australian Government. (2018b). *Through growth to achievement.* https://docs.education.gov.au/system/files/doc/other/662684_tgta_accessible_final_0.pdf

Australian Government Department of Education, Skills and Employment. (2018). *The Australian student wellbeing framework.* https://www.education.gov.au/national-safe-schools-framework-0

Australian Government Department of Education and Training. (2014). *Building education revolution.* https://docs.education.gov.au/category/deewr-program/building-education-revolution

Australian Government National Parks. (2009). *Eucalypts for cold climates. Canberra.* https://www.cpbr.gov.au/gnp/eucalypts-cold-climates.html

Australian Institute for Teaching and School Leadership (AITSL). (2016). *Australian professional standard for principals.* http://www.aitsl.edu.au/australian-professional-standard-for-principals

Australian Institute for Teaching and School Leadership (AITSL). (2017). *Australian professional standard for principals 360 degree reflection tool.* https://www.aitsl.edu.au/australian-professional-standard-for-principals/360-reflection-tool

REFERENCES

Ayres, P., Sawyer, W., & Dinham, S. (2001, April). *Effective teaching and student independence at grade 12* [Paper]. Annual meeting of the American Educational Research Association, Seattle. https://eric.ed.gov/?id=ED453189

Ayres, P., Sawyer, W., & Dinham, S. (2004). Effective teaching in the context of a grade 12 high-stakes external examination in New South Wales, Australia. *British Educational Research Journal, 30*(1), 141–165.

Bagdasarov, Z., Johnson, J. F., MacDougall, A. E., Steele, L. M., Connelly, S., & Mumford, M. D. (2015). Mental models and ethical decision making: The mediating role of sensemaking. *Journal of Business Ethics*, 1–12.

Bagwell, J. (2020). Leading through a pandemic: Adaptive leadership and purposeful action. *Journal of School Administration Research and Development, 5*(S1), 30–34.

Ball, S. J. (2003). The teacher's soul and the terrors of performativity. *Journal of Education Policy, 18*(2), 215–228.

Ball, S. J. (2016). Subjectivity as a site of struggle: Refusing neoliberalism? *British Journal of Sociology of Education, 37*(8), 1129–1146. doi:10.1080/01425692.2015.1044072

Ball, S. J., Maguire, M., & Braun, A. (2012). *How schools do policy: Policy enactments in secondary schools*. Routledge.

Ball, S. J., Maguire, M., Braun, A., & Hoskins, K. (2011). Policy actors: Doing policy work in schools. *Discourse: Studies in the Cultural Politics of Education, 32*(4), 625–639.

Balogun, J., Jacobs, C., Jarzabkowski, P., Mantere, S., & Vaara, E. (2014). Placing strategy discourse in context: Sociomateriality, sensemaking, and power. *Journal of Management Studies, 51*(2), 175–201.

Bandura, A. (2006). Toward a psychology of human agency. *Perspectives on Psychological Science, 1*(2), 164–180.

Baroutsis, A., & Lingard, B. (2017). Counting and comparing school performance: An analysis of media coverage of PISA in Australia, 2000–2014. *Journal of Education Policy, 32*(4), 432–449.

Bartunek, J. M., Krim, R. M., Necochea, R., & Humphries, M. (1999). *Sensemaking, sensegiving, and leadership in strategic organizational development*. In J. A. Wagner III (Ed.), Advances in qualitative organization research (Vol. 2, pp. 36–71). Elsevier Science/JAI Press.

Begley, P. (Ed.). (2010). *Leading with moral purpose: The place of ethics*. Sage Publications Ltd.

Bendikson, L., Robinson, V., & Hattie, J. (2012). Principal instructional leadership and secondary school performance. *SET: Research Information for Teachers, 2012*, 1.

Bendikson, L., Robinson, V., & Hattie, J. (2012). Principal instructional leadership and secondary school performance. *Research Information for Teachers, 1*, 2–8. https://search.informit.org/doi/10.3316/informit.505725715123816

Berkovich, I. (2021). The policy process: Implementation of education policy. In I. Berkovich, *Education policy, theories, and trends in the 21st century* (pp. 41–64). Springer. https://doi.org/10.1007/978-3-030-63103-1_3

Berliner, D. (2011). Rational responses to high stakes testing: The case of curriculum narrowing and the harm that follows. *Cambridge Journal of Education, 41*(3), 287–302.

Bezzina, M. (1989). *Teachers' perceptions and participation in school-based curriculum development*. Macquarie University.

Bezzina, M. (2000). *Catholic education: Corporate commodity or common good* [Paper]. The Inaugural Ann D. Clark Lecture, Parramatta, Sydney, Australia.

Bezzina, M. (2008). Both 'Catholic' and 'school': Leading learning with moral purpose. In A. Benjamin & D. Riley (Eds.), *Catholic schools: Hope in uncertain times* (pp. 220–233). John Garrett Publishing.

Bezzina, M. (2010). Leaders transforming learning and learners: An Australian innovation in leadership, learning and moral purpose. In C. Burford & H. N. Anthony (Eds.), *Global perspectives on educational leadership reform: The development and preparation of leaders of learning and learners of leadership* (Vol. 11, pp. 265–283). Emerald Group Publishing Limited.

Bezzina, M., & Tuana, N. (2014). Moral awareness to action. In C. Branson & S. Gross (Eds.), *The handbook of ethical leadership*. Routledge.

Biesta, G. J. J. (2004). Education, accountability, and the ethical demand: Can the democratic potential of accountability be regained? *Educational Theory, 54*(3), 233–250. doi:10.1111/j.0013-2004.2004.00017.x

Bisel, R. S., & Barge, J. K. (2011). Discursive positioning and planned change in organizations. *Human Relations, 64*(2), 257–283.

Bishop, K., & Limerick, B. (2006). To adopt, adapt or ignore? Challenging corporate type performance measures in state schools. *Leading & Managing, 12*(1), 76–90.

Blase, J., & Blase, J. (1999). Principals' instructional leadership and teacher development: Teachers' perspectives. *Educational Administration Quarterly, 35*(3), 349–378.

Board of Studies Teaching and Educational Standards. (2016). *Teacher accreditation in NSW.* http://www.nswteachers.nsw.edu.au/

Bovens, M. (2007). Analysing and assessing accountability: A conceptual framework. *European Law Journal, 13*(4), 447–468. http://onlinelibrary.wiley.com/doi/10.1111/j.1468-0386.2007.00378.x/pdf

Boyatzis, R. E., Rochford, K., & Taylor, S. N. (2015). The role of the positive emotional attractor in vision and shared vision: toward effective leadership, relationships, and engagement. *Frontiers in Psychology, 6*, 670.

Boyce, J., & Bowers, A. J. (2018). Toward an evolving conceptualization of instructional leadership as leadership for learning. *Journal of Educational Administration*.

Bradbury, A., & Robert-Holmes, G. (2018). *The datafication of primary and early years education: Playing with numbers*. Routledge.

Branch, G. F., Hanushek, E. A., & Rivkin, S. G. (2012). *Estimating the effect of leaders on public sector productivity: The case of school principals*. National Bureau of Economic Research.

REFERENCES

237

Branson, C. M. (2014). The power of personal values. In C. Branson & S. J. Goss (Eds.), *Handbook of ethical educational leadership* (pp. 195–209). Routledge.

Branson, C. M., & Marra, M. (2019). Leadership as a relational phenomenon: What this means in practice. *Research in Educational Administration & Leadership, 4*(1), 81–108.

Branson, C. M, & Marra, M. J. (2020). *An ecological approach to Catholic school reviews: Going beyond verification and accountability to achieve real school improvement.* https://researchonline.nd.edu.au/grace/2020Ireland/paper/20/

Braun, A., Maguire, M., & Ball, S. J. (2010). Policy enactments in the UK secondary school: Examining policy, practice and school positioning. *Journal of Education Policy, 25*(4), 547–560.

Brazer, S. D. (2019). Leaders as bricoleurs: Sensemaking as a pathway to skillful leadership. In B. L. Johnson & S. D. Kruse (Eds.), *Educational leadership, organizational learning, and the odeas of Karl Weick* (pp. 75–93): Routledge.

Breakspear, S. (2012). *The policy impact of PISA: An exploration of the normative effects of international benchmarking in school system performance.* OECD Education Working Papers, No. 71. OECD Publishing (NJ1).

Bridges, E. M. (1967). Instructional leadership: A concept re-examined. *Journal of Educational Administration, 5*(2), 136–147.

Brieve, F. J. (1972). Secondary principals as instructional leaders. *NASSP Bulletin, 56*(368), 11–15.

Brimm, J. L. (1983). What stresses school administrators. *Theory into Practice, 22*(1), 64–69.

Brooker, I. (2002). Botany of the eucalypts. In I. Brooker & D. Kleinig (Eds.), *Eucalyptus* (pp. 17–49). CRC Press.

Brookhart, S. M., & Moss, C. M. (2013). Leading by learning: When principals immerse themselves in learning about formative assessments and how students learn, they become better instructional leaders for teachers. *Phi Delta Kappan, 94*(8), 13.

Brown, G., & Chai, C. (2012). Assessing instructional leadership: A longitudinal study of new principals. *Journal of Educational Administration, 50*(6), 753–772. doi:10.1108/09578231211264676

Bryk, A., & Schneider, B. (2002). *Trust in schools: A core resource for improvement.* Russell Sage Foundation.

Burford, C. (2015). *Taxonomy for discerning value and purpose in educational leadership* [Paper]. The ACEL national conference, Sydney. http://www.acel.org.au/acel/ACEL_docs/Events/Conference%202015%20Presentations/Concurrent/Burford_Charles.pdf

Burford, C., & Pettit, P. (2011). *Leaders as moral agents: Giving purpose to student outcome data* [Paper]. The annual values and leadership conference, authentic leadership: The intersection of purpose, process and context, Victoria, BC.

Burke, C., & Grosvenor, I. (2015). *The school I'd like: Revisited: Children and young people's reflections on an education for the 21st century.* Routledge.

Bush, T. (2003). *Theories of educational leadership and management.* Sage.

Bush, T. (2010). *Theories of educational leadership and management* (3rd ed.). Sage Publications Ltd.

Bush, T. (2019). Models of educational leadership. *Principles of Educational Leadership and Management,* 3–17.

Cairns-Lee, H. (2015). Images of leadership development from the inside out. *Advances in Developing Human Resources, 17*(3), 321–336.

Carnoy, M., Elmore, R., & Siskin, L. (2003). *The new accountability: High schools and high-stakes testing.* Routledge.

Carroll, B., & Levy, L. (2010). Leadership development as identity construction. *Management Communication Quarterly, 24*(2), 211–231.

Carter, M. G. (2015). *A multiple case study of NAPLAN numeracy testing of Year 9 students in three Queensland secondary schools* [PhD thesis]. Queensland Unversity of Technology.

Catasús, B., Mårtensson, M., & Skoog, M. (2009). The communication of human accounts: Examining models of sensegiving. *Journal of Human Resource Costing & Accounting.*

Catholic Education Office Wollongong. (2016). www.ceowoll.catholic.edu.au

Caughron, J. J., Antes, A. L., Stenmark, C. K., Thiel, C. E., Wang, X., & Mumford, M. D. (2011). Sensemaking strategies for ethical decision making. *Ethics & Behavior, 21*(5), 351–366.

Chen, L.-L. (2019). Enhancing teaching with effective data mining protocols. *Journal of Educational Technology Systems, 47*(4), 500–512.

Chennamsetti, P. (2020). Assisting school leaders in overcoming challenges related to COVID-19. *Journal of School Administration Research and Development, 5,* 93–99.

Cherubini, L. (2009). Reconciling the tensions of new teachers' socialisation into school culture: A review of the research. *Issues in Educational Research, 19*(2).

Chitpin, S., & Jones, K. (2015). Leadership in a performative context: A framework for decision-making. *Educational Philosophy and Theory, 47*(4), 387–401.

Chreim, S., & Tafaghod, M. (2012). Contradiction and sensemaking in acquisition integration. *The Journal of Applied Behavioral Science, 48*(1), 5–32.

Cizek, G. J. (2001). More unintended consequences of high-stakes testing. *Educational Measurement: Issues and Practice, 20*(4), 19–27.

Cochran-Smith, M. (2021). Rethinking teacher education: The trouble with accountability. *Oxford Review of Education, 47*(1), 8–24. doi:10.1080/03054985.2020.1842181

Coghill, K., Crawford, D., Cunliffe, I., Grant, B., Hodge, G., Hughes, O., ... Zifcak, S. (2006). Why accountability must be renewed: Discussion paper on reform of

REFERENCES

Government accountability in Australia [Workshop of Parliamentary Scholars and Parliamentarians (7th ed., Wroxton College, Oxfordshire)]. *Australasian Parliamentary Review, 21*(2), 10–48. http://search.informit.com.au/fullText;res= APAFT;dn=200702067

Collin, L. (2017). Quality teaching in our schools. *The Journal for Educators, 36*(4), 29.

Comber, B. (2012). Mandated literacy assessment and the reorganisation of teachers' work: Federal policy, local effects. *Critical Studies in Education, 53*(2), 119–136. doi:10.1080/17508487.2012.672331

Comber, B., & Cormack, P. (2011). Education policy mediation: Principals' work with mandated literacy assessment. *English in Australia, 46*(2), 77.

Connell, R. (2012). Just education. *Journal of Education Policy, 27*(5), 681–683.

Connell, R. (2015). Markets all around: Defending education in a neoliberal time. In In H. Proctor, P. Brownlee, & P. Freebody (Eds.), *Controversies in education* (pp. 181–197). Springer. https://doi.org/10.1007/978-3-319-08759-7_16

Connors, B. (2013). Schoolwide pedagogy: Vibrant new meaning for teachers and principals: Lessons from a successful school system [Book review]. *Leading and Managing, 19*(2), 106.

Conway, J. M., & Andrews, D. (2015). A school wide approach to leading pedagogical enhancement: An Australian perspective. *Journal of Educational Change*, 1–25.

Cook, J. (2006). Reporting to systems and schools. *Professional Educator, 5*(1), 6–10.

Corbin, J., & Strauss, A. (2008). *Basics of qualitative research: Techniques and procedures for developing grounded theory.* Sage Publications Inc.

Corbin, J., & Strauss, A. (2014). *Basics of qualitative research: Techniques and procedures for developing grounded theory.* Sage Publications Inc.

Cornelissen, J. P., Holt, R., & Zundel, M. (2011). The role of analogy and metaphor in the framing and legitimization of strategic change. *Organization Studies, 32*(12), 1701–1716.

Corvellec, H., & Risberg, A. (2007). Sensegiving as mise-en-sens—The case of wind power development. *Scandinavian Journal of Management, 23*(3), 306–326.

Council of Australian Governments. (2012). *Intergovernmental agreements.* http://www.coag.gov.au/

Council of Australian Government's (COAG) Education Council. (2020). *Australian curriculum assessment and reporting authority.* https://www.acara.edu.au/about-us/our-governance

Cranston, N. (2013). School leaders leading professional responsibility not accountability as the key focus. *Educational Management Administration & Leadership, 41*(2), 129–142.

Cranston, N., Reid, A., Keating, J., & Mulford, B. (2011). *The forces and dynamics shaping education.* http://www.agppa.asn.au/content/view/11/15/

Cranston, N., Reid, A., Mulford, B., & Keating, J. (2011). What do we know about the purposes of education and their enactment in Australian primary schools? *The Australian Educational Leader, 33*(3), 20–25.

Crow, G., Day, C., & Møller, J. (2017). Framing research on school principals' identities. *International Journal of Leadership in Education, 20*(3), 265–277.

Crow, G., & Møller, J. (2017). Professional identities of school leaders across international contexts: An introduction and rationale. *Educational Management Administration & Leadership, 45*(5), 749–758.

Dadaczynski, K., & Paulus, P. (2015). Healthy principals – healthy schools? A neglected perspective to school health promotion. In V. Simovska & P. Mannix McNamara (Eds.), *Schools for health and sustainability* (pp. 253–273). Springer. https://doi.org/10.1007/978-94-017-9171-7_12

Danielewicz, J. (2001). *Teaching selves: Identity, pedagogy, and teacher education.* State University of New York Press.

Darling-Hammond, L. (1989). Accountability for professional practice. *Teachers College Record, 91*(1), 59–80.

Darling-Hammond, L. (2010a). *The flat world and education: How America's commitment to equity will determine our future.* Teachers College Press.

Darling-Hammond, L. (2010b). *Performance counts: Assessment systems that support high-quality learning.* Council of Chief State School Officers.

Darling-Hammond, L., Meyerson, D., LaPointe, M., & Orr, M. T. (2010). *Preparing principals for a changing world.* Jossey-Bass.

Datnow, A., & Hubbard, L. (2016). Teacher capacity for and beliefs about data-driven decision making: A literature review of international research. *Journal of Educational Change, 17*(1), 7–28.

DeCourcy, J. (2006). *From academe to classroom: Translating the results of multilevel modeling into changed practice* [Paper]. The ACSPRI social science methodology conference, The University of Sydney.

Dee, T. S., Dobbie, W., Jacob, B. A., & Rockoff, J. (2019). The causes and consequences of test score manipulation: Evidence from the new york regents examinations. *American Economic Journal: Applied Economics, 11*(3), 382–423.

Diamond, J. B. (2007). Where the rubber meets the road: Rethinking the connection between high-stakes testing policy and classroom instruction. *Sociology of Education, 80*(4), 285–313. doi:10.1177/003804070708000401

Diamond, J. B. (2012). Accountability policy, school organization, and classroom practice. *Education and Urban Society, 44*(2), 151–182. doi:10.1177/0013124511431569

Dinham, S. (2005). Principal leadership for outstanding educational outcomes. *Journal of Educational Administration, 43*(4), 338–356. doi:10.1108/09578230510605405

Dinham, S. (2008). *How to get your school moving and improving: An evidence-based approach.* ACER Press.

REFERENCES

Dinham, S. (2016). *Leading learning and teaching*. ACER Press.

Dinham, S., Collarbone, P., Evans, M., & Mackay, A. (2013). The development, endorsement and adoption of a nhational standard for principals in Australia. *Educational Management Administration & Leadership, 41*(4), 467–483. doi:10.1177/1741143213485462

Donaldson, M. L. (2013). Principals' approaches to cultivating teacher effectiveness constraints and opportunities in hiring, assigning, evaluating, and developing teachers. *Educational Administration Quarterly, 49*(5), 838–882.

Donohoo, J., Hattie, J., & Eells, R. (2018). The power of collective efficacy. *Educational Leadership, 75*(6), 40–44.

Donohoo, J., & Katz, S. (2017). When teachers believe, students achieve. *The Learning Professional, 38*(6), 20–27.

Donohoo, J., O'Leary, T., & Hattie, J. (2020). The design and validation of the Enabling Conditions for Collective Teacher Efficacy Scale (EC-CTES). *Journal of Professional Capital and Community, 5*(2), 147–166. doi:10.1108/jpcc-08-2019-0020

Dorbeck-Jung, B. (1997). *Ethics and accountability in a context of governance and new public management* [Paper]. The EGPA annual conference, Leuven, Belgium.

Dowden, T. (2007). Relevant, challenging, integrative and exploratory curriculum design: Perspectives from theory and practice for middle level schooling in Australia. *The Australian Educational Researcher, 34*(2), 51–71.

Drake, T. A., Goldring, E., Grissom, J. A., Cannata, M., Neumerski, C., Rubin, M., & Schuermann, P. (2016). Development or dismissal? Exploring principals' use of teacher effectiveness data. In J. A. Grisson & P. Youngs (Eds.), *Improving teacher evaluation systems: Making the most of multiple measures* (pp. 116–130). Teachers College Press.

Drori, I., & Ellis, S. (2011). Conflict and power games in a multinational corporation: Sensegiving as a strategy of preservation. *European Management Review, 8*(1), 1–16.

Du Plessis, A. E. (2017). *Out-of-field teaching practices: What educational leaders need to know*: Springer.

Dufour, R., & Marzano, R. J. (2011). *Leaders of learning*. Soution Tree Press.

Dufour, R., & Marzano, R. J. (2015). *Leaders of learning: How district, school, and classroom leaders improve student achievement*. Solution Tree Press.

Duignan, P. (2010). *Leading learning in Catholic schools* [DVD]. Duignan Professional and Educational Consulting. www.leadingtoinspire.com.au

Dulude, E., & Milley, P. (2021). Institutional complexity and multiple accountability tensions: A conceptual framework for analyzing school leaders' interpretation of competing demands. *Policy Futures in Education, 19*(1), 84–96.

Dulude, E., Spillane, J. P., & Dumay, X. (2015). High stakes policy and mandated curriculum: A rhetorical argumentation analysis to explore the social processes that shape school leaders' and teachers' strategic responses. *Educational Policy*, 0895904815598396.

Dunford, R., & Jones, D. (2000). Narrative in strategic change. *Human Relations, 53*(9), 1207–1226.

Eacott, S. (2017). A social epistemology for educational administration and leadership. *Journal of Educational Administration and History, 49*(3), 196–214.

Eacott, S., MacDonald, K., Keddie, A., Wilkinson, J., Niesche, R., Gobby, B., & Fernandez, I. (2020). COVID-19 and inequities in Australian education – Insights on federalism, autonomy, and access. *International Studies in Educational Administration*, 6.

Eacott, S., & Norris, J. (2014). Managerial rhetoric, accountability, and school leadership in contemporary Australia. *Leadership and Policy in Schools, 13*(2), 169–187.

Earl, L., & Fullan, M. (2003). Using data in leadership for learning. *Cambridge Journal of Education, 33*(3), 383–394.

Earp, J., & Riley, P. (2018). *The research files episode 41: Principal health and wellbeing.* https://research.acer.edu.au/teacher_audio/22

Edwards-Groves, C., & Kemmis, S. (2016). Pedagogy, education and praxis: Understanding new forms of intersubjectivity through action research and practice theory. *Educational Action Research, 24*(1), 77–96.

Ehrich, L. C., Harris, J., Klenowski, V., Smeed, J., & Spina, N. (2015). The centrality of ethical leadership. *Journal of Educational Administration, 53*(2), 197–214.

Elmore, R. (2005). *Agency, reciprocity, and accountability in democratic education.* Consortium for Policy Research in Education.

Elmore, R., Forman, M. L., Stosich, E. L., & Bocala, C. (2013). *The internal coherence assessment protocol & developmental framework: Building the organizational capacity for instructional improvement in schools.* Harvard University.

Elmore, R. F. (2005). *Accountable leadership* [Paper]. The Educational Forum.

Elmore, R. F. (2005). Accountable leadership. Essays. *The Educational Forum, 69*(2), 134.

Eren, N. (2020). *From cacophony to chorus: How do principals make sense of multiple concurrent interventions?* University of Pennsylvania.

Erikson, J. M. (1964). Nothing to fear: Notes on the life of Eleanor Roosevelt. *Daedalus*, 781–801.

Farrell, C. C. (2014). Designing school systems to encourage data use and instructional improvement: A comparison of school districts and charter management organizations. *Educational Administration Quarterly.* https://doi.org/10.1177/0013161X14539806

Fiarman, S. E. (2019). *Becoming a school principal: Learning to lead, leading to learn.* Harvard Education Press.

Fiedler, F. E. (1964). A contingency model of leadership effectiveness. *Advances in Experimental Social Psychology, 1*(1), 149–190.

Firestone, W., & Shipps, D. (2003). *How do educational leaders interpret the multiple accountabilities that they face* [Paper]. Meeting of the American Educational Research Association, Chicago.

REFERENCES

Firestone, W., & Shipps, D. (Eds.). (2005). *How do leaders interpret conflicting account-ability to improve student learning?* Teachers College Press.

Fisher, Y. (2014). The timeline of self-efficacy: Changes during the professional life cycle of school principals. *Journal of Educational Administration, 52*(1), 58–83.

Ford, T. G., Olsen, J., Khojasteh, J., Ware, J., & Urick, A. (2019). The effects of leader support for teacher psychological needs on teacher burnout, commitment, and intent to leave. *Journal of Educational Administration.*

Franken, M., Penney, D., & Branson, C. M. (2015). Middle leaders' learning in a university context. *Journal of Higher Education Policy and Management, 37*(2), 190–203.

French, J., Raven, B., & Cartwright, D. (1959). The bases of social power. *Classics of Organization Theory, 7*, 311–320.

Fuhrman, S., & Elmore, R. F. (Eds.). (2003). *Redesigning accountability systems for education.* Teachers College Press.

Fullan, M. (2011). *The moral imperative realized.* Corwin Press.

Gannicott, K. (2019). Gonski 2.0 a controlled flight into terrain. *AQ: Australian Quarterly, 90*(1), 21–31. https://www.jstor.org/stable/26563020

Ganon-Shilon, S., & Schechter, C. (2017). Making sense while steering through the fog: Principals' metaphors within a national reform implementation. *Education Policy Analysis Archives, 25*, 105.

Ganon-Shilon, S., & Schechter, C. (2019a). School principals' sense-making of their leadership role during reform implementation. *International Journal of Leadership in Education, 22*(3), 279–300.

Ganon-Shilon, S., & Schechter, C. (2019b). Shared sense-making processes within a national reform implementation: Principals' voices. *Leadership and Policy in Schools*, 1–28.

Gardner, H. (2011). *Frames of mind: The theory of multiple intelligences.* Basic books.

Garn, G., & Cobb, C. D. (2001). A framework for understanding charter school accountability. *Education and Urban Society, 33*(2), 113–128.

Gifford, T. (2010). Judith Wright's poetry and the turn to the post-pastoral. *Australian Humanities Review, 48*, 75–86.

Gillard, J. (2008). *Leading transformational change in schools.* www.deewr.gov.au/Ministers/Gillard/Media/Speeches/pages/Article_081128_133_64

Gioia, D. A., & Chittipeddi, K. (1991). Sensemaking and sensegiving in strategic change initiation. *Strategic Management Journal, 12*(6), 433–448.

Gioia, D. A., & Thomas, J. B. (1996). Identity, image, and issue interpretation: Sensemaking during strategic change in academia. *Administrative Science Quarterly*, 370–403.

Gioia, D. A., Thomas, J. B., Clark, S. M., & Chittipeddi, K. (1994). Symbolism and strategic change in academia: The dynamics of sensemaking and influence. *Organization Science, 5*(3), 363–383.

Giuliani, M. (2016). Sensemaking, sensegiving and sensebreaking. *Journal of Intellectual Capital, 17*(2), 218–237. doi:10.1108/jic-04-2015-0039

Glaser, B. (1992). *Basics of grounded theory analysis: Emergence versus forcing.* Sociology Press.

Gobby, B., Keddie, A., & Blackmore, J. (2018). Professionalism and competing responsibilities: Moderating competitive performativity in school autonomy reform. *Journal of Educational Administration and History, 50*(3), 159–173.

Gold, E., & Simon, E. (2004). Public accountability: School improvement efforts need the active involvement of communities to succeed. *Education Week, 23*(11).

Goldschmidt, P., Roschewski, P., Choi, K., Auty, W., Hebbler, S., Blank, R., & Williams, A. (2005). *Policymaker's guide to growth models for school accountability: How do accountability models differ?* Council of Chief State School Officers.

Gonzalez, R. A., & Firestone, W. A. (2013). Educational tug-of-war: Internal and external accountability of principals in varied contexts. *Journal of Educational Administration, 51*(3), 383–406.

Goos, M., Stillman, G., & Vale, C. (2007). *Teaching secondary school mathematics: Research and practice for the 21st century.* Allen & Unwin.

Gorur, R. (2015). The performative politics of NAPLAN and MySchool. B. Lingard, G. Thompson, & S. Sellar (Eds.), (pp. 30–43). London, England: Routledge. *National testing in schools: An Australian assessment* (pp. 30–43). Routledge.

Grace, G. (1989). Education: Commodity or public good. *British Journal of Educational Studies, 37*, 207–221.

Grant, A. M., & Berry, J. W. (2011). The necessity of others is the mother of invention: Intrinsic and prosocial motivations, perspective taking, and creativity. *Academy of Management Journal, 54*(1), 73–96.

Gray, R. (2002). Thirty years of social accounting, reporting and auditing: What (if anything) have we learnt? *Business Ethics: A European Review, 10*(1), 9–15.

Green Jr., S. E. (2004). A rhetorical theory of diffusion. *Academy of Management Review, 29*(4), 653–669.

Greenleaf, R. K. (2002). *Servant leadership: A journey into the nature of legitimate power and greatness.* Paulist Press.

Grove, D. J., & Panzer, B. (1989). *Resolving traumatic memories: Metaphors and symbols in psychotherapy.* Irvington Publishers, Inc.

Gunzenhauser, M. G. (2003). High-stakes testing and the default philosophy of education. *Theory into Practice, 42*(1), 51–58. doi:10.1207/s15430421tip4201_7

Gunzenhauser, M. G. (2012). *The active/ethical professional: A framework for responsible educators.* A&C Black.

Gurr, D. (2020). Educational leadership and the pandemic. *Academia Letters, 29.*

Gurr, D., & Drysdale, L. (2015). An Australian perspective on school leadership preparation and development: Credentials or self-management? *Asia Pacific Journal of Education, 35*(3), 377–391.

Gurr, D., & Drysdale, L. (2020a). Leadership for challenging times. *International Studies in Educational Administration, 48*(1), 24–30.

Gurr, D., & Drysdale, L. (2020b). School leadership that matters. *Leading and Managing, 26*(1), 54–62.

Halligan, J. (2007). Accountability in Australia: Control, paradox, and complexity. *Public Administration Quarterly, 31*(4), 453–479. http://search.ebscohost.com/login.aspx?direct=true&db=bth&AN=29979979&site=ehost-live

Hallinger, P. (2003). Leading educational change: Reflections on the practice of instructional and transformational leadership. *Cambridge Journal of Education, 33*(3), 329–352.

Hallinger, P. (2018). Bringing context out of the shadows of leadership. *Educational Management Administration & Leadership, 46*(1), 5–24. doi:10.1177/1741143216670652

Hallinger, P., Bickman, L., & Davis, K. (1996). School context, principal leadership, and student reading achievement. *The Elementary School Journal,* 527–549.

Hallinger, P., Gümüş, S., & Bellibaş, M. Ş. (2020). 'Are principals instructional leaders yet?' A science map of the knowledge base on instructional leadership, 1940–2018. *Scientometrics, 122*(3), 1629–1650.

Hallinger, P., Hosseingholizadeh, R., Hashemi, N., & Kouhsari, M. (2018). Do beliefs make a difference? Exploring how principal self-efficacy and instructional leadership impact teacher efficacy and commitment in Iran. *Educational Management Administration & Leadership, 46*(5), 800–819.

Hanushek, E. (2011). *Incentives and test-based accountability in education: A report from the National Research Council.* http://jorgewerthein.blogspot.com/2011/11/incentives-and-test-based.html

Hardy, I. (2014). A logic of appropriation: Enacting national testing (NAPLAN) in Australia. *Journal of Education Policy, 29*(1), 1–18.

Hardy, I., & Lewis, S. (2017). The 'doublethink' of data: Educational performativity and the field of schooling practices. *British Journal of Sociology of Education, 38*(5), 671–685. doi:10.1080/01425692.2016.1150155

Hargreaves, A., & Fullan, M. (2015). *Professional capital: Transformng teaching in every school.* Teachers College Press.

Harris, A., & Jones, M. (2020). COVID 19 – School leadership in disruptive times. *School Leadership & Management, 40*(4), 243–247. doi:10.1080/13632434.2020.1811479

Harris, P., Chinnappan, M., Castleton, G., Carter, J., de Courcy, M., & Barnett, J. (2013). Impact and consequence of Australia's National Assessment Program-Literacy and Numeracy (NAPLAN) – using research evidence to inform improvement. *TESOL in Context, 23*(1/2), 30.

Harrison, J., & Rouse, P. (2014). Competition and public high school performance. *Socio-Economic Planning Sciences, 48*(1), 10–19.

Hasinoff, S., & Mandzuk, D. (2018). *Navigating uncertainty: Sensemaking for educational leaders.* Brill.

Hattie, J. (2015). High impact leadership. *Educational Leadership, 72*(5), 36–40.

Hattie, J., & Timperley, H. (2007). The power of feedback. *Review of Educational Research, 77*(1), 81–112.

Hattie, J., & Zierer, K. (2019). *Visible learning insights.* Routledge.

Hauseman, C. (2020). Strategies secondary school principals use to manage their emotions. *Leadership and Policy in Schools,* 1–20.

Heffernan, A. (2018). *The principal and school improvement: Theorising discourse, policy, and practice.* Springer.

Helms Mills, J., Thurlow, A., & Mills, A. J. (2010). Making sense of sensemaking: The critical sensemaking approach. *Qualitative Research in Organizations and Management: An International Journal, 5*(2), 182–195.

Henebery, B. (2021). In education, accountability has a one-way direction flow-and that's a problem [Press release]. https://www.theeducatoronline.com/k12/news/in-education-accountability-is-a-oneway-direction-flow--and-thats-a-problem/278755

Henson, J. D. (2020). Christian leaders as imitators: Jesus as the ultimate example of leadership. In J. D. Henson (Ed.), *Modern metaphors of Christian leadership: Exploring Christian leadership in a contemporary organizational context* (pp. 289–308). Palgrave Macmillan. https://doi.org/10.1007/978-3-030-36580-6_17

Hersey, B., & Blanchard, K. H. (1988). *Management of organizational behaviour. Utilizing human resources.* Prentice Hall.

Hibbert, P., & Cunliffe, A. (2015). Responsible management: Engaging moral reflexive practice through threshold concepts. *Journal of Business Ethics, 127*(1), 177–188.

Hill, R. C., & Levenhagen, M. (1995). Metaphors and mental models: Sensemaking and sensegiving in innovative and entrepreneurial activities. *Journal of Management, 21*(6), 1057–1074.

Hogan, A., & Thompson, G. (2019). The quasi-marketization of Australian public schooling: Affordances and contradictions of the new work order. *Asia Pacific Journal of Education, 39*(3), 391–403. doi:10.1080/02188791.2019.1598849

Högberg, B., & Lindgren, J. (2021). Outcome-based accountability regimes in OECD countries: A global policy model? *Comparative Education, 57*(3), 301–321.

Holloway, J., Nielsen, A., & Saltmarsh, S. (2018). Prescribed distributed leadership in the era of accountability: The experiences of mentor teachers. *Educational Management Administration & Leadership, 46*(4), 538–555. doi:10.1177/1741143216688469

Honig, M. I., & Hatch, T. C. (2004). Crafting coherence: How schools strategically manage multiple, external demands. *Educational Researcher, 33*(8), 16–30.

Hoogsteen, T. (2020). Collective teacher efficacy: A critical review of education's top influence. *Advances in Social Sciences Research Journal, 7*(6).

Howard, P., O'Brien, C., Kay, B., & O'Rourke, K. (2019). Leading educational change in the 21st century: Creating living schools through shared vision and transformative governance. *Sustainability, 11*(15), 4109.

Hunt, E. K. (2020). *The last discourse: Jesus and sensegiving in the Gospel of John*. Regent University.

Huse, M. (2005). Accountability and creating accountability: A framework for exploring behavioural perspectives of corporate governance. *British Journal of Management, 16*, S65–S79.

Huzzard, T., Hellström, A., & Lifvergren, S. (2014). *System-wide change in cancer care: Exploring sensemaking, sensegiving, and consent* (Research in Organizational Change and Development, Vol. 22). Emerald Group Publishing Limited.

Ieraci, S. (2007). Responsibility versus accountability in a risk-averse culture. *Emergency Medicine Australasia: EMA, 19*(1), 63.

Jaafar, S., & Anderson, S. (2007). Policy trends and tensions in accountability for educational management and services in Canada. *The Alberta Journal of Educational Research, 53*(2), 207–227.

Jacob, B. A. (2005). Accountability, incentives and behavior: The impact of high-stakes testing in the Chicago public schools. *Journal of Public Economics, 89*(5–6), 761–796.

Jäppinen, A.-K., & Maunonen-Eskelinen, I. (2011). Organisational transition challenges in the Finnish vocational education – Perspective of distributed pedagogical leadership. *Educational Studies, 38*(1), 39–50. doi:10.1080/03055698.2011.567024

Jennings, J. L. (2010). School choice or schools' choice? Managing in an era of accountability. *Sociology of Education, 83*(3), 227–247.

Jensen, B., Weidmann, B., Farmer, J., Hunter, A., Romanes, D., & Magee, J. (2013). *The myth of markets in school education*. Grattan Institute.

Johnson, B. L., & Kruse, S. D. (2019). Educational leadership, school organizations, and Karl Weick: An introduction. In B. Johnson & S. D. Kruse (Eds.), *Educational leadership, organizational learning, and the ideas of Karl Weick* (pp. 1–29). Routledge.

Johnson, J. F., Bagdasarov, Z., Harkrider, L. N., MacDougall, A. E., Connelly, S., Devenport, L. D., & Mumford, M. D. (2013). The effects of note-taking and review on sensemaking and ethical decision making. *Ethics & Behavior, 23*(4), 299–323. doi:10.1080/10508422.2013.774275

Johnson, L. F., & Crow, G. M. (2017). Professional identities of school leaders across international contexts. In London, England: SAGE Publications Sage UK.

Juraskova, I., O'Brien, M., Mullan, B., Bari, R., Laidsaar-Powell, R., & McCaffery, K. (2012). HPV vaccination and the effect of information framing on intentions and behaviour: An application of the theory of planned behaviour and moral norm. *International Journal of Behavioral Medicine, 19*(4), 518–525.

Kaufman, T. E., Graham, C. R., Picciano, A. G., Popham, J. A., & Wiley, D. (2014). Data-driven decision making in the K-12 classroom. In J. Spector, M. Merrill, J. Elen, & M. Bishop (Eds.), *Handbook of research on educational communications and technology* (pp. 337–346). Springer.

Kautonen, T., Van Gelderen, M., & Tornikoski, E. T. (2013). Predicting entrepreneurial behaviour: A test of the theory of planned behaviour. *Applied Economics, 45*(6), 697–707.

Keddie, A., Claire MacDonald, K., Blackmore, J., Eacott, S., Gobby, B., Mahoney, C., ... Wilkinson, J. (2020). School autonomy, marketisation and social justice: The plight of principals and schools. *Journal of Educational Administration and History, 52*(4), 432–447.

Kemmis, S., Wilkinson, J., Edwards-Groves, C., Hardy, I., Grootenboer, P., & Bristol, L. (2014). *Changing practices, changing education.* Springer.

Kihlberg, R., & Lindberg, O. (2021). Reflexive sensegiving: An open-ended process of influencing the sensemaking of others during organizational change. *European Management Journal, 39*(4), 476–486.

Klenowski, V., & Wyatt-Smith, C. (2011). The impact of high stakes testing: The Australian story. *Assessment in Education: Principles, Policy & Practice, 19*(1), 65–79. doi:10.1080/0969594x.2011.592972

Klenowski, V., & Wyatt-Smith, C. (2012). The impact of high stakes testing: The Australian story, assessment in education. *Assessment in Education: Principles, Policy & Practice, 19*(1), 65–79. http://dx.doi.org/10.1080/0969594X.2011.592972

Klerks, M. (2013). The effect of school inspections: a systematic review. *School Improvement*, 2–32.

Klinger, D. A., & Rogers, T. (2011). Teachers' perceptions of large-scale assessment programs within low-stakes accountability frameworks. *International Journal of Testing, 11*(2), 122–143. http://dx.doi.org/10.1080/15305058.2011.552748

Knapp, M. S., & Feldman, S. B. (2012). Managing the intersection of internal and external accountability: Challenge for urban school leadership in the United States. *Journal of Educational Administration, 50*(5), 666–694.

Knapp, M. S., Feldman, S. B., & Ling Yeh, T. (2013). Learning-focused leadership in urban high schools: Response to demanding environments. *Journal of School Leadership, 23*(2), 253–286. http://ezproxy.acu.edu.au/login?url=https://search.ebscohost.com/login.aspx?direct=true&db=eue&AN=91978613&site=ehost-live

Koretz, D. (2008). *Measuring up.* Harvard University Press.

Koschmann, T., Kuutti, K., & Hickman, L. (1998). The concept of breakdown in Heidegger, Leont'ev, and Dewey and its implications for education. *Mind, Culture, and Activity, 5*(1), 25–41.

Koyama, J. (2013). Principals as bricoleurs making sense and making do in an era of accountability. *Educational Administration Quarterly.* https://doi.org/10.1177/0013161X13492796

Koyama, J. (2014). Principals as bricoleurs making sense and making do in an era of accountability. *Educational Administration Quarterly, 50*(2), 279–304.

REFERENCES

Kraft, A., Sparr, J. L., & Peus, C. (2015). The critical role of moderators in leader sensegiving: A literature review. *Journal of Change Management, 15*(4), 308–331. doi:10.1080/14697017.2015.1091372

Kraft, A., Sparr, J. L., & Peus, C. (2018). Giving and making sense about change: The back and forth between leaders and employees. *Journal of Business and Psychology, 33*(1), 71–87. doi:10.1007/s10869-016-9474-5

Kruse, S. D. (2019). *Educational leadership, organizational learning, and the ideas of Karl Weick: Perspectives on theory and practice.* Routledge.

Ku, G., Wang, C. S., & Galinsky, A. D. (2015). The promise and perversity of perspective-taking in organizations. *Research in Organizational Behavior, 35,* 79–102.

Kuchapski, R. (2001). *Conceptualizing accountability in education.* hoolboards.ca/old/ResearchAndDevelopment/ResearchReports/Evaluation

Kuntz, J. R., & Gomes, J. F. (2012). Transformational change in organisations: A self-regulation approach. *Journal of Organizational Change Management.*

Lakoff, G., & Johnson, M. (2008). *Metaphors we live by.* University of Chicago Press.

Lambert, K., Wright, P., Currie, J., & Pascoe, R. (2016). Embodiment and becoming in secondary drama classrooms: The effects of neoliberal education cultures on performances of self and of drama texts. *Critical Studies in Education,* 1–19.

Lasater, K., Albiladi, W. S., Davis, W. S., & Bengtson, E. (2020). The data culture continuum: An examination of school data cultures. *Educational Administration Quarterly, 56*(4), 533–569.

Le Fevre, D. M., & Robinson, V. M. (2014). The interpersonal challenges of instructional leadership principals' effectiveness in conversations about performance issues. *Educational Administration Quarterly.* https://doi.org/10.1177/0013161X13518218

Leavell, J. P. (2015). Contolling and informational planned behavior: Self-determination theory and the theory of planned behavior. *Atlantic Marketing Journal, 5*(3), 81–91.

LeChasseur, K., Donaldson, M., Fernandez, E., & Femc-Bagwell, M. (2018). Brokering, buffering, and the rationalities of principal work. *Journal of Educational Administration.*

Leithwood, K. (2005). Understanding successful principal leadership: Progress on a broken front. *Journal of Educational Administration, 43*(6), 619–629.

Leithwood, K. (2018). Postscript: Five insights about school leaders' policy enactment. *Leadership and Policy in Schools, 17*(3), 391–395.

Leithwood, K., & Jantzi, D. (2008). Linking leadership to student learning: The contributions of leaders efficacy. *Educational Administration Quarterly, 44*(4), 496–528.

Leithwood, K., & Riehl, C. (2005). What we know about successful school leadership. In W. Firestone & C. Riehl (Eds.), *A new agenda: Directions for research on educational leadership.* Teachers College Press.

Leithwood, K., Sun, J., & Mccullough, C. (2019). How school districts influence student achievement. *Journal of Educational Administration, 57*(5), 519–539. doi:10.1108/jea-09-2018-0175

Leonardi, P. M., Neeley, T. B., & Gerber, E. M. (2012). How managers use multiple media: Discrepant events, power, and timing in redundant communication. *Organization Science, 23*(1), 98–117.

Leslie, T. (2010). *Gillard stares down teachers over my school.* https://www.abc.net.au/news/2010-03-25/gillard-stares-down-teachers-over-my-school/380010

Lewis, C., Dollery, B., & Kortt, M. A. (2014). Building the education revolution: Another case of Australian Government failure? *International Journal of Public Administration, 37*(5), 299–307. doi:10.1080/01900692.2013.836660

Lewis, S., & Hardy, I. (2015). Funding, reputation and targets: the discursive logics of high-stakes testing. *Cambridge Journal of Education, 45*(2), 245–264.

Lingard, B. (2010). Policy borrowing, policy learning: Testing times in Australian schooling. *Critical Studies in Education, 51*(2), 129–147.

Lingard, B., Martino, W., & Rezai-Rashti, G. (2013). Testing regimes, accountabilities and education policy: Commensurate global and national developments. *Journal of Education Policy, 28*(5), 539–556.

Lingard, B., & Sellar, S. (2013). 'Catalyst data': Perverse systemic effects of audit and accountability in Australian schooling. *Journal of Education Policy, 28*(5), 634–656.

Lingard, B., & Sellar, S. (2016). The changing organizational and global significance of the OECD's education work. In K. Mundy, A. Green, B. Lingard, & T. Verger (Eds.), *Handbook of global education policy* (p. 357). Blackwell.

Lingard, B., Sellar, S., & Lewis, S. (2017). Accountabilities in schools and school systems. In *Oxford research encyclopedia of education.* https://doi.org/10.1093/acrefore/9780190264093.013.74

Lingard, B., Thompson, G., & Sellar, S. (2015). National testing from an Australian perspective. *National Testing in Schools: An Australian Assessment,* 1.

Long, C. E. (2019). *Educational leaders' interpretation of and response to the every student succeeds act and the LOOK act in Massachusetts.* Boston College, Lynch School of Education.

Louis, K. S., & Mintrop, H. (2012). Bridging accountability obligations, professional values and (perceived) student needs with integrity. *Journal of Educational Administration.*

Louis, K. S., & Robinson, V. M. (2012). External mandates and instructional leadership: School leaders as mediating agents. *Journal of Educational Administration, 50*(5), 629–665.

Lovell, C. W. (2009). *Principal efficacy: An investigation of school principals' sense of efficacy and indicators of school effectiveness.* ERIC.

Lowenhaupt, R., Spillane, J. P., & Hallett, T. (2016). Education policy in leadership practice: "Accountability talk" in schools. *Journal of School Leadership, 26*(5), 783–810.

Lunday, J., & Megan, B. (2004). Connecting the dots between intentions, action and results: A multi-pronged approach to ethcial decision making. *Ivey Business Journal Online, March/April*(1), 1–7.

REFERENCES   251

MacBeath, J., Gray, J. M., Cullen, J., Frost, D., Steward, S., & Swaffield, S. (2006). *Schools on the edge: Responding to challenging circumstances.* Sage.

Macpherson, R. J. S. (1995). Introduction. *International Journal of Educational Research, 23*(6), 475–478.

Magee, J. C., Milliken, F. J., & Lurie, A. L. (2009). *Roles, power, and sense-making after 9/11: Differences in the content of attention and construal* [Paper]. The Academy of Management Proceedings.

Maitlis, S. (2005). The social processes of organizational sensemaking. *Academy of Management Journal, 48*(1), 21–49.

Maitlis, S., & Christianson, M. (2014). Sensemaking in organizations: Taking stock and moving forward. *Academy of Management Annals, 8*(1), 57–125.

Maitlis, S., & Lawrence, T. B. (2007). Triggers and enablers of sensegiving in organizations. *Academy of Management Journal, 50*(1), 57–84. doi:10.5465/amj.2007.24160971

Maitlis, S., & Sonenshein, S. (2010). Sensemaking in crisis and change: Inspiration and insights from Weick (1988). *Journal of Management Studies, 47*(3), 551–580.

Maitlis, S., Vogus, T. J., & Lawrence, T. B. (2013). Sensemaking and emotion in organizations. *Organizational Psychology Review, 3*(3), 222–247.

Male, T., & Palaiologou, I. (2012). Learning-centred leadership or pedagogical leadership? An alternative approach to leadership in education contexts. *International Journal of Leadership in Education, 15*(1), 107–118.

Manuel, J., Carter, D., Locke, T., & Locke, T. (2015). "I had been given the space to grow": An innovative model of assessment in subject English in New South Wales, Australia. *English Teaching: Practice & Critique, 14*(2).

Marks, H. M., & Nance, J. P. (2007). Contexts of accountability under systemic reform: Implications for principal influence on instruction and supervision. *Educational Administration Quarterly, 43*(1), 3–37.

Marsh, J. A., Farrell, C. C., & Bertrand, M. (2014). Trickle-down accountability how middle school teachers engage students in data use. *Educational Policy.* https://doi.org/10.1177/0895904814531653

Marsh, J. A., Farrell, C. C., & Bertrand, M. (2016). Trickle-down accountability: How middle school teachers engage students in data use. *Educational Policy, 30*(2), 243–280.

Marsh, S., Waniganayake, M., & De Nobile, J. (2013). Leadership for Learning as an intentional, community-wide activity: The importance of developing a shared language in schools. *School Leadership & Management, 33*(4), 395–411.

Marzano, R. J. (2009). Setting the record straight on "high-yield" strategies. *Phi Delta Kappan, 91*(1), 30–37. https://doi.org/10.1177/003172170909100105

Matthews, P., & Ehren, M. (2021). Accountability and improvement in self-improving school systems. *School Leadership and Education System Reform, 47.*

Maurice, L. (2003). Growing native plants. *Eucalyptus pauciflora.* https://www.anbg.gov.au/gnp/interns-2003/eucalyptus-pauciflora.html

Maxwell, A., & Riley, P. (2017). Emotional demands, emotional labour and occupational outcomes in school principals: Modelling the relationships. *Educational Management Administration & Leadership, 45*(3), 484–502.

Maxwell, J. C. (2014). *The 5 levels of leadership.* BookBaby.

May, P. J. (2007). Regulatory regimes and accountability. *Regulations & Governance, 1,* 8–26. doi:10.1111/j.1748-5991.2007.00002.x

McBrayer, J. S., Jackson, T., Pannell, S. S., Sorgen, C. H., De Blume, A. P. G., & Melton, T. D. (2018). Balance of instructional and managerial tasks as it relates to school leaders' self-efficacy. *Journal of School Leadership, 28*(5), 596–617.

McCollum, D. L., & Kajs, L. T. (2007a). *Examining the relationship between school administrators' efficacy and goal orientations* [Paper]. The Allied Academies International Conference, Academy of Educational Leadership, Proceedings.

McCollum, D. L., & Kajs, L. T. (2007b). School administrator efficacy: Assessment of beliefs about knowledge and skills for successful school leadership. *Advances in Educational Administration, 10,* 131–148.

McGuire, R. (2012). Australian government school principals respond to My School. *Australian Educational Leader, 35*(1), 12–16.

McLeod, S., & Dulsky, S. (2021). Resilience, reorientation, and reinvention: School leadership during the early months of the COVID-19 pandemic. *Frontiers in Education, 6*(70). doi:10.3389/feduc.2021.637075

McMillan, M. R. (2020). *Leading effective inclusive schools: How principals make the difference.* University of North Florida.

McNeil, L. (2000). *Contradictions of school reform: Educational costs of standardized testing.* Routledge.

Milliken, F. J., Magee, J. C., Lam, N., & Menezes, D. (2012). *The lens and language of power: Sense-making gaps in the aftermath of Hurricane Katrina* [Unpublished manuscript].

Ministerial Council for Federal Financial Relations. (2009). *National Partnership agreement (NP).* http://www.federalfinancialrelations.gov.au/content/national_partnership_agreements/education/smarter_schools/literacy_numeracy/national_partnership.pdf

Ministerial Council of Education, Employment, Training and Youth Affairs. (2008). *Melbourne declaration on educational goals for young Australians.* http://www.curriculum.edu.au/verve/_resources/National_Declaration_on_the_Educational_Goals_for_Young_Australians.pdf

Mitani, H. (2018). Principals' working conditions, job stress, and turnover behaviors under NCLB accountability pressure. *Educational Administration Quarterly, 54*(5), 822–862.

Morgan, C., & Shahjahan, R. A. (2014). The legitimation of OECD's global educational governance: Examining PISA and AHELO test production. *Comparative Education, 50*(2), 192–205.

REFERENCES

Moss, P. A. (2013). Validity in action: Lessons from studies of data use. *Journal of Educational Measurement, 50*(1), 91–98.

Mulcahy, D., Cleveland, B., & Aberton, H. (2015). Learning spaces and pedagogic change: envisioned, enacted and experienced. *Pedagogy, Culture & Society, 23*(4), 575–595.

Muñiz, R. (2020). Muddy sensemaking: Making sense of socio-emotional skills amidst a vague policy context. *Education Policy Analysis Archives, 28*, 114.

My School and Beyond. (2009). http://www.acara.edu.au/acara_update_14122009.html

Nardon, L., & Hari, A. (2021). Sensemaking through metaphors: The role of imaginative metaphor elicitation in constructing new understandings. *International Journal of Qualitative Methods, 20*. doi:16094069211019589

National Partnerships: Literacy and Numeracy. (2009).

Nelson, B. S., & Sassi, A. (2005). *The effective principal: Instructional leadership for high-quality learning*. Teachers College Press.

Neumann, E. (2019). Setting by numbers: Datafication processes and ability grouping in an English secondary school. *Journal of Education Policy*, 1–23.

No Child Left Behind Act of 2001, 107–110. (2002).

Noddings, N. (2013). *Education and democracy in the 21st century*. Teachers College Press.

Norris, J. (2017). *From metaphors to mantras – Principals making sense of and integrating accountability expectations: A grounded theoretical model* [Doctor of Education thesis]. Australian Catholic University. https://researchbank.acu.edu.au/theses/661

Norris, J. (2018). *Releasing the accountability squeeze*. https://redthread.blog/2018/05/01/releasing-the-accountability-squeeze-a-leadership-capability-of-the-21st-century/

NSW Education Standards Authority. (2020). *About the HSC*. https://educationstandards.nsw.edu.au/wps/portal/nesa/11-12/hsc/about-HSC

NSW Government. (2020). *Annual reports*. https://education.nsw.gov.au/about-us/strategies-and-reports/annual-reports

NSW Government, Department of Education and Communities. (2010). *NSW Institute of Teachers*. http://www.nswteachers.nsw.edu.au/

Nye, J. (2012). China's soft power deficit to catch up, its politics must be unleash the many talents of its civil society *The Wall Street Journal*. http://online.wsj.com/article/SB10001424052702304451104577389923098678842.html?mod=ITP_opinion_o

O'Connor, P., & McTaggart, S. (2017). The collapse of the broad curriculum: The collapse of democracy. *Waikato Journal of Education, 22*(1).

O'Day, J. (Ed.). (2004). *Complexity, accountability, and school improvement*. Teachers College Press.

Obstfeld, D., Sutcliffe, K. M., & Weick, K. E. (2005). Organizing and the process of sensemaking. *Organization Science, 16*(4), 409+. http://go.galegroup.com/ps/i.do?id=GALE%7CA137212795&v=2.1&u=acuni&it=r&p=AONE&sw=w

OECD. (2013). *Synergies for better learning: an international perspective on evaluation and assessment.* OECD. http://www.oecd.org/edu/school/Synergies%20for% 20Better%20Learning_Summary.pdf

OECD. (2016). *PISA in focus 9.* https://www.oecd.org/pisa/pisaproducts/pisainfocus/ 48910490.pdf

OECD. (2020). *PISA 2018 results, Volume IV.* https://www.oecd-ilibrary.org/docserver/ 48ebd1ba-en.pdf?expires=1598248952&id=id&accname=guest&checksum= 123DB209E4384E4CD9DF2A2949D4FA06

Ofsted. (2011). *School inspections: A guide for parents and carers from September 2009.* http://www.ofsted.gov.uk/resources/school-inspections-guide-for-parents-and-carers-for-inspection-september-2009

Oplatka, I. (2012). Towards a conceptualization of the early career stage of principal-ship: Current research, idiosyncrasies and future directions. *International Journal of Leadership in Education, 15*(2), 129–151. doi:10.1080/13603124.2011.640943

Oplatka, I. (2016). "Irresponsible leadership" and unethical practices in schools: A con-ceptual framework of the "dark side" of educational leadership. In A. Normore & J. Brooks (Eds.), *The dark side of leadership: Identifying and overcoming unethical practice in organizations.* Emerald Group Publishing Limited.

Ozga, J. (2012). Governing knowledge: Data, inspection and education policy in Europe. *Globalisation, Societies and Education, 10*(4), 439–455.

Panzer, B. (1989). *Resolving traumatic memories: Metaphors and symbols in psychother-apy.* Ardent Media.

Penninckx, M. (2017). *Effects and side effects of school inspections: A general framework.* Elsevier.

Penninckx, M., Vanhoof, J., De Maeyer, S., & Van Petegem, P. (2015). Enquiry into the side effects of school inspection in a 'low-stakes' inspection context. *Research Papers in Education.* Advanced online publication.

Pennings, J. M. (1975). The relevance of the structural-contingency model for organiza-tional effectiveness. *Administrative Science Quarterly*, 393–410.

Perryman, J. (2006). Panoptic performativity and school inspection regimes: Disciplinary mechanisms and life under special measures. *Journal of Education Policy, 21*(2), 147–161.

Perryman, J. (2007). Inspection and emotion. *Cambridge journal of education, 37*(2), 173–190.

Perryman, J. (2009). Inspection and the fabrication of professional and performative processes. *Journal of Education Policy, 24*(5), 611–631.

Petridou, A., Nicolaidou, M., & Williams, J. S. (2014). Development and validation of the school leaders' self-efficacy scale. *Journal of Educational Administration.*

Pettit, P. (2009). *From data-informed to data-led? School leadership within the context of external testing* [Doctoral dissertation]. Australian Catholic University.

REFERENCES

Pettit, P. (2010). From data-informed to data-led? School leadership within the context of external testing. *Leading & Managing, 16*(2), 90–107. www.acu.edu.au/leadershipconference2010

Phillips, C. (2014). *Principals' perceived value of data and principals' perceived competency of data use in a rural school division.* Regent University.

Pineda-Báez, C., Bernal-Luque, R., Sandoval-Estupiñan, L. Y., & Quiroga, C. (2019). Challenges facing novice principals: A study in Colombian schools using a socialisation perspective. *Issues in Educational Research, 29*(1), 205–222.

Polesel, J., Rice, S., & Dulfer, N. (2014). The impact of high-stakes testing on curriculum and pedagogy: A teacher perspective from Australia. *Journal of Education Policy, 29*(5), 640–657.

Pollock, K., & Wang, F. (2021). How principals use their time in Ontario, Canada. In M. Lee, K. Pollock, & P. Tulowitzki (Eds.), *How school principals use their time* (pp. 95–109). Routledge.

Pons, X. (2017). Fifteen years of research on PISA effects on education governance: A critical review. *European Journal of Education, 52*(2), 131–144.

Porter, L. W., & McLaughlin, G. B. (2006). Leadership and the organizational context: Like the weather? *The Leadership Quarterly, 17*(6), 559–576.

Power, M. (2000). The audit society – Second thoughts. *International Journal of Auditing, 4*(1), 111–119.

Pratt, M. G. (2000). The good, the bad, and the ambivalent: Managing identification among Amway distributors. *Administrative science quarterly, 45*(3), 456–493.

Prestwich, A., Sniehotta, F. F., Whittington, C., Dombrowski, S. U., Rogers, L., & Michie, S. (2014). Does theory influence the effectiveness of health behavior interventions? Meta-analysis. *Health Psychology, 33*(5), 465.

Qian, H., & Walker, A. (2021). Building emotional principal–teacher relationships in Chinese schools: Reflecting on paternalistic leadership. *The Asia-Pacific Education Researcher, 1–12.*

Queensland Government. (2021). *Reporting, data and research.* https://education.qld.gov.au/about-us/reporting-data-research

Ragusa, A. T., & Bousfield, K. (2017). 'It's not the test, it's how it's used!' Critical analysis of public response to NAPLAN and MySchool Senate Inquiry. *British Journal of Sociology of Education, 38*(3), 265–286. doi:10.1080/01425692.2015.1073100

Rautalin, M., Alasuutari, P., & Vento, E. (2019). Globalisation of education policies: Does PISA have an effect? *Journal of Education Policy, 34*(4), 500–522.

Ravasi, D., & Schultz, M. (2006). Responding to organizational identity threats: Exploring the role of organizational culture. *Academy of Management Journal, 49*(3), 433–458.

Reid, A. (2011, November). The NAPLAN debate. *QTU Professional Magazine.*

Reid, A., Cranston, N., Keating, J., & Mulford, B. (2011). Bringing back the public purposes of education. *Professional Educator, 10*, 20–23.

Reinertsen, N. (2020). *The viability of simulated large-scale marking as professional development for preservice teachers* [Doctor of Philosophy thesis]. Edith Cowan University. https://ro.ecu.edu.au/theses/2320

Richmond, C. (2007). *Teach more, manage less: A minimalist approach to behaviour management.* Scholastic.

Rigby, J. G. (2015). Principals' sensemaking and enactment of teacher evaluation. *Journal of Educational Administration, 53*(3), 374–392.

Rigby, J. G. (2016). Principals' conceptions of instructional leadership and their informal social networks: An exploration of the mechanisms of the mesolevel. *American Journal of Education, 122*(3).

Riley, P. (2017). *The Australian principal occupational health, safety and wellbeing survey 2017 data.* ACU.

Riley, P. (2019). *The Australian principal occupational health, safety and wellbeing survey: 2018 data.* Institute for Positive Psychology and Education (ACU).

Riley, P., See, S.-M., Marsh, H., & Dicke, T. (2021). *The Australian principal occupational health, safety and wellbeing survey 2020 data.*

Robertson, M., Grady, N., Fluck, A., & Webb, I. (2006). Conversations toward effective implementation of information communication technologies in Australian schools. *Journal of Educational Administration.*

Robinson, V. (2011). *Student-centred leadership.* Jossey-Bass.

Robinson, V., Lloyd, C., & Rowe, K. (2008). The impact of leadership on student outcomes: An analysis of the differential effects of leadership types. *Educational Administration Quarterly, 44*(5), 635–674.

Roche, T. (2004). Not just a necessary evil: When teachers embrace standards and testing. *Education Week, 24*(13), 37.

Rogers, S., Barblett, L., & Robinson, K. (2016). Investigating the impact of NAPLAN on student, parent and teacher emotional distress in independent schools. *The Australian Educational Researcher,* 1–17.

Rothstein, R., Jacobsen, R., & Wilder, T. (2009). From accreditation to accountability. *Phi Delta Kappan, 90*(9), 624–629. http://search.ebscohost.com/login.aspx?direct=true&db=ehh&AN=38812143&site=ehost-live

Roueche, J. E., Baker III, G. A., & Rose, R. R. (2014). *Shared vision: Transformational leadership in American community colleges.* Rowman & Littlefield.

Rowe, K. (2005). *Evidence for the kinds of feedback data that support both student and teacher learning* [Paper]. The Australian Council for Educational Research 2005 Conference, Melbourne.

Rumelhart, D. E. (1980a). On evaluating story grammars. *Cognitive Science, 4*(3), 313–316.

Rumelhart, D. E. (1980b). Schemata: The building blocks of cognition. In R. Spiro, B. Bruce, & W. Brewer (Eds.), *Theoretical issues in reading comprehension.* Lawrence Erlbaum Associates.

REFERENCES

Ryu, J., Walls, J., & Seashore Louis, K. (2020). Caring leadership: The role of principals in producing caring school cultures. *Leadership and Policy in Schools*, 1–18.

Sachse, K. A., & Haag, N. (2017). Standard errors for national trends in international large-scale assessments in the case of cross-national differential item functioning. *Applied Measurement in Education, 30*(2), 102–116.

Sahlberg, P. (2007). Education policies for raising student learning: The Finnish approach. *Journal of Education Policy, 22*(2), 147–171.

Salicru, S. (2018). Storytelling as a leadership practice for sensemaking to drive change in times of turbulence and high velocity. *Journal of Leadership, Accountability and Ethics, 15*(2).

Sam, C. H. (2020). What are the practices of unethical leaders? Exploring how teachers experience the "dark side" of administrative leadership. *Educational Management Administration & Leadership.* https://doi.org/10.1177/1741143219898480

Sanders, M. (2018). Crossing boundaries: A qualitative exploration of relational leadership in three full-service community schools. *Teachers College Record, 120*(4), 1–36.

Schechter, C., Shaked, H., Ganon-Shilon, S., & Goldratt, M. (2018). Leadership metaphors: School principals' sense-making of a national reform. *Leadership and Policy in Schools, 17*(1), 1–26.

Schleicher, A. (2012). *Preparing teachers and developing school leaders for the 21st century: Lessons from around the world.* ERIC.

Schoen, L., & Fusarelli, L. D. (2008). Innovation, NCLB, and the fear factor: The challenge of leading 21st-century schools in an era of accountability. *Educational Policy, 22*(1), 181–203.

Schwarzer, R. (2014). *Self-efficacy: Thought control of action.* Taylor & Francis.

Scott, S. (2016). Reconceptualising instructional leadership: Exploring the relationships between leadership, instructional design, assessment, and student needs. In S. Scott, D. Scott, & C. Webber (Eds.), *Leadership of assessment, inclusion, and learning* (Vol. 3, pp. 1–22). Springer. https://doi.org/10.1007/978-3-319-23347-5_1

Seashore Louis, K., Knapp, M. S., & Feldman, S. B. (2012). Managing the intersection of internal and external accountability: Challenge for urban school leadership in the United States. *Journal of Educational Administration, 50*(5), 666–694.

Seashore Louis, K., & Mintrop, H. (2012). Bridging accountability obligations, professional values and (perceived) student needs with integrity. *Journal of Educational Administration, 50*(5), 695–726.

Segal, S. (2010). A Heideggerian approach to practice-based reflexivity. *Management Learning, 41*(4), 379–389.

Sellar, S., & Lingard, B. (2013). The OECD and global governance in education. *Journal of Education Policy, 28*(5), 710–725.

Senate References Committee on Education, Employment and Workplace Relations. (2010). *Administration and reporting of NAPLAN testing.* Senate Printing Unit.

Shaked, H. (2018). Why principals sidestep instructional leadership: The disregarded question of schools' primary objective. *Journal of School Leadership, 28*(4), 517–538. doi:10.1177/105268461802800404

Shapiro, J. P., & Gross, S. J. (2013). *Ethical educational leadership in turbulent times: (Re)solving moral dilemmas.* Routledge.

Shapiro, J. P., & Stefkovich, J. A. (2016). *Ethical leadership and decision making in education: Applying theoretical perspectives to complex dilemmas.* Routledge.

Sharratt, L., & Fullan, M. (2012). *Putting FACES on the data: What great leaders do!* Corwin Press.

Shen, J., Ma, X., Cooley, V. E., & Burt, W. L. (2015). Mediating effects of school process on the relationship between principals' data-informed decision-making and student achievement. *International Journal of Leadership in Education*, 1–29.

Shipps, D. (2012). Empowered or beleaguered? Principals' accountability under New York City's diverse provider regime. *Education Policy Analysis Archives, 20*(1), 1–40.

Shipps, D., & White, M. (2009). A new politics of the principalship? Accountability-driven change in New York City. *Peabody Journal of Education, 84*(3), 350–373. doi:10.1080/01619560902973563

Shore, C., & Wright, S. (2003). Coercive accountability: The rise of audit culture in higher education. In M. Strathern (Ed.), *Audit cultures* (pp. 69–101). Routledge.

Siegel, H. (Ed.). (2004). *What ought matter in public schooling: Judgment, standards, and responsible accountability.* Teachers College Press.

Simon, S., Heck, D., Christie, M., & Farragher, Y. (2019). Leading pedagogical reform: Australian principals tell their stories. *International Journal of Leadership in Education*, 1–24.

Sleeter, C. E. (2007). *Facing accountability in education: Democracy and equity at risk.* Teachers College Press.

Sloan, K. (2008). The expanding educational services sector. *Journal of Curriculum Studies, 40*(5), 555–578.

Smeed, J., Bourke, T., Nickerson, J., & Corsbie, T. (2015). Testing times for the implementation of curriculum change. *Sage Open, 5*(2). https://doi.org/10.1177/2158244015581018

Smeed, J., Spiller, K., & Kimber, M. (2009). Issues for principals in high-stakes testing. *Principal Matters, 81*, 32–34.

Smit, B., & Mabusela, M. (2019). Understanding relational and responsible leadership for school leaders. In J. R. Neikirk & G. W. Noblit (Eds.), *Oxford research encyclopedia of education.* https://doi.org/10.1093/acrefore/9780190264093.013.521

Sonenshein, S. (2006). Crafting social issues at work. *Academy of Management Journal, 49*(6), 1158–1172.

Sosik, J. J., Zhu, W., & Blair, A. L. (2011). Felt authenticity and demonstrating transformational leadership in faith communities. *Journal of Behavioral and Applied Management, 12*(3), 179.

REFERENCES

Spillane, J. P. (2009). Managing to lead: Reframing school leadership and management. *Phi Delta Kappan, 91*(3), 70–73.

Spillane, J. P., & Anderson, L. (2014). The architecture of anticipation and novices' emerging understandings of the principal position: Occupational sense making at the intersection of individual, organization, and institution. *Teachers College Record, 116*, 070306.

Spillane, J. P., Diamond, J. B., Burch, P., Hallett, T., Jita, L., & Zoltners, J. (2002). Managing in the middle: School leaders and the enactment of accountability policy. *Educational Policy, 16*(5), 731–762.

Spillane, J. P., & Lee, L. C. (2013). Novice school principals' sense of ultimate responsibility: Problems of practice in transitioning to the principal's office. *Educational Administration Quarterly.* doi:10.1177/0013161x13505290

Spillane, J. P., & Lowenhaupt, R. (2019). *Navigating the principalship: Key insights for new and aspiring school leaders.* ASCD.

Spillane, J. P., Reiser, B. J., & Gomez, L. M. (2006). Policy implementation and cognition. *New Directions in Educational Policy Implementation,* 47–64.

Spillane, J. P., Reiser, B. J., & Reimer, T. (2002). Policy implementation and cognition: Reframing and refocusing implementation research. *Review of Educational Research, 72*(3), 387–431. doi:10.3102/00346543072003387

Stein, M. K., & Nelson, B. S. (2003). Leadership content knowledge. *Educational Evaluation and Policy Analysis, 25*(4), 423–448.

Steinbauer, R., Rhew, N. D., & Chen, H. S. (2015). From stories to schemas: A dual systems model of leaders' organizational sensemaking. *Journal of Leadership & Organizational Studies.* doi:10.1177/1548051815598007

Stensaker, I., Falkenberg, J., & Grønhaug, K. (2008). Implementation activities and organizational sensemaking. *The Journal of Applied Behavioral Science, 44*(2), 162–185.

Stobart, G. (2008). *Testing times: The uses and abuses of assessment.* Routledge.

Strauss, A., & Corbin, J. (1990). *Basics of qualitative research. Grounded theory procedures and techniques.* Sage Publications.

Strauss, A., & Corbin, J. (1998). *Basics of qualitative research.* Thousand Oaks.

Striepe, M., Clarke, S., & O'Donoghue, T. (2014). Spirituality, values and the school's ethos: Factors shaping leadership in a faith-based school. *Issues in Educational Research, 24*(1), 85–97.

Striepe, M., & O'Donoghue, T. (2014). Servant leadership in a Catholic school: A study in the Western Australian context. *Education Research and Perspectives (Online), 41*, 130.

Sun, J., & Leithwood, K. (2015). Leadership effects on student learning mediated by teacher emotions. *Societies, 5*(3), 566–582.

Supovitz, J., Sirinides, P., & May, H. (2009). How principals and peers influence teaching and learning. *Educational Administration Quarterly.*

Swidler, A. (1986). Culture in action: Symbols and strategies. *American Sociological Review*, 273–286.

Taubman, P. (2009). *Teaching by numbers: Deconstructing the discourse of standards and accountability in education.* Taylor & Francis.

Teddlie, C., & Reynolds, D. (2000). *The international handbook of school effectiveness research.* Psychology Press.

Thayer, L. (1988). Leadership/communication: A critical review and a modest proposal. *Handbook of organizational communication, 231,* 263.

Thayer, L., Goldhaber, G., & Barnett, G. (1988). Leadership/communication: A critical review and a modest proposal. In G. M. Goldhaber & G. A. Barnett (Eds.), *Handbook of organizational communication.* Ablex.

Thessin, R. A. (2019). Establishing productive principal/principal supervisor partnerships for instructional leadership. *Journal of Educational Administration.*

Thessin, R. A., & Louis, K. S. (2019). Supervising school leaders in a rapidly changing world. *Journal of Educational Administration.*

Thessin, R. A., & Louis, K. S. (2020). Is professional learning keeping up. *The Learning Professional, 41*(2), 40–46.

Thiel, C., Bagdasarov, Z., Harkrider, L., Johnson, J. F., & Mumford, M. (2012). Leader ethical decision-making in organizations: Strategies for sensemaking. *Journal of Business Ethics, 107,* 49–64. doi:10.1007/s10551-012-1299-1

Thompson, G. (2015). The challenges of testing accountability: Understanding limitations and negotiating consequences. *Big Fish, Little Fish: Teaching and Learning in the Middle Years,* 139.

Thompson, G., & Mockler, N. (2016). Principals of audit: Testing, data and 'implicated advocacy.' *Journal of Educational Administration and History, 48*(1), 1–18.

Timperley, H., Wilson, A., Barrar, H., & Fung, I. (2007). *Teacher professional learning and development: Best evidence synthesis iteration (BES).* University of Auckland. http://educationcounts.edcentre.govt.nz/goto/BES

Townsend, T. (2019). *Instructional leadership and leadership for learning in schools: Understanding theories of leading* (1st ed.). Palgrave Macmillan.

Tschannen-Moran, M., & Gareis, C. R. (2004). Principals' sense of efficacy: Assessing a promising construct. *Journal of Educational Administration, 42*(5), 573–585.

Underwood, P. R. (2012). Teacher beliefs and intentions regarding the instruction of English grammar under national curriculum reforms: A theory of planned behaviour perspective. *Teaching and Teacher Education, 28*(6), 911–925.

UNSW. (2016). *Arts & social educational leadership.* https://www.arts.unsw.edu.au/future-students/postgraduate-coursework/degrees/educational-leadership/

Utz, S., Schultz, F., & Glocka, S. (2013). Crisis communication online: How medium, crisis type and emotions affected public reactions in the Fukushima Daiichi nuclear disaster. *Public Relations Review, 39*(1), 40–46.

REFERENCES

Valenzuela, A. (2005). *Leaving children behind: How" Texas-style" accountability fails Latino youth.* SUNY Press.

Van Maanen, J. (2010). *Identity work and control in occupational communities.* Cambridge University Press.

Venus, M., Stam, D., & van Knippenberg, D. (2013). Leader emotion as a catalyst of effective leader communication of visions, value-laden messages, and goals. *Organizational Behavior and Human Decision Processes, 122*(1), 53–68. doi:http://dx.doi.org/10.1016/j.obhdp.2013.03.009

Verger, A., Parcerisa, L., & Fontdevila, C. (2019). The growth and spread of large-scale assessments and test-based accountabilities: A political sociology of global education reforms. *Educational Review, 71*(1), 5–30.

Victorian Government. (2021). *The compact.* https://www.education.vic.gov.au/Documents/school/principals/management/thecompact.pdf

Voronov, M. (2008). *Toward a practice perspective on strategic organizational learning.* The Learning Organization.

Walker, A. D., Lee, M., & Bryant, D. A. (2014). How much of a difference do principals make? An analysis of between-schools variation in academic achievement in Hong Kong public secondary schools. *School Effectiveness and School Improvement, 25*(4), 602–628.

Watson, T. J. (1995). Rhetoric, discourse and argument in organizational sense making: A reflexive tale. *Organization Studies, 16*(5), 805–821.

Wayman, J. C., Midgley, S., & Stringfield, S. (2017). Leadership for data-based decision making: Collaborative educator teams. In A. B. Danzig, K. M. Borman, B. A. Jones, & W. F. Wright (Eds.), *Learner-centered leadership* (pp. 189–206). Routledge.

Weick, K. (1993). The collapse of sensemaking in organizations: The Mann Gulch disaster. *Administrative Science Quarterly,* 628–652.

Weick, K. (1995). *Sense-making in prganizations.* Sage Publications Inc.

Weick, K. (2001). *Making sense of the organization.* Blackwell Publishers Inc.

Weick, K., Sutcliffe, K., & Obstfeld, D. (2005). Organizing and the process of sensemaking. *Organization Science, 16*(4), 409–421.

Weick, K. E. (1989). Theory construction as disciplined imagination. *Academy of Management Review, 14*(4), 516–531.

Weiner, J. M., & Woulfin, S. L. (2017). Controlled autonomy: Novice principals' schema for district control and school autonomy. *Journal of Educational Administration.*

Wenner, J. A., & Settlage, J. (2015). School leader enactments of the structure/agency dialectic via buffering. *Journal of Research in Science Teaching, 52*(4), 503–515.

Werts, A. B., & Brewer, C. A. (2014). Reframing the study of policy implementation: Lived experience as politics. *Educational Policy.* doi:10.1177/0895904814559247

Werts, A. B., Della Sala, M., Lindle, J., Horace, J. M., Brewer, C., & Knoeppel, R. (2013). Education stakeholders' translation and sense-making of accountability policies. *Leadership and Policy in Schools, 12*(4), 397–419.

262   REFERENCES

Whelan, A. P. (2000). *A study of Catholic schools' consultants in New South Wales: Their leadership, relationship with principals and influence on schools* [Doctor of Education thesis]. Australian Catholic University. https://acuresearchbank.acu.edu.au/download/7c561924bf92a443b9ffe33f302d600916c5f1d2722f85c77b54fc787b319ee9/10900782/65134_downloaded_stream_359.pdf

Whitby, G. (2013). *Educating Gen Wi-Fi: How to make schools relevant for 21st century learners*. HarperCollins.

White, M. A. (2006). *A case of New York City high school principals' experiences with multiple accountability pressures and accompanying models for decision-making.* Columbia University Teacher's College.

Wilkins, A. (2012). School choice and the commodification of education: A visual approach to school brochures and websites. *Critical Social Policy, 32*(1), 69–86.

Wilkinson, J., Edwards-Groves, C., Grootenboer, P., & Kemmis, S. (2019). District offices fostering educational change through instructional leadership practices in Australian Catholic secondary schools. *Journal of Educational Administration.*

Wilkinson, J., Niesche, R., & Eacott, S. (2018). *Challenges for public education: Reconceptualising educational leadership, policy and social justice as resources for hope.* Routledge.

Willis, A., Hyde, M., & Black, A. (2019). Juggling with both hands tied behind my back: Teachers' views and experiences of the tensions between student well-being concerns and academic performance improvement agendas. *American Educational Research Journal, 56*(6), 2644–2673.

Windle, J. (2009). The limits of school choice: Some implications for accountability of selective practices and positional competition in Australian education. *Critical Studies in Education, 50*(3), 231–246.

Wiseman, A. W. (2010). The uses of evidence for educational policymaking: Global contexts and international trends. *Review of Research in Education, 34*(1), 1–24. doi:10.3102/0091732X09350472

Wong, L.-S. (2019). Administrators' unintentional sensegiving and system reform outcomes. *Education Policy Analysis Archives, 27*(3), n3.

Woodward, R. (2009). *The Organization for Economical Co-operation and Development (OECD)*. London: Routledge.

Wright, J. (2016). *Collected poems*. HarperCollins Publishers.

Wronowski, M. L., & Urick, A. (2019). Examining the relationship of teacher perception of accountability and assessment policies on teacher turnover during NCLB. *Education Policy Analysis Archives, 27*, 86.

Yan, Y. L. (2019). Conceptualization and operationalization of accountability in Canadian education: A systematic review. *Canadian Journal for New Scholars in Education/Revue canadienne des jeunes chercheures et chercheurs en éducation, 10*(1).

REFERENCES

Zajonc, R. B., & Markus, H. (1985). Affect and cognition: The hard interface. In C. Izard, J. Kagan, & R. B. Zajonc (Eds.), *Emotions, cognition and behavior* (pp. 73–102). Cambridge University Press.

Zepeda, S. J., & Lanoue, P. D. (2017). Conversation walks: Improving instructional leadership. *Educational Leadership, 74*(8), 58–61.

Zerubavel, E. (1997). Social mindscapes. *An invitation to cognitive sociology.*

Ziebell, N., Acquaro, D., Tiong Seah, W., & Pearn, C. (2020). *Being a teacher during COVID-19.* https://pursuit.unimelb.edu.au/articles/being-a-teacher-during-covid-19

Zolait, A. H. S. (2014). The nature and components of perceived behavioural control as an element of theory of planned behaviour. *Behaviour & Information Technology,* 1–21. doi:10.1080/0144929x.2011.630419

Index

accountability   X–XIII, 2, 15–18, 24, 26–28, 34, 35, 38, 40, 42–45, 49, 50, 52–54, 57–61, 68, 69, 71–103, 105–117, 120, 122, 123, 126–137, 141, 143, 145, 146, 148, 151, 175, 176, 179–185, 189, 199, 204, 212–214, 219–221, 224–226, 228

accountability mechanisms   XII, 28, 53, 54, 58, 59, 78, 80, 90, 91, 94, 112, 114

accountability stakes   16, 45, 52, 61, 72, 74, 96, 99, 184

accountable   3, 4, 17, 28, 40, 63, 64, 68, 69, 72, 76, 77, 81, 82, 84, 88, 90, 102, 107, 109–113, 121, 122, 128, 129, 136, 140, 141, 159, 174, 184, 190, 191, 195, 200, 202, 204, 209, 218, 224, 226, 230

adaptable   XIII, 63, 67, 79, 226

administrators   X, 4, 62, 67, 85

agile   XIII, 62, 63, 66, 79, 223

anomaly   90, 108, 110, 119, 121, 141, 142, 155, 156

Australian character   230

bureaucratic accountability   73, 83

career pathways   3, 51, 65, 122, 124, 125, 170, 223, 230

collective teacher efficacy   IX, 1, 3, 76

common vision   4

competing priorities   71–73, 77, 202, 213

conjectures   8, 45

consensual validation   1, 17, 25, 27, 110, 171, 174, 175, 196, 200

constraining   16, 17, 21, 27, 121, 133, 161, 162, 166, 173, 180, 185, 212, 213, 219, 220

constraining expectations   17, 20, 174, 180, 216, 219

contextualising   17, 21, 39, 102, 107, 133, 134, 162, 166, 167, 171, 185, 214, 219, 220

contextualising expectations   17, 20, 216, 219

creating coherence   XII, 19–21, 197, 198, 216, 220, 230

credibility   3, 4, 18, 19, 21, 26, 27, 32, 48–50, 96, 117, 124, 138, 143, 144, 146, 163, 168, 176, 182, 188, 195, 196, 201–205, 213, 219, 222–224

cultivating credibility   19, 21, 188, 201–203, 213, 222

cultures of coherence   19, 135, 147, 163, 200, 219

curriculum   51, 52, 57, 58, 60, 61, 64–67, 72, 83, 92, 94–96, 104, 107, 113, 119, 130, 142, 151, 158, 159, 164, 177, 179, 208

decision making   11, 24, 28, 36, 41, 42, 71, 75, 148, 196, 204, 213

defining educational accountability   87

determinants   1, 3, 11, 13, 42–44, 46, 149, 167, 174, 202, 206–208, 210–212, 220

early career   XI, 72, 79, 84, 86, 154, 172, 181, 195, 198, 203, 227

educational accountability   XII, 52–54, 76, 79, 80, 82, 87–89, 92, 94, 96, 98, 112, 123, 132, 182, 189, 200, 206, 210, 211, 219, 230

educational leaders   X, XI, 7, 16, 17, 26, 27, 29, 33–41, 48, 67–69, 72, 76, 77, 82, 84, 89, 95, 97, 148, 162, 178, 188, 190, 191, 201, 214, 216, 217, 221, 224

emotions   2, 4–6, 28, 38, 39, 41, 73, 76, 77, 85, 98, 104, 114, 115, 122, 126, 161, 182, 184, 185, 190, 195, 217

enactment   12, 18, 20, 26, 27, 43, 45, 72, 74, 75, 86, 100, 135, 143, 151, 166, 176, 191, 192, 197, 203, 213, 216, 221, 229

energising   30, 31, 33, 46, 48–50, 187, 192, 195, 198, 199

envisioning   29, 31, 40, 45, 187, 192

ethical accountability   84

ethical dilemmas   117

eucalypt   X–XIII, 2–5, 7–9, 11, 12, 21, 100, 215, 227, 228, 230

eucalyptus leadership model   X, 2, 5, 8, 12–14, 16, 21, 22, 45, 51, 74, 79, 80, 100, 101, 190, 214, 215, 218, 219, 221–224, 227–230

eucalyptus pauciflora   228

external demands   XI–XIII, 4, 8–10, 12–19, 21, 40, 41, 48, 52, 62, 73, 76–80, 100, 112, 135, 156, 164, 166, 168, 174, 180, 182, 184–189, 191, 192, 195, 197, 203, 213, 214, 219–222, 225–227, 229

INDEX

faith-based 57, 69–71
first nation 231
first nation peoples 231
framing 40, 100, 132–134, 162, 166, 180, 184, 185, 211, 219, 220, 226
framing expectations 18, 20, 21, 162, 211, 216, 219

high stakes XI, 15, 17, 45, 52, 58, 61, 72, 74, 77, 80, 85, 94–99, 161, 164, 170, 184
high velocity X, XI, 3, 9, 180, 223, 226

indigenous 2, 5, 6
instrument confusion 56
intentional influence 11, 191

languaging learning 135, 138, 139
leader credibility 146
leader identity 79, 135, 145, 160, 163, 178, 181
leader self 28, 31, 181
leadership 2, 5, 8, 12–14, 16, 21, 22, 45, 51, 74, 79, 80, 100, 101, 190, 214, 215, 218, 219, 221–224, 227–230
leading XII, 65, 68, 71, 72, 77, 110, 129, 135, 138, 139, 141–144, 146, 156, 159, 163, 164, 175, 176, 178, 179, 181, 200, 202, 205, 208–210, 213, 218, 222, 223, 225
learning IX–XIII, 2–4, 13, 14, 17–21, 26, 28, 36, 39, 40, 48–50, 52, 55, 58–60, 62–71, 73, 75–79, 81, 83–86, 90–95, 97, 101, 103, 104, 108–131, 135–147, 150–165, 172–181, 184, 188, 189, 191–194, 196–214, 216–230
legitimacy 36, 38, 48, 177, 195
legitimate power 36–38, 48–50, 196, 202, 203
linguistic devices 32, 180
loosening 25, 26, 196, 198

mantras 18, 32, 35, 135, 137, 138, 158–160, 162, 163, 180, 183, 188, 189, 191, 197, 212, 213, 219–221, 223, 226, 230, 231
memo 13–15, 35, 104, 110, 111, 117, 118, 129, 131, 133, 154
memoing 101
metaphors XI, XIII, 2, 5, 13, 19, 32, 124, 125, 135–137, 145, 146, 158–160, 162–164, 180, 181, 183, 189, 190, 198, 208, 213, 215, 217, 219–221, 223, 226–228, 230, 231

moderators 18, 21, 31, 33, 34, 38, 200–202, 205, 207
moral accountability 84
moral purpose 13, 84, 128, 129, 153, 165, 188, 191
motivation 4, 28, 41, 46, 49, 50, 138, 163, 194, 195, 199, 203, 227

narratives 2, 5, 18, 22, 32, 35, 50, 73, 85, 119, 135–139, 158–160, 163, 180, 183, 189, 190, 197, 199, 208, 215, 219–221, 223, 226, 230, 231

ongoing projects 20, 25, 27, 46, 166, 174, 175, 192, 196, 198, 208, 216

performative cultures 19, 69, 90, 98, 156, 163, 217, 222, 223, 225
personal accountability 85, 86, 109
personal identity 20, 25, 27, 28, 48, 49, 172, 175, 179, 181, 197, 216
persuasive accounts XII, 16, 18, 20, 21, 190, 206, 216, 219, 220
plausibility 18, 20, 22, 25, 27, 32, 46, 50, 166, 176, 182, 185, 197, 198, 216
policy to practice 74, 167, 185
principals IX–XIII, 3–5, 12, 15, 17, 18, 23, 24, 26–28, 31, 42–45, 48–50, 53–76, 78, 80, 82, 83, 88, 93, 97–107, 109–128, 130–161, 163–167, 169–207, 209–214, 219–231
prioritising expectations 16, 102, 121, 162, 174, 180, 220
problem re-namers 23
professional accountability 71, 84
Pseudo-NAPLAN 67, 96, 170
psycho-social processes XI, 2, 5, 7, 130, 132, 227
purposes of schooling 28, 110

reciprocal relationships 2, 4–7, 41
reciprocity 4, 6, 211
referents 27, 43–46, 48, 49, 107–110, 112, 113, 118, 122, 143, 160, 171, 174, 177, 180, 183, 202, 209–213, 219, 222, 224, 225, 227
retrospect 17, 20, 24, 25, 27, 46, 48, 174, 175, 216
re-visioning 30, 31, 33, 48, 49, 192, 195, 199

266 INDEX

salient cues 20, 25, 27, 46, 174, 175, 216
schema 18, 29, 35, 36, 38, 39, 41, 79, 105,
126, 130–132, 134, 140, 142, 161, 171, 176,
180–183, 185, 196, 199, 220, 226
school leaders IX–XIII, 1–24, 26–32, 36, 40,
42, 45, 46, 48, 51–69, 71–92, 98–100, 129,
166–207, 211–215, 217–230
school systems IX–XII, 3, 11–13, 17, 21, 28, 31,
54–57, 59, 63–71, 74, 77, 81, 83, 84, 89,
91, 92, 94–96, 99, 100, 107–109, 112–115,
117–123, 125, 126, 128–130, 133, 134, 136,
137, 142, 144, 145, 147–151, 171, 173–181,
183–187, 190, 191, 193, 197, 200, 201, 208,
209, 212–214, 220, 222, 224, 225, 229, 230
sense breaking 39, 40
sense leaders 9–11, 18, 19, 28, 29, 31–35, 157,
215, 216, 218, 219, 221, 228, 231
sense receiving 39
sensegiving XI, XII, 1, 2, 4, 7–13, 15, 16, 18–20,
22–24, 28–32, 35–41, 45–50, 100, 134,
135, 143, 147, 157–159, 164, 165, 180, 182,
187–191, 193–195, 197, 199, 202, 203, 206,
207, 213, 217–222, 225, 227, 230
sensegiving acts 9, 11, 16, 18, 19, 29–32, 35–38,
46, 134, 135, 143, 147, 157–159, 164, 165,
182, 187, 189–191, 193–195, 197, 199, 202,
203, 206, 207, 217, 218, 230
sensemaking XI, XII, 1, 2, 4, 5, 7–20, 22–40,
45–50, 73, 80, 100, 110, 121, 131, 133, 135,
146, 157–162, 166, 168, 171–176, 178–182,
185–190, 197, 201, 203, 206–208, 211,
213–216, 218–231
sensemaking devices 2, 5, 160, 180, 181, 230
sensemaking-for-self 9–11
shared vision 32, 192, 206, 223
signalling 29–31, 45, 49, 50, 146, 147, 163, 187,
191, 192, 197, 198, 208

sites of struggle 81
social context 1, 17, 18, 20, 25, 27, 46, 49, 87,
110, 166, 171, 174, 175, 178, 179, 198, 216
social identity 5, 198
soft power 54–56

teacher receptivity 17, 20, 162, 163, 167, 171,
216
teachers IX–XIII, 1–4, 9, 14–17, 19, 20, 26–29,
31, 32, 34–41, 44, 46, 53, 54, 56, 61–67,
69, 70, 73–82, 84–86, 89, 91–93, 95, 98,
100–103, 105, 106, 108, 112, 113, 115–120,
122–125, 130, 135–137, 139–156, 158,
160–164, 167–172, 175–179, 181, 183–185,
187, 189–206, 208, 209, 213–220,
222–225
teaching IX–XIII, 3, 4, 9, 13, 14, 16, 18–21,
28–31, 36, 38–40, 48, 56, 61–72, 75–78,
81, 84, 86, 91, 93, 95, 96, 98, 101, 103, 106,
107, 119, 122–126, 135, 137, 138, 141–150,
152, 153, 155, 156, 159–161, 163–165,
169–171, 173, 176, 177, 179, 181, 183, 185,
187, 188, 191–194, 196, 200–206, 208–211,
213, 214, 216–227, 230
theoretical IX–XII, 1–4, 7–14, 16, 18, 19, 21,
22, 24, 32, 33, 43, 48, 51, 80, 100, 101, 183,
187, 189, 190, 192, 206, 213, 215, 218, 219,
221, 222, 229
theoretical relationships 11, 13, 19, 189, 206
theories 1, 5, 8, 41, 167, 178, 221, 230
theory construction 8
theory of planned behaviour XI, 2, 8, 11, 12,
20, 22, 23 41–43, 74, 221
typology, accountability 82, 86

vision 4, 20, 32, 101, 110, 122, 135, 138, 144, 158,
159, 163, 165, 167, 181, 188, 189, 191

Printed in the United States
by Baker & Taylor Publisher Services